Lost Patrols

Submarine Wrecks
of the
English Channel

By

Innes McCartney

With a Foreword by Jak Mallmann-Showell

Published in 2003 by
Periscope Publishing Ltd.
33 Barwis Terrace
Penzance
Cornwall TR18 2AW

www.periscopepublishing.com

A CIP record for this book is available from the British Library

ISBN No 1-904381-04-9

Printed in England by Antony Rowe Ltd
Eastbourne

Cover photography by John Hammond
Cover design by Innes McCartney

"There is no margin for error in submarines. You are either alive, or dead" - Max Horton

This book is dedicated to the 3,308 submariners who lie buried within the submarine war-graves mentioned in its pages.

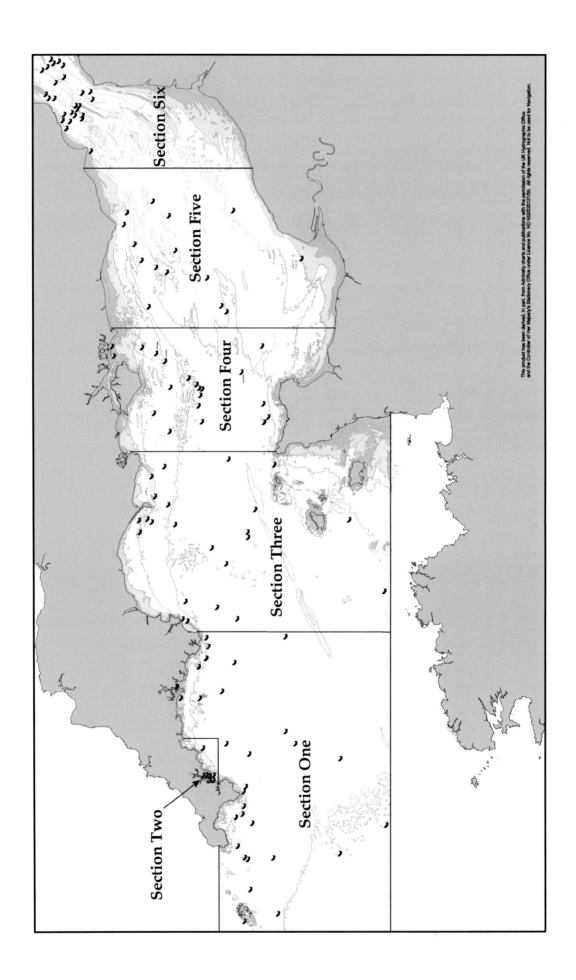

Section Six

Section Five

Section Four

Section Three

Section Two

Section One

Foreword

By Jak Mallmann-Showell

The recent history of the English Channel is just as murky as its waters and consequently eminent historians have got away with feeding their public a vast assortment of emotional twaddle. Finding the truth has been difficult, especially as officialdom does not appear too keen on clarifying data or sorting fact from fiction. This new book by Innes McCartney is a most welcome illumination of the gloomy darkness that still hangs over these shallow coastal waters. For the first time in more than half a century, the majority of submarine wrecks in the English Channel have been positively identified by an enthusiast, and throw an intriguing new light on the battles that raged so close to land. Although such identification might sound to be an easy task, it must be remembered that some previous researchers couldn't distinguish between First and Second World War U-boats nor work out the nationality from the remains. Therefore this work makes a significant contribution to the study of the wars at sea.

One exciting point about this book is that it focuses firmly on the men who served in the boats rather than describing anonymous pieces of bent steel. Writing a large number of such narratives can be most daunting and Innes McCartney has made a stupendous effort in bringing these wrecks back to life. One often gets the impression he was on board during the fateful voyages, which abruptly ended so many young lives.

The greatest plus point, however, must be that the author actually visited the wrecks and can therefore provide accurate sinking positions. This has made it possible to dispel earlier woolly theories about some losses. This is rather important, especially for battles fought towards the end of the war, where a variety of sources have provided contradicting theories of what might have gone on. Interestingly enough these earlier ideas have not been dismissed out of hand, but the author has made a considerable effort to explain why some of them cannot be correct. It also needs to be emphasised that many of the new ideas were not conceived in isolation and eminent historians, such as Dr. Axel Niestle, have provided unflagging help in unravelling or deepening the mysteries of the shallow seas.

The solid information in this book is wrapped up well in fascinating stories and a wealth of interesting narrative, making it a jolly good read. Therefore it will appeal to anyone studying the war at sea, divers who are contemplating exploring the Channel and armchair enthusiasts who want to smell the sea from the comfort of their armchair. The book also contains a fascinatingly wide variety of rare photographs, which help to bring the past back to life and will make it easy to visualise the men who now lie on the bottom of the English Channel.

Jak P. Mallmann Showell

Acknowledgements

The author wishes to acknowledge assistance given by many people in helping me with this project. At the risk of missing out the names of some, the following have helped make this work possible. They are not listed in any order.

Patricia McCartney, the late Gus Britton, Debbie Corner, Margaret Bidmead, George Malcolmson, Peter Gange, Glynis Furze, Nelson McEachan, Yvonne Oliver, Horst Bredow, Bob Peacock, Dave Batchelor, Gifford Pound, Simon Bird, Tony Hilgrove, Tomas Termote, Dave Saywell, Martin Woodward, Mark Webster, Peter Gilson, Kendall McDonald, John Ovenden, Alan Yeend, Bill Reid, Dave Wilkins, Alan Dunster, Gerry Dowd, Kate Tildesley, James Travers, Tim Bonetto, Graham Knott, Peter Webb, Steve Johnson, Nick Bright, Ivan Warren, the late Andy Smith, Dr Ian Buxton, Edwyn Gray, Dr Axel Niestlé, Jak Mallmann-Showell, the late Eddie Cheeks, Yves Dufeil, Simon Mills, Keith Forward, Captain John Moore, Seaford Museum and all of the divers who have supported my research by coming on submarine expeditions over the last eight years

Contents

Illustrations   8

Introduction   9

Section one – Submarine Wrecks of the Southwest   19

Section two – The Falmouth U-boats   51

Section three – Submarine Wrecks Around Lyme Bay   59

Section four – Submarine Wrecks Around the Isle of Wight   99

Section five – Submarine Wrecks off Sussex   123

Section six – Submarine Wrecks of the Dover Straits   141

Appendices   164

Bibliography   171

Index   176

Illustrations

The publishers wish to thank the following for their permission to use the photographs and drawings in this book. Page numbers are given for ease of reference.

- The U-boot Archiv, Alternbruch, Germany: pages 20, 21, 22, 23, 25, 26, 27, 28, 29, 30, 31, 32, 33, 34, 36, 37, 38, 39, 40, 59, 62, 63, 64, 66, 68, 69, 70, 71, 99, 100, 101, 102, 103, 104, 106, 107, 109, 112, 114, 120, 123, 124, 125, 126, 127, 128, 132, 133, 142, 143, 145, 147, 148, 150, 153, 158, 159, 160, 161, 168, 169
- The Royal Navy Submarine Museum, Gosport UK: pages 41, 42, 43, 44, 45, 56, 47, 49, 74, 75, 78, 79, 82, 83, 84, 85, 86, 87, 115, 117, 118, 135, 136, 137, 163
- Innes McCartney: pages 4, 18, 50, 56, 58, 77, 89, 90, 91, 98, 122, 140 and back cover illustration
- Peter Gilson: pages 52, 53, 54, 55, 56, 57
- Imperial War Museum, London UK: pages 81, 110, 130, 149
- Marius Bar, Toulon France: pages 88, 119, 138
- John Hammond: page 94 and cover photograph
- Dave Saywell: pages 76, 91
- The Seaford Museum, Seaford UK: page 105
- Ian Bailey: page 103
- Cate Groom: page 89
- Martin Woodward: page 95
- Simon Mills: page 36
- H.J. Spornhauer: page 38
- Edwyn Gray: page 48

Introduction

The purpose of this book

This book has been written to appeal to the naval enthusiast and the recreational diver. It deals with the ultimate fate of all the known submarines sunk in the English Channel and serves as a guide to where they are located. A potted history of each submarine is given along with the tale of its loss and any known information as to its condition today.

Divers will especially enjoy the wreck information and positional data. Historians will undoubtedly find many of the submarine profiles both unique and challenging, for this book contains the revised fates of several submarines, where recreational divers have discovered the truth surrounding their losses. This information is being placed in the public domain for the first time.

Hunting and identifying submarine wrecks

Wreck diving is truly one of the most exciting pastimes around today. The ability to descend into the depths and visit examples of the most lethal craft built by human hand makes the sport what it is; exhilarating, addictive, awe-inspiring and sometimes terribly moving.

The one nation that has had far more experiences of the potency of the submarine than any other is Great Britain. Twice in the last century she fought long and deadly battles with these underwater foe, the outcomes of which were far more important to her survival than any other theatres of war. For an island nation to lose the sea-lanes would have meant collapse and defeat. To keep them open, Britain paid a cruel human price. In World War Two alone, more than 30,000 merchant seamen were killed.

The German U-boats, which sought to strangle Britain into defeat, were initially successful in both wars. However, ultimately they were defeated, after suffering appalling casualty rates, unequalled in any other field of conflict. In World War Two, 32,000 German submariners died.

In both wars, the waters of the English Channel became a killing ground for merchant seamen, sailors and submariners alike. They died in often pitiless duels to the death. There are no headstones for these brave men. In many cases, the locations where their vessels sunk are unknown or have been simply guessed at. In the two world wars, 2,828 German submariners were killed in the Channel, or attempting to enter it.

The infancy of submarine technology, inexperience in operational doctrine and the underwater environment meant that in peacetime, submariners were also to die in scores of tragic accidents. Channel waters have claimed the graves of 355 British and French submariners in this way.

An experienced wreck diver and photographer, the author is also a post-graduate historian. He has devoted much of his diving to the search, location and identification of the submarine wrecks that lie in the Channel. This book is a summary of his findings to date.

During the last eight years, he has built up a detailed archive of information on the submarine losses in the Channel. He has dived and filmed many of the known wrecks. Moreover, he has located and filmed 18 previously unidentified submarine wrecks. Although not all can be given a specific identity yet, the ones that have been mark the graves of at least 552 submariners. This is a sizable contribution to our understanding of the rich marine heritage that lies in the waters of the English Channel.

To the reader on this subject, it may appear strange that in a confined body of water, such as the Channel, the locations and identities of all of the wrecked submarines is not known. This section attempts to explain why this is the case and outlines the role played by historians and amateur divers in furthering our knowledge of the fates of so many forgotten souls.

The submarine wrecks in this book

The submarine wrecks covered in this book are the ones that have been lost in the area of sea bounded by the following: 6 deg 50 min West, 1 deg 55 min East, 49 deg 0 min South. The northern boundary to the west of Britain is 50 deg 0 min North. To the east of Britain it is 51 deg 15 min North. This area is referred to in the book as the 'Channel'. If a submarine wreck is known to (or thought to) have been lost within these boundaries, it will be covered in this book.

Within the six geographical sections are the histories of 121 submarines and submarine wrecks. Some have been located and identified. Some have not been. There are also submarine wrecks in this book, which have not been located yet. The appendices also deal with the fates of another 37 submarines that may lie (or briefly lay) in the waters of the Channel. In total therefore, up to 158 submarines have sunk in Channel waters. This figure could be a little high as the ten U-boat wrecks, which are unidentified will, hopefully, in time, be associated with some losses, so far unaccounted for.

However, the simple fact remains that it has been the unpaid and unrecognised contribution of amateur divers that has slowly closed the gap between the desktop research of the historians and the realities of submarine warfare.

A brief note on wreck positions

Each submarine covered in this book has some positional data appended to it. Where known, the historical and physical positions of the wrecks are published here. The author believes that this information should reside in the public domain. It serves no one if the information is hidden. By publishing so much positional data, it is hoped that this work will be both informative and useful to wreck researchers and divers, who now have the opportunity to become engaged in furthering the knowledge laid out in this book. More importantly, the positional information will hopefully allow historians to examine the evidence and assimilate its contents into future works of naval history.

It has been with reluctance, therefore, that some positions in this book have been withheld. This has only been done to respect the wishes of several people who have been of considerable assistance during this project.

Historical loss sources only tell half the story

Of the submarines covered in this book, over 60percent of them are U-boats lost on patrol. Therefore it is with the analysis of U-boat losses that we turn to now. Beyond that, a further examination of the other causes of submarine wrecks in the Channel will be covered.

Military analysts, writers and historians have produced much literature on the history of U-boat losses during the last century. All of these sources, even the latest and the most diligently researched are not accurate. They cannot be, because without physical evidence, the analysis of many U-boat losses is based on best estimates and supposition. A brief history of U-boat loss analysis is given below.

A brief history of U-boat loss registers

During both wars, the combatants attempted to calculate the effectiveness of their naval operations by keeping detailed records on most aspects of the conflicts at sea. Allied naval intelligence and German U-boat command were no different. Detailed lists exist of reported allied ASW (Anti-Submarine Warfare) attacks. Lists of the dates U-boats were posted missing also exist. Despite major intelligence breakthroughs by both sides in both conflicts, neither side could ever have been able to draw up a comprehensive list of U-boats destroyed.

However, at the end of these conflicts, lists of sunken U-boats were compiled. Their accuracy varies from unreliable to extremely methodical.

At the end of World War One, the allies produced lists of the U-boats they believed to be destroyed and where and how these losses had taken place. This appears to have been done with little or no reference made to German reports and records, possibly because they were unobtainable at the time. The errors held within them not surprisingly are many. The most commonly used text from this period today is Gibson & Prendergast's *'The German Submarine War'*, published in 1931 and based almost entirely on the British wartime record. While this is an excellent account of the war against the U-boat, it cannot be relied upon when researching U-boat losses simply because it is based on only half of a story.

Starting at the same time, Konteradmiral Arno Spindler began work on his five-volume history *'Der Handelskrieg mit U-Booten'*. Never published in English, this monumental work was not completed until 1966. In the same year, Erich Gröner's *'Die Deutschen Kriegshiffe 1815-1945'* was also published. Both of these books provided historians with the German perspective of U-boat losses during World War One.

The American historian R.M. Grant wrote by far the most useful sources of information on U-boat losses 1914-18. His two books *'U-boats Destroyed'* 1964 and *'U-boat Intelligence'* 1969 (both republished by Periscope Publishing Ltd in 2002) mark the hiatus of studies in this area. They are simply the finest texts available to the historian and wreck researcher. Grant was able to gain access to many intelligence records which had not been consulted previously and had the added bonus of being able to consult Gröner's and Spindler's works as well as the standard British sources. Regardless of the hype, most subsequent works on this topic have been based squarely on Grant's studies.

At the end of World War Two, the allies captured the War records of the Kriegsmarine (and the Imperial German Navy) at Tambach Castle. So, from the outset, the allied naval intelligence had access to the full story of U-boat losses, from both sides of the conflict. However, by the end of the war, the assessors, who had worked hard to determine each U-boat sinking up to around January 1945, were moved on to other tasks. The record for the last few months of the war was cobbled together with a process inconsistent with what had happened previously. Moreover, all undetermined losses were then matched, with the best-looking ASW reports, regardless of merit, to produce a finished picture. For those studying U-boat losses in the Channel, this is particularly frustrating, because so many took place late in the war.

With few exceptions, the lists of U-boats destroyed as listed by Stephen Roskill's *'The War at Sea'* 1961 and the Admiralty commissioned study by Kriegsmarine staff officer Gűther Hessler, *'The U-boat War in the Atlantic'* have been used as the basis of most studies since.

However, in 1998 German historian, Axel Niestlé, published a major revision of the World War Two U-boat loss register. *'German U-boat Losses During World War Two'* was the culmination of a decade's study into this topic and it exposed around 20percent of all assessments as erroneous. Not surprisingly this book has now become the standard work on the subject. The author has been fortunate to be able to call upon Dr Niestlé's superb knowledge and expertise while searching for sunken U-boats and attempting to identify them. His assistance has been invaluable.

Physical evidence of destruction and the sunken U-boat

Ever since the British Admiralty first began to assess the losses of U-boats, forensic evidence of destruction has been at the heart of its analysis. In World War One especially, divers were employed to visit U-boat wrecks to gather intelligence and to identify them. Readers of this book will become familiar with the work of the legendary Cmdr. Damant.

The evidence-gathering concept became so well embedded within Admiralty circles, that by World War Two, a classification scheme, based upon verifiable evidence came into use.

The grading scheme, which came to be used by all of the allies, is complex and does not need full explanation here. However the grading of an 'A' is crucial. It is only in these cases that a U-boat was confirmed sunk. The 'A' grade was only given when a prisoner, human remains or substantial wreckage was in evidence.

Assessments 'B' to 'G' were given according to the evidence of a U-boat being damaged in the reported ASW attack. Other grades were awarded if a submarine was considered not to have been present, or there was not enough information to make an assessment.

This obsession with physical evidence is as it should be. For it is only the presence of evidence of this nature that ensures that the submarine has indeed been destroyed. Especially in World War Two, submarines were attacked while submerged. Physical evidence therefore is absolutely necessary to guarantee destruction. However, it didn't always appear.

One somewhat unsavoury aspect of the use of evidence to confirm kills was the common practice · of 'tin opening'. After a submarine had bottomed (presumably sunk), the wreckage was often liberally plastered with depth charges, in order to bring evidence to the surface. This occurred frequently in the shallow waters of the Channel, especially in World War Two. Some of the wrecks bear testament to this treatment.

Even so, of the 41 U-boats thought lost in the Channel in the Second World War, only 19 were classified as 'A' grade losses. Dr Niestlé has already challenged some of these, as well as the 22 losses with other grades.

Evaluation without physical evidence

Attempting to evaluate U-boat losses without physical evidence is fraught with difficulties. There are several reasons for this, some of which are:

- The best ASW attack may not necessarily destroy a U-boat: A 'perfect straddle' of depth charges, as seen by the tail gunner of an aircraft, may in fact have fallen short, or may have perfectly straddled a whale or other non-sub target.
- A poorly executed ASW attack could destroy a U-boat: See *U672* (Wreck No 3/9) – In this instance the crew survived although the submarine was wrecked by the 'speculative' firing of a hedgehog. If the crew had not survived, it is certain that this attack would have gone unnoticed. It certainly would not have been classified as 'A'- U-boat destroyed.
- An ASW attack can be carried out on a previously destroyed U-boat wreck. This is almost certainly the reason why the destruction of wreck No 5/8 went undetected until located by recreational divers. The assessors may well have assumed that the 'attack', which sunk this U-boat, was delivered against the wreck of *U741* (see No 5/6). Not all assessments were catalogued and written up.
- U-boats can sink in accidents, far from areas of conflict. There are four submarine wrecks on the bottom of the Channel that were sunk, simply as the result of diving accidents. They happen, and there is no reason to assume that some U-boats did not succumb to them too. This is especially so when sabotage by the dockyard workers of occupied countries are taken into consideration. In the Channel, at least one U-boat was lost by accident when *UC69* collided with *U96* (see No 4/12).
- U-boats can strike mines, far from allied view. The mine probably claimed far more U-boats than originally credited with. In the Channel, *U480* was mined (see No 4/1) when the assessment committee claimed it met another fate. In this case, it was the author who was able to adjust the loss register by identifying the wreck.

In the author's experience, any assessment from either war which cannot be denoted as an 'A' grade sinking is highly suspect. The evidence amassed within these pages should be enough to convince sceptics that the proceedings of the assessment committee (and its equivalents during and after World War One) although conducted with great thoroughness simply do not stack up against what is being found on the seabed.

While this may come as a surprise to many, it should not. Without ample evidence, how can any attempt to examine U-boat losses be anything more that 'educated' guesswork?

The physical evidence, which is making the difference these days, is the evidence being found by amateur divers. In all, recreational divers have been responsible for 17 unassailable *changes* to the record of U-boat losses in the Channel. These are all outlined in this book.

On top of this, it is recreational divers that are confirming many of the submarine sinking positions found in loss registers. This too is a valuable contribution to codifying what, up to now, has in many cases been little more than supposition.

In recent years, it has been the evidence found by divers that has made the most valuable contribution to the re-assessments of many U-boat losses. Furthermore, diving evidence continues to show the relative futility of "desktop" re-assessments conducted without reference to hydrographic and diving sources.

Peacetime losses and disposals

Leaving operational U-boat losses aside for a moment, there are four other contributing factors that add to the numbers of submarine wrecks that litter the seabed of the Channel. They are:

- Nine lost as the result of peacetime accidents. These wrecks belong to the British and French navies. They were sunk in a combination of diving accidents and collisions. 355 submariners died in this way.
- 24 submarines lie on the seabed of the Channel, because they were essentially dumped there when they no longer served any useful purpose. These wrecks are a combination of obsolete British designs and surrendered World War One U-boats.
- Seven more submarines were lost in the Channel while being towed to breakers yards. These wrecks are a combination of British and German submarines.
- One was deliberately sunk while filmmaking; The British submarine *H52* (see No 1/28) was sunk while making the silent film 'The Q-Ships'.

Another unique contribution to the history of submarine losses is made in this book. For the first time, the correct disposals of 10 World War One U-boats are related. Divers made two of these discoveries. The author during detailed archival research made the other eight.

In 1921, the Royal Navy dumped eight surrendered U-boats from World War One in the Channel. The fates of these vessels were clearly not made available to the historians of the day, who concluded that they must have been left to rot on Britain's 'east coast', like several others were. In the Medway today, the remains of some of the surrendered U-fleet of World War One can still be seen.

By dumping these submarines, they were fortuitously saved from the breaker's torch. When combined with the submarines that were lost on tow to destruction in the same yards, many historically significant submarine designs were 'accidentally' saved for posterity. This fact was recognised in 1982, when the wreck of *Holland 1* was raised from the seabed of the Channel to be preserved (see Appendix 3).

Submarine wrecks and the role of the recreational diver

This book supports the contention that recreational diving contributes significantly to the development of our knowledge of the underwater world. The study of submarine wrecks is a small field in a much larger patchwork of diving activities.

However, in all cases the rewards to the diver who enters the sea with the purpose of learning, discovering and reporting findings is immense. The satisfaction gained by the author when the identification of a new submarine wreck is made is immeasurable.

Wreck divers can peer into the ocean's depths and see maritime and naval history in an utterly unique way. Shipwrecks are fascinating places. The author has met many people who cherish those brief moments of exploration of our maritime past above all but the most fundamental of acts of existence.

The author genuinely believes that the ability of divers to share this fascination with non-divers, through talks, photographs, videos and books like this, is the key to the survival of our sport. It is with this in mind that this section deals with the most important issues of diving, researching and reporting findings relating to submarine wrecks.

The location and discovery of a new submarine wreck is a rare event. It can be a very exciting moment in the career of any diver. In most cases at least one member of the diving team will take up the challenge, report the finding and help work out what it might be. The pages of this book are scattered with the accounts of divers that have done this. In all of these satisfaction felt by those involved has been immense. In what other sport can such discoveries be made?

Not every diver wishes to be a wreck hunter, but all divers have a duty to understand what he or she is looking at. Otherwise, what is the point?

Archival research

For those divers wishing to locate new wrecks, the archives are places where the best information can be found. The author located HMS *M1* almost entirely from archival material (see No 1/26), which was not available in any published source.

Archival work can be frustrating, but the nuggets of information that can be found, can make the investment of much time well worth the effort. During the course of the project that culminated in this book, the author has spent considerably more time searching through primary source documentation than diving the wrecks. This is one of the prices to be paid for the thrill of genuine exploration.

The archival sources of information used in writing this book are listed in the bibliography. To learn which museum, library or archive may hold what you are looking for, it is best to get on the phone and make inquiries. Once the relevant place to go has been established, then a visit in person is always worthwhile. Once there, if the pockets are large enough, photocopy everything relevant.

Those that were there

Over the past few years, the author has met and spoken with countless numbers of ex-submariners and other servicemen. There simply isn't any substitute for first hand knowledge. As in any other aspect of life, there are those who are genuinely interested and those that are not.

However, perseverance will yield results. Veterans from both sides of the Battle of the Atlantic have been able to furnish the author with a greater understanding of the technologies, operational doctrine, living conditions, morale and many other factors to do with the war at sea.

Sadly, the chance to contact survivors of the specific wrecks mentioned in this book has been scant. This is primarily because high proportions of the war losses were sunk with their entire crews. Distance and language differences have also contributed to make this a difficult journey. However, the author was finally able to make contact with an English-speaking veteran of a U-boat sunk off Ireland in 1945. His knowledge of the times made his contribution to the author's understanding of this period immeasurable. A few hours on the telephone yielded a greater understanding of events than any book could ever impart.

Those who were there can relate a personal and real-life version of events that simply transcends any other form of learning. It is essential to the healthy development of the sport of recreational diving, that those survivors, and their relatives are increasingly offered the opportunity to be engaged in the exploration of our past. The choice to get involved is theirs, but the hand of friendship should always be there.

Identifying submarine wrecks

One of the frustrating aspects of the research that has gone into this book has been the quality of feedback from divers that have visited some of the wrecks mentioned. While a high proportion of wreck divers can tell one sort of ship from another, most see one submarine to be exactly the same as any other. Nothing could be further from the truth.

The following section contains some guidelines for divers who visit or discover unidentified submarines to help focus upon which type they may have located. It should not be considered as 100percent reliable and many other key pieces of information can also come into play. However, all of the following information can be extremely useful.

Design features

A submarine wreck contains all of the information needed to tell what it is, without the need to necessarily bring items to the surface. The following design features, where present, are the important ones to record or remember. These seven key features will nearly always ensure that at least the class of submarine can be identified:

- Deck cannon: the presence of a deck cannon on a submarine wreck in the Channel will almost always point to the vessel being German and from World War One. The diameter of the muzzle or the shells fired is useful in determining its possible age.
- Smaller calibre weapons: the presence of 20mm or 37mm guns can point to the submarine being of late World War Two vintage.
- Torpedo tubes: the number of torpedo tubes found at the bow and the stern is important to record. It can help identify the class of submarine located. The diameter of the tubes is also important.
- Hatches: the number of hatches can help as above.
- Propellers and rudders: the number of propellers and the material (bronze or steel) can help identify the class of vessel and its age. U-boats of World War One tended to have their number stamped on the hub of the propeller.
- Mine chutes: the presence, location and number of mine chutes.
- Schnorchel mast – the presence of a schnorchel would identify the wreck as a late World War Two U-boat.
- Position of hydroplanes: this can tell the diver how the submarine was manoeuvring at the moment of destruction.

Forensic evidence

As important as attempting to establish the key design features of the submarine, recording the condition of the wreck and the way it is laid out on the seabed is essential. Key things to remember include:

- Deck cannon ammunition: if fired shells are present, then the U-boat was certainly on patrol or returning from patrol. If only live ones are present, then it is possible that the U-boat was sunk on its way to its designated patrol area;
- Open hatches: these can point to the possibility of survivors. The wreck could then be traced as an 'A' grade sinking.
- Damage: the type of damage and its location are key pieces of information when trying to establish the destruction of submarines. The damage from mines, ramming, depth charges and hedgehogs are different and can be analysed. Even no damage at all is a valuable clue.
- Evidence of salvage: the removal of the conning tower was a common practice among Navy divers, as it allowed easier access to the submarine's interior to divers in standard dress. The absence of propellers can point to the submarine being towed to the breakers when it sunk.
- Periscopes or schnorchel extended: this can indicate that the submarine was sunk while at periscope depth.

Recording and reporting

Ultimately what is found needs to be recorded. Before using video, the author used to make a drawing of each wreck visited as soon as the diving suit was off and the kettle on. This is the best way to describe all that has been seen and the way all items co-relate. Better still is video and stills photography. This really can help in identifying what is there.

The author has no need to advise divers on reporting what they find. The booklet *Underwater Finds* covers all of the salient issues and is available free of charge from the major diving organisations, English Heritage, DCMS, CADW, Historic Scotland, Environment and Heritage Centre, NAS, Council for British Archaeology, The National Trust and Maritime and Coastguard Agency.

Finders of submarine wrecks anywhere, are positively welcome to contact the author via the publishers.

This book is not definitive

While the culmination of eight years of work has gone into this book, it can in no way be claimed to be the end of the story. It is in fact an interim report, which will be updated in the years to come. The reader will notice that many of the wrecks mentioned have still to be located, and more still cannot certainly be stated to have been lost in the Channel. It is certain that by the time this book is published, our knowledge will have expanded; such is the pace of discovery at present.

The author intends to continue working on this project in the years to come and over time to get closer to a final solution to the many questions which the research to date has yielded. It goes without saying that any discovery made in the Channel, which is not included in this book, would be of immense interest.

It may be that at the end of the day, some of the locations will never be known. However, the more discoveries that are made, the easier the process of elimination becomes to make our understanding of the known wrecks greater.

A note on photograph selection

The photographs which accompany each submarine profile have been selected to both illustrate the main submarine classes covered in this book and to reflect the personal impact of submarine losses. With this in mind, most U-boat photos have been selected from Horst Bredow's unique collection held at the U-Boot Archiv in Altenbruch, Germany. This collection has been assembled in the large part by the donation of personal photographic collections from veterans and their families. They offer a rare human dimension to what would otherwise be a repetitive parade of photographs of submarines.

The photos of the British submarines featured in this book have mostly come from the Royal Navy Submarine Museum, Gosport and have been selected as far as is possible to illustrate the wide-ranging types of British submarine classes lost in the Channel.

Finally – exploding some myths

The introduction to this book has covered the key aspects that govern the search location and identification of submarine wrecks. As a means of summarising its contents the following myths will be exposed.

"The historical record tells us all we need to know about submarine wrecks"

As this chapter has shown, the historical loss register for operational U-boats is not accurate. The loss register for British submarines is little better. It just so happens that in the waters of the Channel, there are few British submarine wrecks and with one exception, HMS D3, (see No 5/14) they have all been found. If this book were about submarine wrecks in the Mediterranean, then this picture would be very different.

However, the proper examination of sites by divers who report what they know will help to increase the accuracy of all loss registers in the future. This is one of the key motivations behind this book.

When the reader begins to look through some of the stories of the submarines wrecked in the Channel, he or she should pay a little attention to feelings of the relatives of those that were lost. One case in particular points to the personal and human dimensions of the sinking of any vessel at sea.

Martin Woodward, a diver, located HMS *Swordfish* (see No 4/16) in 1983. Previously lost, position unknown, the finding of this submarine brought much solace to the families of the bereaved. A memorial service was held near the wreck and now, each year on the anniversary of its loss, the relatives of some of the crew gather together around a small brass 'W' from the wreck, on display at Mr Woodward's museum, to remember. Previously, their loved ones had no place of remembrance in either space or time, regardless of what the history books said.

"All submarine wrecks are war-graves"

In Channel waters, over 20 percent of the submarine wrecks are not war-graves. In the waters around Northern Ireland, this figure could be as high as 95 percent, because of Operation Deadlight (the disposal of the surrendered U-boat fleet in 1945-6) and in other areas, submarines that are not war-graves will also be found.

However, what is absolutely certain, is that until identified, all submarine wrecks should be *assumed* to be war-graves. It is up to divers, working with historians and museums to identify which are which.

"Surveys of the seabed tell us all we need to know about submarine wrecks"

Surveys find wrecks – divers identify them. Sadly, the practice in the past has been for survey information on the location of submarine wrecks to be married with information in loss registers. All this results in is confusion.

Surveys produce accurate information on the positions of wrecks. Where they have been conducted in recent years, using side-scanning sonar, it is possible that the type of vessel can be guessed at. That is, as far as survey information will take anyone.

The use of a diver (or ROV) is the only way to really know what is there. Around the British Isles recreational divers have made the vast majority of underwater finds. On many occasions, the wrecks have been found using information from the Hydrographic Office's survey information. This has been, and will always be a welcome contribution to our knowledge of what is on the seabed.

"*UB39* was sunk near the Isle of Wight"

According to British histories of U-boat losses in World War One, UB39 was sunk by the Q-ship, *Glen* 20 miles south of The Needles on 17th May 1917. There is a charted position so ascribed and the author has met people who have gone looking for her.

However, the fact is that (see No 6/23) we don't know where *UB39* lies with certainty. *Glen's* attack was on *UB18*, which survived and got safely home. A perusal of Gröner, Spindler or Grant would have saved the searchers a day at sea!

Do your research – let it be a lesson to us all!

Innes McCartney – December 2002

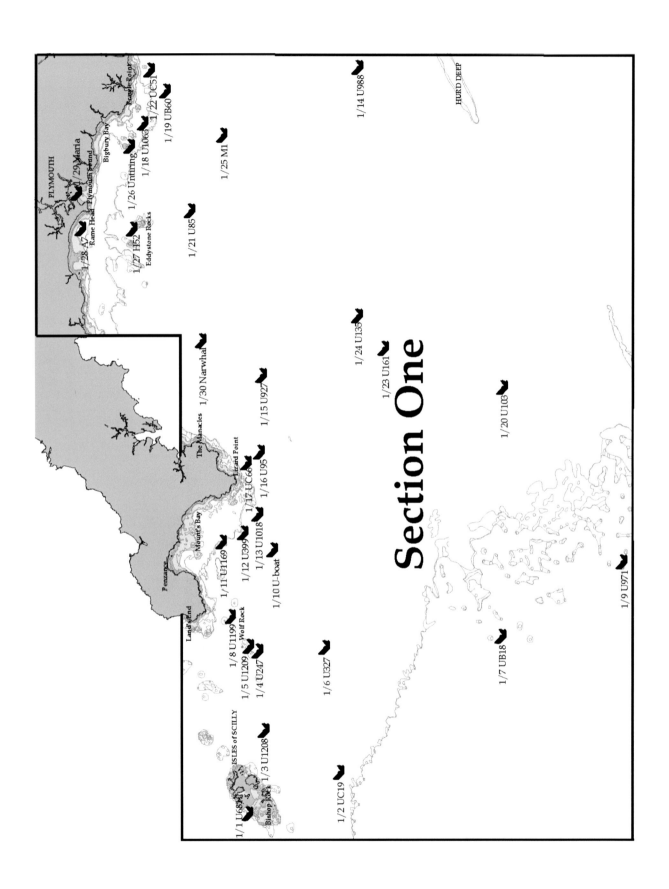

Section One

PLYMOUTH
Beacle Point
1/22 UC51
1/19 UB60
1/29 Maria
Bigbury Bay
1/18 U1063
1/26 Untiring
Plymouth Sound
1/28 A7
Rame Head
1/27 H52
Eddystone Rocks
1/21 U85
1/25 M1
1/14 U988
HURD DEEP
1/30 Narwhal
The Manacles
1/15 U927
Lizard Point
1/16 U95
1/17 UC64
1/13 U1018
1/12 U399
1/11 U1169
Mount's Bay
1/10 U-boat
Penzance
Land's End
1/8 U1199
Wolf Rock
1/5 U1209
1/4 U247
1/6 U327
1/24 U135
1/23 U161
1/20 U103
1/9 U971
1/7 UB18
ISLES of SCILLY
1/3 U1208
1/1 U681
Bishop Rock
1/2 UC19

Section 1

Submarine Wrecks of the Southwest

With at least 31 submarine wrecks to be located and explored, the Southwest section of this book is the largest. Moreover, it offers the diver and the submarine historian a very varied selection of wrecks.

As far as is known, the world's first submarine fatality took place in this area, when Mr John Day descended into the depths in 1774 in Plymouth Sound. His craft, the Maria has never been found.

In fact, Plymouth has long played a part in the development and operation of British Submarines. It is no surprise therefore that five British submarine wrecks lie in the waters of this section. Among these are two war-graves, HMS *A7* and HMS *M1*. They were both lost in peacetime accidents and, naturally made headline news at the time. In recent times, both of these wrecks have been in the newspapers again, one for being discovered, the other for sadder reasons.

Since World War One, when the U-boat first became a major threat to the survival of the British Isles, they have used this area as a major killing ground of merchant vessels. In so doing many have been lost as well. For most of World War One, the U-boats could use the Dover Straits. Therefore this area became a transit zone for operations off Ireland's south coast, the Western Approaches and elsewhere.

During World War Two many U-boats were sunk in this area, either on patrol within it, or attempting to enter the Channel through it. The Dover Straits were closed to U-boats early in the war and therefore any U-boat ordered into the Channel had to pass through the western Channel to enter and leave its designated patrol area. Of the confirmed losses, high proportions were killed here, while attempting to reach their areas of operation. The density of U-boat losses around Land's End is virtually unique. The process of locating and identifying these wrecks is far from finished.

The Southwest remains one of the least explored areas of the Channel. It is worthy of note that in the next few years, more of the submarines lost in these waters will be found. There are several interesting targets here including rare design types, submarines commanded by war criminals and Q-ship victims. These offer the experienced diver (for many of the wrecks are deep) great adventure and the ability to contribute to the process of setting straight the historical record of submarine losses.

No 1/1, *U681* – Ran Aground

Class: VIIC	**Built at:** Howaldtswerke-Hamburg
Length: 67.1m	**Displacement:** 871t
Date sunk: 10th March 1945	**How sunk:** Depth charges from US Liberator
Historic Position: 49 53N; 06 31W	**Known Position:** 49.52.47 N; 06.38.689W?
Crew losses: 11 (from 49)	**Commander:** Olzs. Werner Gebauer

U681 could be considered by some to be an unlucky U-boat. However, the fact that the majority of her crew survived her sinking could also be construed as the opposite.

Under the command of Olzs. Werner Gebauer, the type VIIC U-boat was on her first war patrol when she was lost. She had left the Norwegian base of Horten on 14th February 1945 to operate in the Channel. This was Gebauer's first patrol in command of a U-boat, although he had service experience on *U212* (also lost in the Channel, see wreck No 5/2). He was probably the most experienced crewman on board. Whether it was inexperience, or for some other reason, on 10th March 1945, while rounding the Scillies to enter the Channel, *U681* ran into Bishop Rock while running submerged at 25 metres.

In a desperate attempt to get her off the rock, much damage was done to the propellers and hull of the submarine. One of her saddle tanks had been pushed inwards creating a pressure build-up, which forced tons of diesel fuel into the U-boat. Although the bulkhead doors were shut, in only a few minutes the crew in the control room were wading in three feet of fuel. Gebauer had no option but to surface.

He planned to head for Ireland on diesel power as fast as he could make the vessel run. Internment in an Irish compound would have been better than being imprisoned in an English POW camp, and having to endure the interrogation that would obviously follow. The plan could have succeeded. However, a Liberator of 103 Squadron, US Navy, spotted *U681*. The Liberator attacked the surfaced submarine and dropped a stick of depth charges, running in from astern. Gebauer gave

U681's Commander whilst watch officer on U212 (U-Boot Archiv)

the order to abandon ship as some crewmen fired the 37mm AA gun in a vain attempt to fend off the attacking aircraft. With the U-boat severely damaged, the crew abandoned *U681*, as Lt. Field in the Liberator came in to make a second attack to ensure the U-boat's destruction.

U681 was seen to sink stern first by Lt. Field who guided the Second Escort Group to the scene, where all but 11 of the crew were rescued.

Technical divers first visited this wreck in 1999 at a depth of 90 metres. A life raft was recovered and declared to the Receiver of Wreck. At the time of writing this book, it was being conserved at the Duxford Museum. It is understood that the German authorities were keen to show that there were two sides to the conflict at sea. By the time *U681* was lost, it was a very one-sided affair.

No 1/2, *UC19* – Depth Charge Victim

Class: UCII (UC16 series)	**Built at:** Bhlom & Voss – Hamburg
Length: 49.35m	**Displacement:** 493t
Date sunk: 6th Dec 1916	**How sunk:** Explosive sweep from HMS *Ariel*
Historic Position: 49 41N; 06 30W	**Known Position:** 49.39.9N; 06 21.2W?
Crew losses: 25 (all crew lost)	**Commander:** Olzs. Alfred Nitzsche

UC19 was of the small UCII class, of which around 73 were built. Primarily designed as minelayers, this coastal type of U-boat also carried torpedoes. The UC classes operated extensively in the Channel.

UC19 left Zeebrugge on 27th November 1916 to operate in the western Channel area. Clearing the Dover Straits, she headed westward and was in her area of operation for a few days. She had accounted for several vessels previous to her loss. The last of these was thought to be the Russian sailing ship *Ans*, which was destroyed using explosives. Unfortunately for *UC19*, the P&O vessel *Kashmir* witnessed the act and immediately sent out a warning by radio. This attracted the destroyer HMS *Ariel*, under the command of Lt. Chas Blackman.

Later that day, HMS *Ariel* spotted *UC19*'s conning tower. At the same moment the U-boat spotted the destroyer and dived. HMS *Ariel* ran to the area where the U-boat had dived and dropped a depth charge, which did not explode. However, the destroyer then ran out her paravane and detonated it at around 30ft. The explosion that followed contained much oil and bubbles. In all likelihood it destroyed the U-boat right there. This was a very rare success for the explosive paravane.

Some British histories attribute the loss of this vessel to an attack by HMS *Llewellyn* on 4th December in the Dover Straits. This cannot be so, because she should have been in her operational area by then. The attack by HMS *Ariel* has also been accredited by similar sources with the destruction of *UB29* (see No 6/26). However, this U-boat is now thought to have perished in the Dover Straits on 13th December.

There is a reasonable likelihood that a U-boat will be located in the future near the historical position given here. Only then, will we be sure which submarine was destroyed during this attack. The best current information suggests that there is a possible submarine wreck at 49 39.9; 06 21.2W in a charted depth of 100m.

No 1/3, *U1208* - Lost on First Patrol

Class: VIIC	**Built at:** Schichau - Danzig
Length: 67.1m	**Displacement:** 871t
Date sunk: 24th February 1945	**How sunk:** D/Cs HMS *Duckworth* and *Rowley*
Historic Position: 49 46N; 05 47W	**Known Position:** 49 51.820N; 06 06.806W
Crew losses: 49 (all crew lost)	**Commander:** KKpt. Georg Hagene

U1208 was on its first patrol when she was sunk, in all probability in the western Channel. She sailed from Kristiansand, Norway on 14th January 1945 to operate in British coastal waters. The allies intercepted her passage report on 31st January. Nothing else is presently known about what happened to her.

The position given above was historically attributed to the sinking of *U480* on 24th February 1945.

*U1208's officers during her commissioning.
The Commander is second from left. (U-Boot Archiv)*

However, the author identified the wreck of *U480* off the Dorset coast (see wreck No4/1) in 1998.

The sinking report for the position above remained as viable as others reported in this area. The attack is known to have produced tins of dried egg, several loaves of brown bread and a Nazi forage cap. An echo sounder trace made at the time seemed to show a U-boat on the bottom. Although not conclusive, the evidence seemed to suggest that a U-boat would be found in this area.

The wreck was persistently reported as being a submarine. The last occasion was in 1988. Rumours of a ROV survey also circulated. Finally, local diver Gifford Pound confirmed this in July 2002. He describes the wreck as being a U-boat, which has been hit on the top, forward of the conning tower. Peering into the control room, Gifford reports that the interior is very silted. She is heavily netted, but the presence of anti-aircraft guns means that with great certainty we can deduce that a late World War Two U-boat lies in this position.

Dr Axel Niestlé believes now that the wreck is most probably that of *U1208*, which was almost certainly destroyed in this area in late February 1945. However, it remains possible that this could be the wreck of *U927* or *U683*, which could also have been nearby at the time.

No 1/4, *U247* – 48 Hour Hunt

Class: VIIC	**Built at:** Germaniawerft - Kiel
Length: 67.1m	**Displacement:** 871t
Date sunk: 1st September 1944	**How sunk:** D/Cs from Canadian frigates
Historic Position: 49 54N; 05 49W	**Known Position:** 49 53.9N; 05 49.7W?
Crew losses: 52 (all crew lost)	**Commander:** Olzs. Gerhard Matschulat

The sinking of *U247* shows clearly how effective the anti-submarine forces in the Channel had become by the closing years of World War Two. On 31st August 1944, at 18:45, the 9th Escort Group, which was made up of six Canadian frigates, was sweeping along the convoy route between Land's End and Hartland point, when an interesting contact was picked up. Three frigates, HMCS *Port Colbourne*, HMCS *Swansea* and HMCS *St John* stayed in the area to see if they could identify what had been found. What was to follow was a long and determined hunt for a U-boat that stood little chance of escape after she had been detected; she was *U247*.

U247 was on her second patrol and had departed from Brest on 26th August to operate in the

Channel. Her previous patrol had taken her north of Scotland, where she had sunk a fishing trawler using her anti-aircraft armament. This made her one of the last U-boats to sink a vessel by gunfire. This act can be considered to have been either extremely brave, or very foolish, because at the time the skies around the British Isles were swarming with ASW (Anti Submarine Warfare) aircraft. Either way, this incident led to the deaths of most of the trawler's crew. Survivors stated that the submarine had been firing at them as well as the vessel. This incident was played out at the Nuremberg trials in an attempt to convict Admiral Dönitz

U247's crew, note the enhanced anti-aircraft armament added to all late-war U-boats. (U-Boot Archiv)

of ordering his men to commit war crimes. Olzs. Gerhard Matschulat, *U247*'s commander was not there to testify, as we shall see.

On her second and final patrol, *U247* had just entered the Channel when she was located. At 21:15 on the same evening, HMCS *Swansea* located the target again and a single depth charge was dropped, because it was not certain whether this contact was a shoal of fish. However, HMCS *St John* saw oil bubbling up and the attack was pressed home with hedgehogs, increasing the oil patch. However, at this point, contact with the target was lost. Ordered to stay in the area, the frigates searched for the U-boat until 01:55 on 1st September, when the target was relocated and ascertained to have bottomed. Three attacks followed, during which the weather worsened to force eight gales. The difficulties this caused meant that the contact was lost.

The seabed in this area is littered with wreckage and many obstructions were located before the target was found again at 14:04. At this point, depth charges dropped opened up the U-boat and much debris came to the surface, confirming that *U247* had been destroyed. This included a certificate for the 10 millionth revolution of *U247*'s diesel engines, a door panel, clothing and other paperwork. A further attack was made to ensure *U247* had been sunk.

The wreck of *U247* was located in the 1960s and was still giving off oil. It is thought to lie at 49 53.9 N; 05 49.7W, very close to the original position and in a depth of 68 metres. At some point, its existence in this area will be confirmed by divers and the final resting place of 52 submariners will be known for sure.

No 1/5, *U1209* – Collided with Wolf Rock

Class: VIIC	**Built at:** Schichau - Danzig
Length: 67.1m	**Displacement:** 871t
Date sunk: 18th December 1944	**How sunk:** Ran aground
Historic Position: 49 55N; 05 48W	**Known Position:** Unknown?
Crew losses: 9 (from 53)	**Commander:** Olzs. Ewald Hulsenbeck

In a remarkable similar event to the loss of *U681*, *U1209* also ran into a submerged rock in the Land's End area, like so many hundreds of vessels have done since man took to the sea around Cornwall.

U1209 was also on her first patrol when she foundered. She had left the Norwegian base of

Three of the fortunate survivors of U1209 aboard HMCS Ribble, shortly after their rescue. (U-Boot Archiv)

U1209's surviving crew bury their comrades the day after the collision. (U-Boot Archiv)

Farsund on 26th November 1944 and had made the transit to the entrance to the Channel. Her orders were to patrol off Cherbourg and she must have been heading in that direction when she struck Wolf Rock on 18th December. With the boat severely damaged, she surfaced and scuttled. The crew found it hard to keep the boat afloat while they evacuated and survivors reported that three of the crew failed to emerge from the submarine as she sank. Another six drowned in the heavy seas during the next two hours.

The astonished lighthouse keeper on Wolf Rock radioed an emergency transmission, which attracted the attention of two Canadian corvettes and some British motor vessels, which managed to pluck 44 survivors from the water in a bad sea state. Olzs. Ewald Hulsenbeck was among them. However he died, along with the chief engineer Hans-Georg Claussen, probably of exposure, shortly after being rescued.

Days after the sinking of *U1209*, the German U-boat command ordered an emergency change of Enigma machine settings. This may well have been the result of the interception of the radio transmissions from the Wolf Rock lighthouse, which would not have been encoded.

The survivors reported having been treated well by the Canadians. They were allowed to bury Hulsenbeck and Claussen at sea, the following day. The interrogation of the survivors is remarked upon in the U-boats situation reports during this period. It relates that they unanimously aired their contempt for the commander, who they depicted as an "incompetent and harsh coward". Later placed in British captivity, it was not until April 1948, that the crew of *U1209* was returned to Germany. Some opted to make their homes in the UK.

In 1996, local diver Gifford Pound reported locating a U-boat at 49 57.8N;05 42.7W. However, it is not known at present whether this U-boat is *U1209*, or *U1199*. Its location being nearer to the sinking position of *U1199* means probably, that *U1209* is still to be located.

No 1/6, *U327* – Lost on First Patrol

Class: VIIC/41	**Built at:** Flenderwerft - Lübeck
Length: 67.23m	**Displacement:** 860t
Date sunk: 27th February 1945	**How sunk:** D/Cs from 2nd Escort Group
Historic Position: 49 46N; 05 47W	**Known Position:** Unknown
Crew losses: 46 (all crew lost)	**Commander:** Klt. Hans Lemcke

Like so many other U-boats of this era, *U327* failed to return from its first patrol. She had been ordered into the western Channel and was not heard from again. In 1945, the destruction of *U327* was classified as 'B' (U-boat probably sunk) at this position, following a well-executed attack by HMS *Lauban*, HMS *Loch Fada* and HMS *Wild Goose*, with all three vessels working together to locate and destroy a submerged target. This was achieved using depth charges, hedgehogs and squid.

In 1992, Dr. Axel Niestlé re-assessed this attack and credited it instead to the destruction of *U1208*. However, due to the identification by the author of *U480* off the Dorset coast, the original loss position of *U480*, which was designated as a definite kill (and has subsequently been dived and discovered to be a U-boat) had to be re-evaluated. *U1208* is now thought by Dr Niestlé to have been destroyed there (see wreck No 1/3).

This has meant that *U327* has now been re-assessed again, back in favour of this position, where she was originally thought destroyed in 1945. If this tells us anything, it shows that diving evidence is vital to making a steadfast re-assessment, because in many cases the paper trail does not contain enough evidence to warrant so many changes.

Interestingly, there is an unidentified U-boat wreck to the east (see wreck No 1/10). This may turn out to be the mysterious *U327*, or one of the other U-boats still unaccounted for, such as *U740*, *U683*, *U1055* and *U650*.

No 1/7, *UB18* - Rammed

Class: UBII (UB18 series)	**Built at:** Blohm & Voss - Hamburg
Length: 36.13m	**Displacement:** 292t
Date sunk: 9th December 1917	**How sunk:** Rammed by Trawler
Historic Position: 49 17N; 05 47W	**Known Position:** Unknown
Crew losses: 24 (all crew lost)	**Commander:** Olzs. G. Niemayer

UB18 was of the small, coastal UBII design and was the first of that class to be constructed. Commissioned in December 1915, she had been in service for nearly two years when she left Zeebrugge on 1st December to patrol in the western Channel. During her service life she had been responsible for sinking many ships, especially under the command of Otto Steinbrink, one of the aces of World War One. It is also known that *UB18* had sunk the British submarine HMS *E22* off Great Yarmouth in April 1916, while Steinbrink was in command.

On this, her last patrol, it is known that she cleared the Dover barrage, because she was seen off Start Point on 4th December by *U84*. However, her movements after that time are a little unclear. The official German history ascribed the sinking of *UB18* to being rammed. The trawler *Ben Lawer* was escorting a coal convoy in the western entrance to the channel on the early morning of 9th December when she spotted a U-boat coming to the surface. The trawler immediately rammed the submarine, catching her behind the conning tower. The U-boat submerged, or sank. In the darkness of night, it was probably difficult for

The little UB18 sets out for sea. (U-Boot Archiv)

the trawler to know specifically. However, the measure of the damage done to the submarine can be estimated by the fact that the trawler was so badly damaged that she hardly made it back to port.

The Admiralty originally thought *UB18* was lost off Start Point, although it was later agreed that the U-boat sunk there on the 17th November was *UC51* (see wreck No 1/22). However, in 2000 another U-boat of World War One vintage was found near the wreck of *UC51*. This could be *UB18*, assuming she survived being rammed here and moved back to that area. However, it is more likely to be the wreck of *UB60*.

No 1/8, *U1199* – Depth Charge Victim

Class: VIIC	**Built at:** Schichau - Danzig
Length: 67.1m	**Displacement:** 871t
Date sunk: 21st January 1945	**How sunk:** D/Cs from 14th Escort Group
Historic Position: 49 57N; 05 42W	**Known Position:** 49 57.8N; 05 42.7W?
Crew losses: 46 (from 47)	**Commander:** Klt. Rolf Nollman

Klt. Rolf Nollman of *U1199* was born in France – well, Lorraine, when it was a German province. Apart from this curio, he is also known because of his expert use of the schnorchel. On its first patrol, *U1199* conducted a 50-day stretch, operating entirely on the device - a record at the time. Many U-boat commanders distrusted it, although it was the saviour of many boats in this last period of the U-boat war. However, Nollman embraced the technology straight away and was glowing in his praises.

U1199 was sunk on its second patrol while operating in the Channel. She had left Bergen on New Year's Day, 1945 and made a successful transit to her area of operations in the Western Approaches. On the 21st January, *U1199* located the coastal convoy, TBC43 and torpedoed the 7,176 ton steam freighter, *George Hawley*. She was taken under tow, but became a total loss.

However, Nollman did not have long to savour his success. The supporting escort group hunted him down. HMS *Icarus* and HMS *Mignonette* were on hand to destroy her with depth charges. The position given for the destruction of this vessel is in a depth of around 70 metres. It therefore is quite extraordinary that one crew member was able to survive. Oblt. Friedrich Claussen was plucked from the seas over the wreck. During his initial interrogation, he gave the boat's number as 91 and the commander's name as 'Norman'. It didn't take the British long to work out that the submarine sunk was *U1199*, because they already knew she was operating in the Cornwall area.

In 1996, a local diver, Gifford Pound reported finding a U-boat at 49 57.8N;05 42.7W. The most likely identity of this wreck is Nollman's *U1199*.

No 1/9, *U971* - U-Zeppelin

Class: VIIC	**Built at:** Blohm & Voss - Hamburg
Length: 67.1m	**Displacement:** 871t
Date sunk: 24th June 1944	**How sunk:** Combined Air & Sea attacks
Historic Position: 49 01N; 05 35W	**Known Position:** 49 00.9N; 05 34.1W?
Crew losses: 1 (from 53)	**Commander:** Olzs. Walter Zeplien

Olzs. Walter Zeplien's distinctive name meant that when it came to making a pennant for his first command, *U971* the crew naturally painted a Zeppelin on the conning tower.

U971 was ordered to attack shipping in the western Channel area and left on her first patrol on 8th June 1944, two days after the Normandy Landings had begun. *U971* had been based at Kristiansand in Norway and had a long voyage around Great Britain to get to her operational area.

Operation Neptune, the allied sea effort to protect the Normandy landings was at its height. The ASW effort around the south coast of England was at its most intense at this time. Therefore, any penetration into the Channel would be a very dangerous undertaking, even for an experienced crew. Nevertheless, *U971* pressed on towards her objective with the stoicism that defines the U-boat men of the era. Even before reaching southern Ireland, *U971* had been approached by aircraft on two occasions and had had to outrun a suspicious-looking naval vessel.

U971 at her commissioning ceremony, note the difference between the naval and civilian salute of the time. (U-Boot Archiv)

However, it was on 20th June that things started to go wrong. On that day, she survived a scrape with a Wellington. The boat was badly damaged, with three torpedo tubes out of action. On 21st June she was attacked twice, once by a Sunderland and then by a Halifax, again shaking up the boat. At this point, Zeplien changed course and headed toward the Brittany coast, thinking that air defences in this area would be lighter. By now, *U971* had only two functioning torpedo tubes. He attempted to use these on 24th June, when two warships were sighted. However, the torpedoes were damaged and did not run correctly.

By now, continuing the patrol had become pointless, and Zeplien decided to make for Brest, which was some 60 miles away. So at 07:30 on 24th June he surfaced and began to make the run for safety. However, it was only 20 minutes before the first aircraft appeared, forcing the U-boat under. One hour later the batteries failed. The crew was issued with potash and went to their bunks as the boat waited for nightfall to surface and try the run to Brest again. Within the hour though, depth charges began raining down. These continued all day. It seems that Zeplien attempted to find out what was happening by coming to periscope depth at around 15:45. Unfortunately, the periscope was spotted and immediately attacked by a Liberator, which dropped smoke when the U-boat dived. This led the Escort Group, consisting of the British destroyer HMS *Eskimo* and the Canadian destroyer, HMCS *Haida* right to the bottomed submarine. The game was up. From 16:30 to 18:30 the depth charges came down again, steadily closing on the hapless U-boat. The salvo dropped at 18:25 was the first to damage her. It took out the starboard diesel and because there was no battery power, underwater movement was impossible. Water began to enter the pressure hull. After all the secret papers and gear had been destroyed, the crew was issued with a bottle of beer each. This was drunk while they stood knee-deep in water. Zeplien thanked them for their loyalty then blew the tanks with the last of the air aboard and *U971* rushed to the surface.

The destroyers heard the sound of the tanks being filled and knew the U-boat was about to breach. As the bows of the submarine broke the surface, Oerlikon fire was commenced, ripping into the U-boat's hull. This was suspended, once it was obvious that the crew were abandoning her. Whalers were lowered in an attempt to get aboard the submarine before she sank, but this was unsuccessful. One member of Zeplien's crew had been killed and 26 injured as they escaped the doomed submarine. They waited for rescue, each sitting in a one-man life raft. The life rafts later became prized trophies of war by HMCS *Haida's* crew. The prisoners of war were later landed at Plymouth. They had, at least, survived the war.

The credit for sinking *U971* was shared between the destroyers and the Liberator 0/311. The aircraft was from a Czech squadron operating as the Cork Air/Sea Patrol.

U971's commader, Walter Zeplien (U-Boot Archiv)

There is a charted wreck at 49 00.9;05 34.1W. Although there is no evidence that this is a submarine, its location is but half a mile from where *U971* was finally sunk. In a general depth of 102 metres and in a very remote location, a very determined team of divers would be needed to identify this one.

No 1/10, Unidentified Submarine Wreck

Class: U-boat	**Built at:** Unknown
Length: Unknown	**Displacement:** Unknown
Date sunk: Unknown	**How sunk:** Unknown
Historic Position: N/A	**Known Position:** 49 51.25N;05 29.86W
Crew losses: Unknown	**Commander:** Unknown

In 1976, the Risdon Beazley salvage company reported a submarine wreck at the location given above. Local diver Gifford Pound, who dived on the wreck site in 1997, confirmed this. The wreck conforms to being that of a U-boat. The outer casing has deteriorated and the pressure hull can be seen quite clearly. The cladding around the conning tower is gone and the periscope standards are clearly visible.

As to the identity of this wreck? Well, sadly there are many possible candidates. Aside from the submarines that may have been sunk in the channel, (see Appendix 2) there are a number of historic sinking positions that have not yielded a wreck as of yet. Possible candidates include *U1169* and *UC66* among many others. However, the presence of ferrous propellers points to a late World War Two U-boat.

Further examination of this site could help to reduce the number of possible candidates. However, the wreck lies in 80 metres, in an area of poor visibility, so this is not for the faint-hearted.

No 1/11, *U1169* – A Case of Mistaken Identity

Class: VIIC/41	**Built at:** Dandier Weft - Dazing
Length: 67.23m	**Displacement:** 860t
Date sunk: 29th March 1945	**How sunk:** D/Cs HMS *Duckworth*
Historic Position: 49 58N; 05 25W	**Known Position:** Unknown
Crew losses: 49 (all crew lost)	**Commander:** Olzs. Heinz Goldbeck

The original sinking location allocated to *U1169* is not in the Channel. It is at 52 03;05 53W and it was originally claimed that she was mined. The original sinking location for *U246* was always given at the historical position given in the box above (now thought to be *U1169*). However, due to the ongoing work of Dr. Axel Niestlé, the pre-eminent historian of World War Two U-boat losses, these original assessments have been changed.

On 20th April 1945, the destroyers HMS *Hesperus* and HMS *Havelock* were credited with the destruction of *U242* at 53 42;04 53W. However the evidence they supplied for the destruction of the U-boat included personal belongings for the crew of *U246*. Niestlé noticed this in 1991, and the official record was altered. But if she wasn't *U246*, what was sunk at 49 58;05 25W? The answer seems to be *U1169*, which was supposed to be operating in the Channel and not near 52 03;05 53W, the mining position. The U-boat lost at that position is now thought to be *U242*. This is one of many cases of mistaken identity that Dr. Niestlé has corrected.

On the bridge of U1169, note the binoculars mounted on the UZO pillar. These were used for surface firing, suggesting this photo was taken during the boat's working-up. (U-Boot Archiv)

The famous frigate, HMS *Duckworth*, carried out the attack that sank the U-boat that is now thought to be *U1169*. The frigate recorded a trace of an object 24 feet high on the bottom, following a successful hedgehog attack. However, bad weather prevented further action. At the time, the attack by HMS *Duckworth* was first assessed, it was given a 'B' rating, meaning possible kill, but not sufficient evidence for positive identification.

However, as yet there is little evidence to suggest that divers in this area have located a U-boat near the sinking position. Indeed the position marked on the Admiralty chart of the area as possibly a submarine has now been made 'position approximate'. Some other U-boat wrecks have shown up nearby, but they tend to better fit being the wrecks of *U399* and *U1018*. This is because there were survivors from these two, ensuring that their wrecks are definitely in the area. It is quite possible the 'attack' on *U1169* was actually an attack on the wrecks of these other two U-boats.

Either way, Heinz Goldbeck and his brave crew disappeared after 8th March 1945. It was its first patrol. An unlucky boat, three crew members had been killed during training.

No 1/12, *U399* – Sunk the SS James Eagan Layne

Class: VIIC	**Built at:** Howaldtswerke - Kiel
Length: 67.1m	**Displacement:** 871t
Date sunk: 26th March 1945	**How sunk:** Hedgehogs from HMS *Duckworth*
Historic Position: 49 56N; 05 22W	**Known Position:** 49 56.4N; 05 22.5W
Crew losses: 46 (from 47)	**Commander:** Olzs. Heinz Buhse

Like so many of the U-boats lost during this period of World War Two, *U399* was on its first patrol when she was destroyed. She had sailed from Horten in Norway on 26th February. After entering the Channel, *U399* was initially successful in her operations.

On 21st March 1945 she attacked and critically damaged the Liberty Ship, *James Eagan Layne*. This is one of the most popular dive sites in the UK and was the first wreck the author ever dived! The reason why *U399* was not immediately located and destroyed, as so many other U-boats were after attacking convoys in this period of the war, was that she followed the *James Eagan Layne* as she foundered and lay next to the wreck for over 30 hours before continuing her patrol. While this may have inevitably given the U-boat some confidence, her next attack was not to be so successful.

On the bridge of U399, note the large insulators on the jumper wire and the UZO mounting. (U-Boot Archiv)

On 26th March *U399* attacked convoy No. BTC 108 and put a torpedo into the Dutch motor-coaster *Pacific* of 362 tons. Within 15 minutes, the U-boat was to be destroyed. Three frigates from the 3rd Escort Group were trailing the convoy and now moved in for the kill. While HMS *Rowley* and HMS *Essington* dropped charges to the landward and seaward respectively (to encourage the U-boat to stay in its original area), HMS *Duckworth* entered the attack area. She quickly obtained a good sonar contact, which showed the submarine moving across the tide at a depth of 60 metres. The frigate destroyed the *U399* with a single hedgehog attack.

A massive air bubble rose from the wrecked submarine, inside which there were two men. One was pulled from the sea alive. Subsequently, the wreck was subject to 'can opening' by depth charges and hedgehogs, until sufficient evidence of a kill was established.

There is a known U-boat wreck at 49 56.4N; 05 22.5W. In all likelihood, it is the wreckage of *U399*. Local diver, Gifford Pound, has reported that this wreck is quite intact. However, *U1018* was lost nearby, so this could be her. It would mean that the wreck at 49 56.7N; 05 20.2W could be *U399*. Either way, the wreck of *U1169*, if she was destroyed around these parts, is still to be found (see No 1/11).

No 1/13, *U1018* – Destroyed by Squid

Class: VIIC/41	**Built at:** Blohm & Voss - Hamburg
Length: 67.23m	**Displacement:** 860t
Date sunk: 27th February 1945	**How sunk:** Squid attack from HMS *Loch Fada*
Historic Position: 49 56N; 05 20W	**Known Position:** 49 56.7N; 05 20.2W
Crew losses: 51 (from 53)	**Commander:** Klt. Walter Burmeister

Divers who have been on excursions from Plymouth may well have dived on the wreck of the *Persier*. It is a popular dive in the area. It was sunk by *U1018* while she was on its first and last patrol. Within 16 days of this success, all but two of *U1018*'s crew were dead and the submarine had joined the *Persier* on the bottom of the Channel.

U1018 had left its Norwegian base of Horten on 21st January 1945. She had passed along the western side of Great Britain and began operations in the Western Approaches in mid-February. She sank the *Persier* on 11th and proceeded westward.

At 10:09 on 27th February, a ship in convoy BTC81 exploded after being hit by a torpedo. The 1,317- ton steam freighter, *Corvus* was lost. However, somewhere ahead of the convoy was a powerful division of the 2nd Escort Group that turned to find the U-boat, as did the 14th Escort Group, which had been supporting a neighbouring convoy. Between them, they employed six ships to hunt down the raider. There was little chance of escape for its hapless crew.

At 11:24 a squid attack by HMS *Loch Fada* was carried out. As the ship passed over the launch point, a bubble appeared with five struggling men in it. Two of them were picked up and were to be the only survivors from *U1018*. The others were not seen again. Further attacks were carried out on the wreck site, but little more came to the surface.

There is a known U-boat wreck at the position given above. It was dived on and investigated by local diver Gifford Pound. It lies in 60 metres of water and has been a

U1018 at her commissioning, note the camouflage-netting overhead intended to hide her from allied aircraft. (U-Boot Archiv)

charted wreck for many years. Gifford reports that this wreck is very badly damaged. It is possible to swim under her and look up through the conning tower.

No 1/14, *U988* – Sunk After a Successful Patrol

Class: VIIC	**Built at:** Blohm & Voss - Hamburg
Length: 67.1m	**Displacement:** 871t
Date sunk: 29th June 1944	**How sunk:** Combined Air and Sea Attack
Historic Position: 49 37N; 03 41W	**Known Position:** 49 36.39N; 03 39 94W?
Crew losses: 50 (all crew lost)	**Commander:** Olzs. Erich Dobberstein

During the training and working-up phase of the life of this U-boat, it was sadly in a collision with *U983*, which sank, killing five of its crew. This unlucky event was not the last to befall *U988*. Her young commander, Olzs. Erich Dobberstein, was to be given a job of immense difficulty on his first and only patrol. His initial successes were to end in the destruction of the U-boat.

On 22nd May 1944 *U988* left Norway for a war patrol. Initially, this was to be in the North Atlantic. She made her passage report on 6th June, stating she had arrived on station. However, on 8th June, she was ordered into the Channel. D-Day two days before had led U-boat command to alter *U988*'s orders. At this time allied ASW forces were at their most concentrated in the Channel, making it an extremely dangerous place for a U-boat to operate.

At the time, the Admiralty attempted to piece together what happened to *U988* after she was sent to the Channel. It seemed as if she got into her operational area in the Baie de Seine and was successful in fatally damaging the Corvette HMS *Pink* on 27th June and the steamer *Maid of Orleans* on 29th. *U988* was also credited with the destruction of the freighter *Empire Portia* from convoy FMT22 on 29th June. However, these losses have not been firmly attributed to *U988*, because she did not return from this patrol to make a report.

It was assumed that while making her way to Lorient, where she was ordered to go at the end of her patrol, a Liberator of 224 Squadron damaged her, while south of Start Point on 29th June. The Liberator guided the escorts HMS *Dommet*, HMS *Essington*, HMS *Cooke* and HMS *Duckworth* to the area, where in the morning of 30th June, they attacked a target and were rewarded with 'some evidence of destruction on the surface'. However, when assessed at the end of the war, this sinking was classified as 'B' grade – U-boat possibly sunk, but not enough evidence for confirmed kill.

The crew of U988 aboard the Blohm & Voss depot ship in Hamburg. Her Commander is sitting between the two civilians. (U-Boot Archiv)

It is quite possible that the wreck of *U988* lies elsewhere. She would be an excellent candidate to be one of the two unidentified VIICs the author's diving team found in the area north of the Baie de Seine. In fact, their positions are very near where *Maid of Orleans* and HMS *Pink* were attacked, (see Nos 5/7 and 5/8).

However, there is a charted wreck designated as *U988* at 49 36.39;03 39 94W. The reports of what it may be are confused. She was located during the 59 - day search for HMS *Affray* in 1951, although it appears that she was not examined. Until divers investigate this position, in a depth of 70 metres, the mystery surrounding *U988* will continue. Alternatively, this could be the final resting place of *U441*.

Erich Dobberstein was only 25 years old when *U988* was destroyed with all hands.

No 1/15, *U927* - Air Victim?

Class: VIIC	**Built at:** AG Neptun - Rostock
Length: 67.1m	**Displacement:** 871t
Date sunk: 24th February 1945	**How sunk:** Air attack by Warwick
Historic Position: 49 54N; 04 45W	**Known Position:** Unknown
Crew losses: 47 (all crew lost)	**Commander:** Klt. Jurgen Ebert

Klt. Ebert takes command of the new U927. (U-Boot Archiv)

Klt. Jurgen Ebert was a new U-boat commander taking a new crew on an operational patrol for the fist time, when *U927* slipped its mooring at Kristiansand, Norway on 31st January 1945. This was to be the U-boat's only patrol. At present, it is thought that *U927* made it into the Channel and was operating there into late February.

The official historical analysis of the sinking of *U927* shows that she was lost southeast of Falmouth. On the evening of 24th February 1945, a Leigh-Light equipped Warwick (K) of 179 Squadron detected the schnorchel head of a U-boat by radar. Piloted by Flt. Lt. Anthony G. Brownsill, the Warwick picked out the schnorchel using the Leigh-Light and ran in to attack at an altitude of 75 feet. A perfect straddle was made with six depth charges. Brownsill was later awarded the DFC for this attack.

Partly because no more was ever heard from the submarine, Brownsill was credited with sinking her, although it was only allocated 'B' classification. This meant that she was 'probably' sunk, but no evidence of a kill was produced.

From the point of view of divers, the question is, is she really there? The answer at the moment seems to be that this is very unlikely, although not impossible. The area around the potential wreck site was surveyed in 1973 and after an extensive search no wreck was located. With no other evidence available at the moment, the presence of the wreck of *U927* at this location must be considered suspect.

No 1/16, *U95* – Or *U93*?

Class: MS (*U93* series)	**Built at:** Germaniawerft - Kiel
Length: 71.55m	**Displacement:** 1000t
Date sunk: 7th Jan 1918	**How sunk:** Rammed by SS *Braeneil*
Historic Position: 49 57N; 05 09W	**Known Position:** Unknown
Crew losses: 43 (all crew lost)	**Commander:** Klt. A. Prinz

The large ocean-going U95 at sea. (U-Boot Archiv)

In the early hours of 7th January 1918, the 424-ton steamer *Braeneil* was making for Rouen, from Swansea. She had just passed the Lizard at 04:15 when she sighted a surfaced submarine 100 yards in front of her. She headed straight for her and rammed her ahead of the conning tower, sending her into the deep for the last time. To ensure the submarine was totally wrecked, SS *Braeneil* then reversed over the doomed vessel. As she passed over the spot where the submarine had once been, 'foreign' voices were heard from the water – clear evidence of a U-boat sinking.

The Admiralty thought so, and awarded £1,000 to the crew of the steamer and the captain was given the DSC.

Although, while it is likely that a submarine was indeed sunk at this location, its identity seems to have become confused as historians in the years that followed attempted to reconcile anti-submarine attacks with U-boat losses. German historians have nearly always claimed that this sinking accounted for *U95*. However, most British sources have claimed that *U93* (See Appendix 1) was lost here. While this could be explained as a simple typing (or handwriting) error somewhere in the past, it is known that both of these submarines were at sea at this time, having left port within a day of each other.

The most detailed survey of U-boat losses in World War One probably lies in R.M. Grants book 'U-Boat Intelligence'. The loss register in this book states the submarine lost here was *U95*. However, in his previous work 'U-Boats Destroyed', he claimed she was *U93*. It is not clear why he reversed the identities of these losses. It is certainly true that both U-boats were operational in the Channel. *U95* had made a safe passage report and *U93* apparently exchanged recognition signals with *UC17* on 5th January.

It is interesting to note that the position given for the SS *Braeneil's* ramming in most official U-boat histories actually plots on land at 49 59;05 12W! The alternative British position given above is in the right area.

Until either *U93* or *U95* is located and positively identified, the mystery of which U-boat was sunk is likely to remain unsolved as there appears to be little fresh evidence for historians to consider.

No 1/17, *UC66* – Sunk by a Trawler?

Class: UCII (UC65 series)	**Built at:** Blohm & Voss - Hamburg
Length: 50.35m	**Displacement:** 508t
Date sunk: 12th June 1917	**How sunk:** D/C from Trawler *Sea King*
Historic Position: 49 56N; 05 10W	**Known Position:** Unknown
Crew losses: 23 (all crew lost)	**Commander:** Olzs. Herbert Pustkuchen

The minelayer *UC66* left Zeebrugge on 22nd May 1917 to lay mines off Swansea and Milford Haven. Nothing more was ever heard of her. Furthermore, it is thought that she did not lay her mines in the areas she was ordered to.

The Admiralty was certain that *UC66* had made it through the Dover barrage and was operating for a time in the Channel. She is supposed to have sunk ships there during late May.

The official sinking of this U-boat has always been attributed to the trawler *Sea King*, under the command of Lt. Godfrey Herbert. His vessel had been fitted with a hydrophone, so that she could drift, engines off, and listen for U-boats running submerged, or laying mines.

UC66 in port, note the external torpedo tube on the casing next to her mine chutes. (U-Boot Archiv)

The Navy was aware that U-boats used the southern point of the Lizard as a convenient resting area, where they could lie in wait for unescorted merchant ships entering the Channel. *Sea King* had been assigned to patrol this area and in an attempt to stir-up any submerged U-boats, a depth charge was dropped randomly and was rewarded with a surfacing U-boat. This was promptly attacked as she dived and was depth-charged. The resultant explosion was thought to have ignited the submarine's mines, destroying her.

Although this attack was in all likelihood a well-carried-out affair, no U-boat has been found at this location, although it could be that she has yet to be located. Importantly, it is interesting to note that *UC66* would have been expected back at base by 8th June. This sinking on 12th June seems improbable when this is considered. The Admiralty noted this in its monthly anti-submarine reports at the time and gave four alternative sinking positions, as well as the one noted above.

Her commander, Herbert Pustkuchen had been in command of *UB29* when she had torpedoed the cross-Channel packet *Sussex* on 24th March 1916. Although the ship reached port, 25 Americans had been killed. This incident, among others led to the abandonment of unrestricted submarine warfare for the second time.

Some sources also say that *UC66* had previously sunk the White Star Liner, *Afric,* south of Plymouth. It is also interesting to note that in April 1917, she survived an attack by the British submarine HMS *D3* (see wreck No 5/14).

No 1/18, *U1063* – Destroyed by Squid

Class: VIIC/41	**Built at:** Germaniawerft - Kiel
Length: 67.23m	**Displacement:** 860t
Date sunk: 16th April 1945	**How sunk:** Squid & D/Cs of HMS *Loch Killin*
Historic Position: 50 08N; 03 52W	**Known Position:** 50 08.94N; 03 53.47
Crew losses: 29 (from 46)	**Commander:** Klt. H Stephan

The destruction of *U1063* is a perfect example of the type of U-boat kill that guarantees the presence of a wreck to dive on. This is because there were survivors from the sinking. The assumption has always been made that the crew of a submarine will not evacuate, until they absolutely have to. In these cases, there is always a wreck to locate and explore.

HMS Loch Killin. (U-Boot Archiv)

U1063 was a newly-commissioned type VIIC/41. This variant of the VIIC workhorse of the U-boat fleet was slightly longer, but benefited from lighter equipment and a hardened pressure hull, giving deeper diving depths. *U1063* was on her first patrol when she was destroyed. She had left her base of Horten in Norway on 11th March 1945 to patrol in the Channel. These orders were altered, giving *U1063* a patrol area to the south of Ireland, with the discretion to approach more dangerous locations if conditions seemed favourable. This is quite probably why *U1063* was sunk off the Devon coast. If Karl-Heinz Stephan had known that 54 percent of all the U-boats at sea in April 1945 were to be destroyed, he may have had second thoughts.

On April 16th *U1063* was attempting to make a fix of her position by periscope when she was detected. Unfortunately, she was too near the coastal convoy TBC128, southwest of Salcombe. The experienced frigate HMS *Loch Killin* detected her schnorchel and periscope by radar and ran in to make an attack with Squid. The third wave brought the U-boat to the surface. HMS *Loch Killin* raked *U1063* with gunfire as the crew abandoned the submarine. This resulted in only seventeen of the crew being plucked from the water, of which six were wounded. The commander was not among the living. Under interrogation, the survivors questioned Stephan's order to abandon ship, because they did not think the damage to the submarine warranted it.

The survivors of U1063 are brought ashore blindfolded. (U-Boot Archiv)

U1063 makes an excellent dive today. Lying in a general depth of 58 metres, local diver Tony Hilgrove describes her as being generally intact. She has a list of 45 degrees to starboard and some hatches are open. Remarkably, Tony reports that the sky observation (search) periscope and schnorchel are in the raised position, as they were when *U1063* was detected. The only major blast hole is in the bows, where it is possible to peer into the forward torpedo room.

No 1/19, WW1 U-boat - *UB60*?

Class: UBIII?	**Built at:** Unknown
Length: Unknown	**Displacement:** Unknown
Date sunk: Uncertain	**How sunk:** On tow or mined?
Historic Position: Start Point	**Known Position:** 50 08.01N; 03 47.73W
Crew losses: assume all	**Commander:** Unknown

During the summer of 2000, a group of divers from Salcombe, led by Bill Reid, an experienced Salcombe diver, located a submarine wreck at the location given above. It has been identified as being of World War One vintage by the presence of a deck gun. WW2 U-boats did not carry them in the Channel, so it is an easy way to tell which era a U-boat is from. The following day the diving team found another, which has been identified by the author as *UC51*.

There is a distinct possibility that the wreck could be *UB60*, lost on tow after World War One. *UB60* was commissioned on 6th June 1917 and was used exclusively as a training boat throughout World War One. She surrendered on 26th November 1918 and was transferred to Britain for disposal. Being in a reasonable condition, she was placed on the "for sale list" by the Admiralty. It appears she was on her way to the breakers when she foundered off Start Point on 12th June 1919.

It is known that between 5th and 11th November 1917, 680 deep mines were laid to the south of Start Point as a U-boat trap. This trap accounted for *UC51* (see No. 1/22) and could also have accounted for a wartime loss, if the wreck turns out not to be *UB60*.

The Admiralty originally believed the U-boat sunk off Start Point was *UB18*. However, a sea-boot with the name Metzger was pulled from the water. Ewald Metzger was a crewman aboard *UC51*. *UB18* was seen off Start Point by *U84* on 4th December and then nothing more was ever heard of her. At present there is another plausible explanation for her loss (see No 1/7). However, it is possible that *UB18* was lost here instead.

An alternative possibility lies in the depth-charge attack made 2.5 miles south of Prawle Point on 20th August 1917 by the trawler *Lois*. Oil did come to the surface and a wreck was snagged at this location, although the Admiralty was not certain at the time that a U-boat had been destroyed.

For other U-boats thought to have been lost in the Channel, see Appendices 1 and 2.

No 1/20, *U103* - Sunk by a Leviathan

Class: MS (U99 series)	**Built at:** AG Weser - Bremen
Length: 67.6m	**Displacement:** 952t
Date sunk: 12th May 1918	**How sunk:** Collision with SS *Olympic*
Historic Position: 49 16N; 04 51W	**Known Position:** Unknown
Crew losses: 9 (from 44)	**Commander:** Klt. Claus Rücker

The story of the sinking of *U103* is one of the most interesting submarine losses of all time. It is utterly unique, being the only time in the history of submarine warfare up to that date that a U-boat had succumbed to a passenger liner. The liner in question was none other than the sister-ship of the SS *Titanic*. Her other sister, HMHS *Britannic* had been sunk by mines laid by *U73* in 1916, but revenge was to be exacted here.

SS *Olympic* was operating as a troopship, bringing American doughboys over from the US to the trenches in France. US destroyers based in Ireland were escorting her, when in the early hours of 12th May 1918 she sighted a surfaced U-boat 500 yards ahead. Gunners aboard the White Star liner promptly opened fire. The massive ship turned to ram, as the submarine immediately crash-dived to 30 metres and turned to a parallel course. However, almost immediately afterwards, the submarine collided with *Olympic*.

The large ocean-going U103 - note the two deck-guns. (U-Boot Archiv)

The huge liner had struck the U-boat abaft the conning tower and the suction from her propellers drew the submarine towards them. Seconds later *Olympic's* port side propeller sliced through the pressure hull, critically damaging the U-boat. Tanks were blown and the crew of the U-boat scuttled and abandoned their vessel.

The *Olympic* hardly stopped to see the result of her handiwork, but continued on to Cherbourg. However, the US destroyer *Davis* homed in on a flare and was rewarded with the site of a sinking submarine, surrounded by its crew attempting to save themselves. The destroyer was able to pick up 31 survivors. The U-boat turned out to be *U103*, under the command of Klt. Claus Rücker.

Under interrogation, it transpired that the U-boat had manoeuvred into a firing position and was preparing to torpedo the *Olympic* when, it seems the crew could not flood the two stern torpedo tubes. While attempting to redress this problem, *U103* was spotted and fired upon, forcing her to dive.

Although the *Olympic* suffered superficial damage to her bows, it was likely that the damage that crippled the U-boat came from her enormous port side propeller, into which the submarine had been drawn, while submerged. This was of particular interest to the Admiralty, because *Olympic* had been involved in a collision with the cruiser HMS *Hawke* in 1911. That incident was thought to have been caused by the suction from the liner's propellers. SS *Olympic* was also to collide with the Nantucket lightship in 1934, sending her to the bottom of the Atlantic Ocean with its entire crew. In 1914, the *Olympic* had also been on hand to attempt to rescue the battleship HMS *Audacious*, after she had been mined off Lough Swilly.

Klt. Claus Rücker was on the Admiralty's wanted list. In 1917 he had sunk the fishing vessel *Victoria*. The crew was allegedly massacred for resisting attack.

Of more interest is the state of mind of the commander at this stage of the war. Rücker was a seasoned veteran of the U-boat campaign. He had been a serving commander since its outbreak and the accounts of survivors from *U103* tend to show that the signs of stress were beginning to show on him. He had become a nervous and irritable individual, often

The bows of Olympic showing the damage she sustained ramming U103. (Simon Mills)

short-tempered and then regretful. While his state of mind was known, it appears as if he had been given an extended time in command in order to win the 'Pour le Mérite', which he would have been close to, having sunk in excess of 200,000 tons of shipping.

From a historical perspective, *U103* remains one of the unique stories of U-boat losses during World War One.

No 1/21, *U85* - Q-ship Victim

Class: MS (U81 series)	**Built at:** Germaniawerft - Kiel
Length: 70.06m	**Displacement:** 946t
Date sunk: 12th March 1917	**How sunk:** Gunfire from Q-ship *Privet*
Historic Position: 50 02N; 04 13W	**Known Position:** 50 02.47N; 04 06.85W?
Crew losses: 38 (all crew lost)	**Commander:** Klt W. Petz

On 12th March 1917, *U85* fell victim to the Q-ship *Privet*. Until the adoption of the convoy system, Q-ships were one of the only ways the Royal Navy was able to bring gunfire to bear on surfaced U-boats. Q-ships were usually merchant vessels that had been taken over by the Admiralty. They were then armed with any combination of guns, depth charges and torpedoes that could be hidden from view behind the innocuous-looking items usually associated with innocent-looking merchant vessels. Their crews were all drawn from naval service, but dressed to look like merchant seamen, some even as women.

Q-ships deliberately sailed through areas where there was known U-boat activity in attempts to lure U-boats into making attacks on them. Once under fire, smoke machines were used to make it look as if the 'merchant' vessel was damaged. A 'panic party', specially trained to mimic an inexperienced

U85's conning tower. Note the helm, a feature of World War One-era U-boats. (U-Boot Archiv)

and undisciplined merchant crew would then descend into the lifeboat (sometimes over-turning one by 'accident' to keep up the ruse) and row away from the ship. This was done in the hope that the U-boat would then close on the stricken vessel to identify her and speak to the ship's 'master' in the lifeboat.

Meanwhile the Q-ship's commander, gun and torpedo crews crouched, hidden behind false facades, waiting their chance to surprise the seemingly victorious submarine. Timing was critical, because it only took a few seconds for a U-boat to crash-dive. She could then simply torpedo the Q-ship into oblivion. The shorter the range - the greater the accuracy. Hence, the greater the chance of destroying the submarine. When the Q-ship commander felt the time was right, the false gun coverings fell away, the White Ensign ran up the mast and the Q-ship's gun crews opened fire, hopefully peppering the submarine and sending her to the bottom.

Q-ships destroyed at least 11 U-boats during World War One. Of course, once the Germans knew of the existence of these vessels, then U-boat commanders became much more cautious when approaching innocent-looking merchant ships, often torpedoing them without warning or firing at them at long range, until they were totally destroyed. To ask a naval crew to remain hidden while their vessel is torn apart by torpedo and shellfire, is the unique feature of these vessels. It is no wonder that the successful commanders, men like Gordon Campbell and F. H. Grenfell, became national heroes.

The Q-ship *Privet* was a smallish steamer of 803 tons. She was steaming from Land's End to Alderney on 12th March 1917 when a U-boat attacked her. A torpedo passed underneath her and presently the submarine surfaced and began to fire accurately at her from long range. One round exploded among the 'panic party' causing several casualties, another destroyed *Privet's* steering gear. Shells punctured *Privet's* hull in several places and she was compelled to radio an SOS signal. However, the U-boat had now closed to a range where the Q-ship could surprise her and she opened fire with two of her 12-pounders, striking the submarine in the conning tower area on at least three occasions. The U-boat crash-dived, but it was too late, the fragile craft was seen to attempt to rise and then slide back underwater, stern first. There were no survivors. Lt. Cmdr. Matheson was awarded the DSO in this action and *Privet's* crew received a bounty of £1,000.

However, *Privet* was so badly damaged that she too sank in Cawsands Bay, while being towed into Plymouth. She was raised and re-commissioned. She claimed *U34*, the last Q-ship victim of the war, two days before the Armistice, although some sources doubt that the U-boat was destroyed on that occasion.

R.M. Grant has alternatively given the position of this attack as 49 52;03 20W. Although, at present no submarine matching the description of *U85* has been found at either location. The wreck at 50 02.47N 04 06.85W is reputed to be the ill-fated *U85*.

No 1/22, *UC51* - Mine Victim

Class: UCII (UC49 series)	**Built at:** Germaniawerft - Kiel
Length: 52.69m	**Displacement:** 511t
Date sunk: 17th November 1917	**How sunk:** Mined
Historic Position: 50 08N; 03 42W	**Known Position:** 50 11.52N; 04 17.18W
Crew losses: 29 (all crew lost)	**Commander:** Olzs. H. Galster

UC53 at sea, (UC51 was identical) - note the raised forward section that incorporated her mine chutes. (U-Boot Archiv)

Ernst Sprenger, on the left, died on UC51. His brother Karl, on the right served on U101 and survived the war. (H. J. Spornhauer)

Between 5th and 11th November 1917, 680 deep mines had been laid south of Start Point, as a U-boat trap. She did not have to wait long for its first victim. On 17th November, the trawler *Lois*, patrolling around the minefield witnessed a huge explosion, followed by the sight of a U-boat struggling to surface, but wallowing and then rolling over and sinking.

Then, a mine appeared on the surface, which was promptly destroyed. Oil and other debris also began to float around the trawler. Pieces of wood, human entrails and a sea-boot were also seen. The name inside the boot was read as 'Meegzer', but turned out to be from Ewald Metzger, a crew member of *UC51*.

This wreck was located in July 2000 by a diving team led by Bill Reid, who has dived the waters around Salcombe for many years. The author visited the site in August of the same year and confirmed that the wreck is of a UCII-class submarine lying mostly intact in 68 metres. She is a superb example of this class of vessel, with the only damage being to her stern, where she clearly detonated a mine. There is a net-cutter on her bows and alarmingly, her mine chutes are still full! It is clear therefore, that *UC51* was on her way to complete a mission when the very weapon she was attempting to deploy against her enemy destroyed her.

In a rare co-incidence, a week after the dive, the author was contacted by one of the crew's (Ernst Sprenger) great-nephews, Hans Spornhauer, inquiring as to whether we had found *UC51* during the course of the research which makes up this book. The author was able to confirm this and to swap some information and photographs. Ernst Sprenger had been at his sister's wedding the day before *UC51* left on her last patrol. Ernst's brother, Karl (seen on the right in the previous photo) was also serving in U-boats. He survived and died in 1972. Such are the fortunes of war.

No 1/23, *U161* - Unwanted War-Prize

Class: MS (U160 series)	**Built at:** Bremer Vulcan & Schiffbau, Bremen
Length: 71.55m	**Displacement:** 1002t
Date sunk: 30th June 1921	**How sunk:** Dumped
Historic Position: 49 33.7N; 04 42.5W	**Known Position:** 49 34.397N; 04 46.305W
Crew losses: None	**Commander:** None

The large U161 seen in 1918. (U-Boot Archiv)

U161 was a brand-new submarine when she surrendered to Britain on 20th November 1918. One of the latest and largest classes of U-boat built in World War One, she was an example of just how far submarine design advanced during the war period. Her construction was a precursor to the successful Type IX series of the Second World War.

As a prize of war, *U161* was put on Britain's for sale list in 1918 and she was laid up, awaiting a buyer. However, by the summer of 1921, the Admiralty seemed keen to finally get rid of the surrendered submarines still in its possession. There seems to have been an agreement that all the surrendered German submarines were to be destroyed, or scrapped after the war. Nearly three years had passed since the end of hostilities. So in a precursor to Operation Deadlight at the end of the Second World War, the surviving U-boats were taken out to sea and unceremoniously dumped in deep water.

This was the fate of *U161*. On 30th June, her rusting hulk was towed out to the position given above and deliberately sunk. She was one of at least nine U-boats disposed of in this way in the Channel during July 1921.

In 1991, a wreck was located at 49 34.397N;04 46.305W. It appears as if this could turn out to be *U161*.

No 1/24, *U135* - Unwanted War-Prize

Class: U-ship Project 42 (U135 series)	**Built at:** Kaiserliche Werft - Danzig
Length: 83.5m	**Displacement:** 1534t
Date sunk: 30th June 1921	**How sunk:** Dumped
Historic Position: 49 38.5N; 04 33.0W	**Known Position:** Unknown
Crew losses: None	**Commander:** None

U135 at sea in 1918. (U-Boot Archiv)

Designed for deep-water patrolling, the U-ship Project 42 produced a large and extremely powerful submarine raider (or U-Cruiser), which had a very potent operational range of 10,000 miles. This class was to be heavily armed. In photos of these vessels, it seems that the gunnery team had been equipped with sophisticated range finders for the 105mm deck-gun. The Project 42 class of vessel would have been extremely dangerous to allied shipping if it had become operational during World War One. Luckily for the allies none of the class was to see service.

U135 had been commissioned in June 1918, and surrendered in November. She became a British war-prize and was put up for sale. Having not attracted the interest of ship-breakers by the summer of 1921, she was towed out of Devonport and deliberately sunk in the Channel on 30th June 1921, alongside *U161* (see No 1/23). This was seemingly done as part of a final clearance of the U-boats languishing in the Channel dockyards. Another cluster of seven U-boats met the same fate in waters south of the Isle of Wight (see Nos 4/6 - 4/11 and 5/9). The French Navy disposed of two more off Cherbourg (see Nos 4/20 and 4/21).

This rare class of U-boat would make an interesting find for divers and historians. However, as yet, little is known of her exact whereabouts, as far as the author is aware.

No 1/25, HMS *M1* – Supergun Submarine

Class: M-Class	**Built at:** Vickers – Barrow-in-Furness
Length: 89.6m	**Displacement:** 1946t
Date sunk: 12th November 1925	**How sunk:** Collision with SS *Vidar*
Historic Position: off Start Point	**Known Position:** Withheld on Request
Crew losses: 69 (all crew lost)	**Commander:** Lt.Cmdr. Alec M. Carrie

Of the three M-Class submarines built, two have come to lie in the waters of the Channel. The third, HMS *M3* was scrapped in the 1930s. The first of the M-Class submarines to be lost was the first one to be built - HMS *M1*. Just over six years later, HMS *M2* was also lost. A full description of the design features of the M-Class is given in the HMS *M2* profile (see No 3/21).

The M-Class 'submarine monitors' form a unique branch in the development of the British submarine. Although other nations experimented with the idea of a submarine with the firepower of a warship, the 12-inch gun on the M-Class makes it unique in the history of submarine development.

After her completion in 1918, HMS *M1* toured the Mediterranean and Black Sea. The deployment of such a powerful British submarine in the eastern Mediterranean at that time was intentional. Its presence was aimed at giving a powerful reminder of Royal Navy firepower in an uncertain post-war world.

In 1920, HMS *M1* returned to the UK where she was used on trials. This included using surrendered U-boats for gunnery practice. During 1924, all of the M-Class submarines were painted in differing paint schemes, in an attempt to see which was the most difficult to be spotted from the air. It was then that HMS *M1* received its distinctive 'wavy line' colour scheme, which can be seen on many

The giant M1 docked in Italy. (Royal Navy Submarine Museum)

photographs of her.

It seems that HMS *M1* was a popular submarine with her crew. There are many reasons for this. The massive gun turret acted as a superb spray deflector for the bridge watch and was reputed to be the driest in the submarine service. The massive 17-ton gun gave the *M1* a fast diving speed for such a large submarine. She was able to fully submerge in 80 seconds. Because the gun barrel was closed at either end, when underwater she became positively buoyant by 15 tons, which led to excellent handling and depth keeping. Internally, she was spacious too, offering a higher than normal degree of comfort at the time.

HMS *M1* has the dubious distinction of being the only submarine in history to have anchored itself to the seabed by firing its main armament. On firing practice, the tampion, which kept water out of the muzzle of the main gun, was accidentally left closed. When the gun was fired, the barrel ruptured and a large section of it flew off and sank in front of the submarine. Battleship-sized guns of the time were wound with cable. This unravelled and was still attached to the submarine and the gun muzzle as it lay on the seabed! The use of a hacksaw to cut the cable enabled HMS *M1* to return to port, wiser for the event. Fortunately, there were no injuries.

On 12th November 1925, under the command of Lt.Cmdr. Alec M. Carrie, HMS *M1* was to take part in exercises where she was to make simulated attacks against a 'convoy'. This was to be carried out in concert with HMS *M2*, HMS *L22* and HMS *L23*. HMS *L17* was acting as a convoy escort.

At 4.45pm HMS *M1* was seen to spot the convoy and to dive. She was seen broaching several times, as if making dummy gun attacks. The minesweeper HMS *Newark* was the last ship to positively see HMS *M1*. That evening, she did not return to port.

Immediately, a search for her was undertaken using the most up to date technology available. The search, using four Navy vessels initially lasted for two days. This was conducted using simple magnetometers and a 'Chernikeef' log for position fixing. Although this technology is extremely simple by the standards of the day, the Navy vessels did in actual fact locate the wreck of HMS *M1*. It just so happened that they had no way of knowing this.

On 24th November, HMS *Rocket* carried out another search of the same area. In this instance also, the wreck of HMS *M1* was located. During all

HMS M1 (on the right) with M3 alongside. (Royal Navy Submarine Museum)

searches made, three distinctive 'wrecks' were located in similar positions. Although one of them was HMS *M1*, there was no possible way of ascertaining this for certain.

Curiously, one of the three positions was noted to have been giving off oil. For an inexplicable reason, no thought was given to this critical piece of information (see loss of HMS *A7* No 1/29). We know now that the oil was coming from the wreck of HMS *M1*. This is particularly saddening, because there is evidence to suggest that some of the crew had survived the sinking and were attempting to communicate to the surface vessels by the use of 'Fessenden' underwater wireless telegraphy. When this was reported to the Admiralty, it was taken extremely seriously and a rigorous search of Navy records was made to ensure that the signals did in fact, come from the wreck of HMS *M1*. The Admiralty went as far as to check with the French Navy and the operators of ocean liners too. It concluded that survivors inside HMS *M1* had indeed been attempting to communicate with their potential rescuers. The conditions under which these survivors perished do not bear thinking about.

The simple reality was that the technological challenge of locating and diving on the wreck was too great for the time. Moreover, no submarine in 1925 had been fitted with underwater submarine escape equipment. HMS *M2* was the first to be fitted with the DSEA (Davis Submerged Escape Apparatus) system, and it was installed in 1932.

Standard diving dress was not regularly used at the depths in which HMS *M1* was thought to lie. However, armoured dress was available. Otto Kraft, a diving contractor was enlisted to help. Using armoured dress, several dives were made to 250ft, but the wreck of *M1* was not located, probably due to the difficulties of position fixing out of sight of land.

The mystery of how HMS *M1* was sunk was solved without the need for diving. On 19th November, a Swedish collier, SS *Vidar* entered Värta harbour. She had felt an 'underwater explosion' near Start Point at the time of HMS *M1*'s disappearance. It wasn't until the captain of SS *Vidar* heard a German news report of the loss of HMS *M1* that he felt the need to report the incident.

On 20th November, a diving inspection of SS *Vidar* found that her bows had been bent and showed evidence of collision. During a later inspection, paint that matched the special colour scheme of HMS *M1* was found on SS *Vidar's* hull plating. The reason why HMS *M1* had been lost was now known. With this in mind, and reluctantly acknowledging the chance of locating the wreck was low, further searches for HMS *M1* were abandoned. HMS *M1* simply became a statistic in the long list of tragic peacetime submarine accidents.

Many of the countless thousands of recreational divers who have visited the wreck of HMS *M2* have thought about the whereabouts of HMS *M1*. The 29 years that separates the diving of HMS *M2* to the discovery of HMS *M1* by the author, saw the development of the necessary deep diving techniques and technology which now enables recreational divers to descend to 75metres, or more.

In actual fact, the first claim made to the finding of HMS *M1* was in 1967! A diving contractor, Silas Oates made this claim, after one of his divers stumbled across the wreck of a submarine in around 150ft off Start Point. There was considerable media attention at the time, but the claim was never substantiated. It seems that they probably discovered the wreck of *U1063* (see No 1/18), the schnorchel resembling HMS *M1*'s main gun.

With the necessary training and experience to hunt for HMS *M1*, in 1997 the author turned his attentions to this task. The trail was a cold one and the first pieces of useful evidence came from the

official records of the search for HMS *M1*, which are held in the Public Records Office. Other anecdotal sources of information came from many different places, including the Royal Navy Submarine Museum. In 1998, the author discussed a search for HMS *M1* with Weymouth-based charter boat operator, Graham Knott. The pair decided to pool their knowledge and come up with a 'hit list' of positions. On 18th June 1999, the author's diving team visited the site of the first position on the list.

In 78 metres of water, off Start Point, the wreck of HMS *M1* was seen for the first time since she sank 74

A view from the bridge - the simplest gun sight for the largest gun ever mounted on a submarine! In the raised position it indicated that the hydraulic tampion in the gun's muzzle was opened. (Royal Navy Submarine Museum)

years previously. Lying upright on the seabed in near darkness she was the most remarkable diving discovery of that year. The wreck was largely intact. In fact all of the features that could be associated with HMS *M1* were there. This included her massive gun turret, smaller foldaway gun and hatches. The torpedo tube configuration matched that of the M-Class, as did all other features. The only thing missing from the wreck itself was the 12-inch gun and its turret. However, the breech assembly and much of the turret plating was seen to be lying off the wreck on the port side.

With the wreck on video, the author took the evidence to the Royal Navy Submarine Museum, which confirmed to the delight of the diving team that they had discovered the wreck of HMS *M1*. This was a tremendous achievement for a group of amateur divers and ranks among the author's proudest diving achievements.

No 1/26, HMS *Untiring* – aka *Xifias*

Class: U-Class	**Built at:** Vickers – Barrow-in-Furness
Length: 59.6m	**Displacement:** 740t
Date sunk: 25th July 1957	**How sunk:** As Sonar target
Historic Position: 50 12.36N; 04 00.36W	**Known Position:** 50 12.802N; 04 00.669W
Crew losses: None	**Commander:** None

There are two British U-Class submarine wrecks in the Channel (see No 4/18 HMS *Upstart*) and both of them were sunk as sonar targets in 1957. Of the two, HMS *Untiring* is deeper and in much better condition.

The history of the U-Class submarines marks one of the great chapters in the history of the British submarine service. Their story is bound up in the struggle for ascendancy in the Mediterranean in World War Two. In particular, the U-Class submarines will always be associated with the 10th Flotilla that was, for a large part of the fighting, based in Malta. There it suffered the same hardships, which befell the populace of this brave little island.

Completed in June 1943, HMS *Untiring* was to be one of the last of the U-Class submarines to see action in the Mediterranean. Nevertheless, she operated on 14 separate patrols and accounted for on average a ship a patrol, no mean feat at the time. This was because, as the axis was losing the war, targets became rare, and when encountered, they were usually heavily escorted, making them dangerous to attack.

HMS Untiring *in 1944. Note the letters depicting her name on the conning tower, a feature of British Submarines of this period. (Royal Navy Submarine Museum)*

On her first patrol, HMS *Untiring* was sent to intercept a U-boat that was heading for the base at Toulon. HMS *Unseen* had already attempted an attack on her. The following morning the submarine was heard approaching and HMS *Untiring*, in its first torpedo firing of the war, lined up an attack. Four torpedoes were fired in a 'spread' and at the correct juncture, an explosion was heard. Celebrations broke out aboard, as the crew believed they had sunk a U-boat. It wasn't until returning to base in Algiers that HMS *Untiring* learned that the U-boat had reported being fired at and making a lucky escape.

The U-boat in question was *U616* under the command of the experienced commander Siegfried Kiotschka. He was a wily submariner who held the coveted Knight's Cross. On this occasion, his life and that of his crew was saved by the quick thinking and sharp eyes of his watch officer Karl Boch. *U616* was able to avoid the onrushing torpedoes and escape. Kiotschka was captured a few months later, after the longest submarine hunt of World War Two.

In subsequent patrols, HMS *Untiring* was more successful, she accounted for several ships, including ASW vessels, ammunition lighters and in a memorable attack, she sank an enemy minesweeper in Monaco harbour. This was a particularly audacious and tricky attack, which involved slotting a torpedo through the harbour gates. After seeing the first one run up the breakwater, it took not an inconsiderable degree of courage to circle around and try again. The second attempt was successful, sinking the target and shaking up the Monaco harbour front into the bargain.

HMS Untiring's crew with their Jolly Roger in 1944. (Royal Navy Submarine Museum)

At the end of the war, both HMS *Upstart* and HMS *Untiring* were leased to the Greek Navy. HMS *Untiring* went under the name of Xifias. The two submarines were returned to the UK in 1952. In 1957, it was decided that these two antiques could be best used as sonar training targets. On 25th July 1957, HMS *Untiring* was sunk off Start Point to fulfil this role.

Today, the wreck of HMS *Untiring* lies in 55 metres of water. She sits proud of the shingle seabed, apparently upright. By all reports she makes a great dive, in an area where the visibility can be exceptional.

No 1/27, HMS *H52* – The Film Star

Class: H-Class	**Built at:** HM Dockyard - Pembroke
Length: 52.05m	**Displacement:** 500t
Date sunk: 3rd January 1928	**How sunk:** Making the film 'The Q-Ships'
Historic Position: N of Eddystone	**Known Position:** 50 11.52N; 04 17.17W
Crew losses: None	**Commander:** None

H52 at sea with her loading davit erected. (Royal Navy Submarine Museum)

At the outbreak of World War One, Britain did not possess a modern, small submarine for coastal defence. This was a serious problem, because the coastal areas of the UK came under attack from U-boats and elements of the High Seas Fleet. Furthermore, the deployment of coastal defence submarines could be utilised to sink enemy merchant vessels in the North Sea.

Without a design ready, Admiral 'Jackie' Fisher desperately searched for a solution to this problem. The answer was found by utilising an existing design, an American one. A deal was struck between the Bethlehem Steel Corporation and the Admiralty to build the 'H'-Class in the United States. However, due to trading restrictions at the time (the US was still a neutral power), production was switched to Vickers shipyard in Canada.

The first H-Class submarines proved to be of immense utility. They were of good design and became universally popular with their crews. A total of 35 of this class were finally completed for the Royal Navy. For its designers, the H-Class was also successful, because several of the world's navies purchased it. The last H-Class submarines were still in service in Chile in the 1950s.

The H-Class was the first class of British submarine to carry four bow torpedoes, making it the most powerful submarine Britain possessed during World War One. Twenty of the H-Class were completed in time to see action. Five were lost during the war, of which only one was due to the enemy. The other four were lost in various accidents, two of them in the Channel, although these were later raised (see Appendix 3).

After the United States had entered the war, production was also brought to Britain. HMS *H52* was built at HM Dockyard Pembroke. She was launched on 13th March 1919 and completed in December of the same year. Built too late to see service in the war, HMS *H52*, like others of her class, became key vessels

The result of collision - H52 was lucky to survive after being hit by a ship. (Royal Navy Submarine Museum)

in the post-war submarine service. HMS *H52* was used primarily for training purposes and probably as a test-bed for new submarine technologies.

During one exercise, HMS *H52* had a very lucky escape when she was hit by a surface vessel while running submerged. Extensive damage was done to her bridge and conning tower and her main periscope was bent.

It may have been a result of this damage that the decision to sell HMS *H52* was made. She was sold on 9th November 1927 to New Era Productions. This was a film company that was making 'The Q-Ships'. HMS *H52* was (somewhat) disguised to look like a U-boat and was sunk off the Eddystone Lighthouse by gunfire in January 1928 during filming. Presumably, the lighthouse provided for a high camera angle. A popular dive around Weymouth, the wreck of the *Amy* was also sunk during the course of making this film.

A silent movie, 'The Q-Ships' is interesting to see and is still available on video from some specialist suppliers. Although not entirely historically accurate, it is quite fascinating to see the little *H52* masquerading as one of the 'Hun pirates'!

Today the wreck of *H52* lies in the waters, just northwest of the Eddystone Lighthouse. She is resting in 60 metres of water and is not dived on frequently. Diving reports seem to suggest that the gunfire damage to her is largely to the bow area. Furthermore, there is evidence to suggest that some other salvage work may have taken place on her in the past.

1/28, HMS *A7* – Diving Accident

Class: A-Class	**Built at:** Vickers – Barrow-in-Furness
Length: 30.3m	**Displacement:** 207t
Date sunk: 16th January 1914	**How sunk:** Diving accident
Historic Position: Whitesand Bay	**Known Position:** 50 18.48N; 04 17.92W
Crew losses: 9 (all crew lost)	**Commander:** Lt. G. M. Welman

HMS *A7* is one of three A-Class submarines that lie on the bottom of the Channel. Unlike the other two, HMS *A3* and HMS *A1* (See Nos 4/16 and 4/18), this wreck is a war grave. She is another example of the tragic number of HM submarines lost to accidents in peacetime.

One of the later versions of the British A-Class, HMS *A7* was launched on 23rd January 1905 and completed in April. She did not have to wait long to witness the sinking of her sister, *A8* (see Appendix 3). This occurred on 5th June 1905.

Like the other A-Class submarines, HMS *A7* was used predominately for coastal defence and for training. It was while on a training exercise that *A7* was to be lost.

On 16th January 1914, HMS *A7* and four other submarines were undertaking dummy torpedo attacks against the gunboat HMS *Pygmy* and the depot ship HMS *Onyx*. As HMS *Pygmy* made a run in front of HMS *A7*, the submarine dived to commence an attack. The attack failed and HMS *A7* never resurfaced.

When she failed to return to base, a search was launched. Although the approximate position of the wreck was known and the area where air bubbles were seen was buoyed, it took another six days before the submarine was located. In this instance, she was found because of a small trail of oil on the surface. This lesson was clearly forgotten during the search for HMS *M1*, some 15 years later (see No 1/26).

When divers visited the wreck, they found HMS *A7* lying at an angle of 35 degrees, with her bows pointing toward the surface. Clearly something had gone terribly wrong during her dive. In order to ascertain what had happened, salvage was attempted. On three separate occasions, cables were attached to the wreck and attempts were made to pull her clear of the mud. They all failed, even the 14,000-ton battleship HMS *Exmouth* used her powerful capstans to try and release the submarine from the seabed's grip. The submarine's hull was damaged during these attempts and reluctantly, all further salvage efforts were abandoned.

HMS A7 with experimental hydroplanes forward of the conning tower. (Royal Navy Submarine Museum)

The wreck of HMS *A7* appears to have been first visited by sport divers in the early 1980s. Since then, it seems she became a popular dive for Plymouth-based dive boats. The author visited this wreck in June 1994, when diving aboard the Plymouth charter boat 'Cee King', captained by Richard King. It was dusk when we dived and at the depth of 43 metres, the ghostly outline of a White Ensign, fluttering in the current greeted the divers.

As part of the celebrations for the 50th Anniversary of the D-Day landings, Navy divers had attached the flag to HMS *A7*'s periscope. A moving tribute to the 9 crew members that remain buried inside the wreck of the submarine.

Like the other A-Class wrecks, HMS *A7* makes an interesting dive, although the wreck itself is small. She is now lying flat on the seabed and her major point of interest is her little conical conning tower, with its beautifully sculptured hatch and little portholes.

In 1999, HMS *A7* was in the news when a local diver was given a police caution for the offence of theft by finding. The police had seized HMS *A7*'s compass binnacle from his possession. This marked the first case in which a diver risked prosecution for removing artefacts from an official war grave.

Partly in response to this, in late 2001 the Ministry of Defence listed 16 war graves as controlled sites under the 1986 Protection of Military Remains Act. HMS *A7* was on the list. In order to dive on this wreck in the future, permission will need to be sought and a licence granted.

No 1/29, *Maria* – World's First Submarine Death

Class: N/A	**Built at:** Unknown
Length: Unknown	**Displacement:** 50t
Date sunk: 20th June 1774	**How sunk:** Diving accident
Historic Position: Plymouth Sound	**Known Position:** near Drake's Island
Crew losses: 1 (all crew lost)	**Commander:** John Day

Of all of the tales related in this book, surely none can compare to the comedic and yet tragic tale of Mr. John Day and his 'submarine' *Maria*.

The year was 1774 and Mr Day, a wagon maker, decided to enter the race to build a practical submarine. He claimed to have used a pond near Yarmouth to descend to 30 feet in his prototype and spend 24 hours on the bottom, before rising again to the surface.

On the back of this great success, Mr Day entered into business with an investor, Christopher Blake, to make a larger 'submarine' in which he could descend to 130ft in full view of the public and stay down for 12 hours. Mr Blake backed the scheme with £350 and promised Mr Day 10percent of all the revenues he would make on the bets laid on Mr Day's dive.

John Day duly purchased the 50-ton vessel, *Maria* and modified her to his specifications, so that she would act as a submersible. This included placing 75 empty barrels in her hold as buoyancy and 30 tons of stone ballast, which could be dropped to allow the submarine to rise. The entire vessel was painted bright red, doubtless to add some sense of occasion to the spectacle.

On 20th June, Mr Day was ready and in front of a crowd of onlookers, *Maria* was towed into position. The depth was checked as being 130 feet and the brave submariner entered his craft with a candle, a box of biscuits and a bottle of water. The hatch was closed and the submarine immediately submerged, for its first and only time. John Day had become the first man (of many hundreds) to die in a submarine accident.

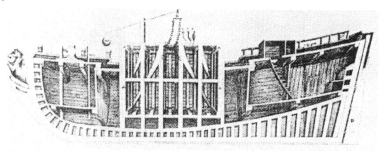

The Maria, in which John Day plunged to his death. (Edwyn Gray)

It must be considered as certain that *Maria* simply imploded on its way to the bottom. Mr Blake hurriedly departed the scene and although salvage was attempted, neither Mr Day nor his submarine was ever seen again. To this day, the wreckage of this historic part of submarine history has not been found.

There may be a good reason for this. Mr Edwyn Gray, a renowned author and submarine historian, who initially unearthed this story, has some doubts as to its validity. However, Mr Kendall

McDonald, author of several books on shipwrecks is positive that the story is genuine. He believes that the wreck will be found near Drake's Island.

Originally published in a magazine of the period, it could be possible that the tale is not entirely accurate. The author wishes to thank Mr Gray for his permission to relate this tale and for his analysis of the event so described. Until the wreck is located, the story remains a curious anecdote in the annals of submarine losses.

No 1/30, HMS *Narwhal* – Last Submarine Sunk in the Channel

Class: Porpoise Class	**Built at:** Vickers – Barrow-in-Furness
Length: 89.5m	**Displacement:** 2030t (surfaced)
Date sunk: 3rd August 1983	**How sunk:** Training facility
Historic Position: 15m S of Falmouth	**Known Position:** 50 00.78N; 04 41.36W
Crew losses: None	**Commander:** None

HMS *Narwhal* is the youngest of all of the submarines that lie on the bottom of the Channel. She was sunk in 1983 as a diving and submarine escape training facility. She lies in a depth of 80 metres.

This submarine was commissioned in 1959 and served until 1974. During this time, she was active all around the world. She took part in exercises and travelled extensively to British and allied bases globally.

HMS Narwhal at Gosport. (Royal Navy Submarine Museum)

The high points in her service career came first in March 1963, when she spent a month under the Arctic ice cap, a significant achievement. HMS *Narwhal* also made an entire circumnavigation of South America in the first four months of 1969. During this cruise, she took part in exercises with the navies of Peru, Chile and Argentina.

In April 1974 she suffered damage to her starboard external tanks and was withdrawn from service. She remained in reserve and in 1980 was deliberately sunk in Weymouth Bay as part of a submarine salvage exercise. She was raised later in the same year.

Local diver, Mr Gifford Pound, has dived this wreck in the last few years. He was out diving charted 'marks' and investigating what they might be. Not knowing that HMS *Narwhal* had been sunk at the location he dived, he was extremely surprised to find the wreck of an immense black rubber-coated submarine! Gifford reports that the wreck is upright and very intact. She would make an interesting technical diving target.

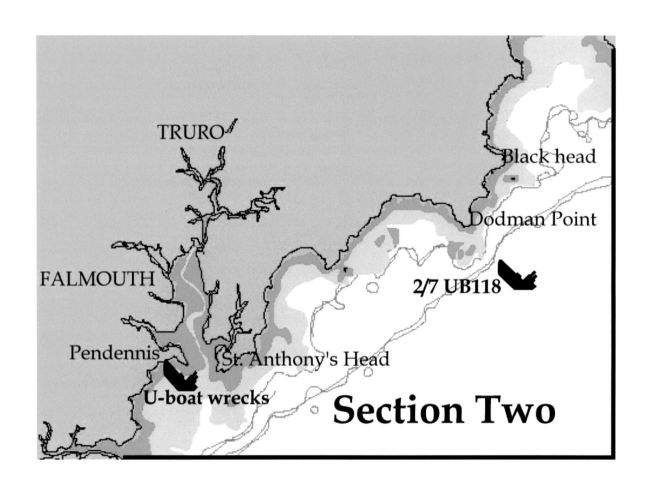

TRURO

Black head

Dodman Point

FALMOUTH

2/7 UB118

Pendennis

St. Anthony's Head

U-boat wrecks

Section Two

Section 2

The Falmouth U-boats

At the end of World War One, 105 U-boats were allocated to Great Britain as war reparations. Some of these submarines were initially used for testing and several were put on display to the general public. However, it was always intended that the majority of these war prizes should be sold for scrap. This was a good idea. However, it did not take too long at war's end for scrap prices to slump. By 1920, the Admiralty seemed to be having difficulties disposing of the proportion of submarines it had left.

Moreover, the submarines had not been kept in a decent state of repair. Their batteries had been allowed to run down and basic maintenance had been ignored. This was partly due to the downscaling of the Royal Navy personnel pool during 1919 and 1920 and the amount of home leave granted to trained submariners directly after the war.

It is known now that several were simply dumped in the Channel, some in the river inlets of the Kent coast and perhaps others elsewhere. Some were also allocated to Falmouth, along with the U-boat tender vessel, *Cyclops*. These were to be used for explosive testing and gunnery practice. This section relates the stories and fates of these submarines and tells the story of how Falmouth ended up becoming a U-boat graveyard, where several of these vessels can still be seen today.

During 1921 a total of nine of the surrendered U-boat fleet were allocated to Falmouth. It is known that eight of these vessels arrived. One U-boat foundered on the way from Devonport. This was, in all probability *UB118*, which broke its towing line near Dodman Point and was sunk by gunfire on 25th November 1920 (see No 2/7).

Of the eight that made it to Falmouth, two were taken out into Falmouth Bay and were sunk by gunnery shortly after they arrived. The author has not been able to identify which U-boats these were, despite some considerable effort. Wherever they were sunk, they don't appear to have been located and it must be assumed that they were later scrapped. There is no doubt that the remaining six U-boats were destined for the same fate. However, while moored at Gyllyngvasse, a severe winter storm broke their moorings and drove them ashore; one on Gyllyngvasse beach and five on the rocks surrounding Pendennis Point.

The submarines instantly became a tourist attraction, with many visitors wandering the seafront to stare at these monsters of the deep that so nearly defeated Britain in World War One. A roaring trade was made for a little while, taking visitors out to the submarines by boat.

It seems that around this time, the *Cyclops* was returned to the Admiralty for disposal. She had served her purpose as a U-boat depot and repair ship when her escorting submarines had been blown ashore.

Due in part to low scrap prices, the only salvage seriously undertaken on the vessels was by locals who searched through the wrecks for souvenirs and non-ferrous metal. However, with the advent of World War Two, the demand for scrap increased and the vessels were broken up where they lay by Marine Salvage of Penzance. This was not a particularly difficult undertaking, as the submarines were exposed at low tide, as the last of their remains are today. However, the wrecks were still being worked on even after the war and are known to have had several owners during this period. They last changed hands as late as 1983.

Today, the remains of the submarines can make an interesting shore dive. Best dived when the kelp that covers the wreckage is not in full bloom, much can still be seen. This includes the tubular pressure hulls and other recognisable items. Maximum depth is around 12 metres.

No 2/1, *UB86*

Class: UBIII (UB80 series)	**Built at:** AG Weser - Bremen
Length: 55.85m	**Displacement:** 647t
Date sunk: Unknown	**How sunk:** Blown ashore
Historic Position: Unknown	**Known Position:** Falmouth Bay
Crew losses: None	**Commander:** None

This submarine was commissioned into the German Navy on 10th November 1917. Under the command of Klt. Hans Trenk, *UB86* was to conduct a total of five successful war patrols before she surrendered in Wilhelmshaven a year later.

After the storm – a UB-boat lies awash. (P Gilson)

Her areas of operation covered the North Sea, North Channel, North Cornwall and Firth of Forth. During these patrols she sank seven ships, totalling over 13,000 tons. These included the 684-ton *Dalegarth Force*, 1,701-ton *Gregynog*, and 1,567-ton *Helene*.

UB86 appears in the lists of U-boats under British control on 21st February 1919, when she was recorded to have been moored in Harwich.

No 2/2, *UB97*

Class: UBIII (UB88 series)	**Built at:** AG Vulcan - Hamburg
Length: 55.52m	**Displacement:** 640t
Date sunk: Unknown	**How sunk:** Blown ashore
Historic Position: Unknown	**Known Position:** Falmouth Bay
Crew losses: None	**Commander:** None

The stern of a UB-boat wrecked at Pendennis. (P Gilson)

This submarine was commissioned on 25th July 1918 and was still under training when the war ended. This was essentially a new U-boat when she was transferred to Britain.

UB97 appears in the lists of U-boats under British control on 21st February 1919. She was recorded as moored in Harwich at this time.

No 2/3, *UB106*

Class: UBIII (UB103 series)	**Built at:** Blohm & Voss - Hamburg
Length: 55.3m	**Displacement:** 649t
Date sunk: Unknown	**How sunk:** Blown ashore
Historic Position: Unknown	**Known Position:** Falmouth Bay
Crew losses: None	**Commander:** None

It seems that *UB106* had a personality of its own, preferring to be wrecked than to be used as an operational weapon of war. After her commissioning on 7th February 1918, she was ordered to join the Flanders Flotilla. However, she sank on 15th March 1918 in the Baltic while working-up. It is believed that this was the result of an accident. Her entire crew was killed.

High and dry – two U-boats at Pendennis. (P Gilson)

The submarine repair and salvage vessel *Vulcan* (sister-ship to *Cyclops*) raised her three days later. She was in the process of being overhauled when the war ended.

She is recorded as having been moored in Harwich on 21st February 1919.

No 2/4, UB112

Class: UBIII (UB103 series)	**Built at:** Blohm & Voss - Hamburg
Length: 55.3m	**Displacement:** 649t
Date sunk: Unknown	**How sunk:** Blown ashore
Historic Position: Unknown	**Known Position:** Falmouth Bay
Crew losses: None	**Commander:** None

A partially dismantled UB-boat at low tide. (P Gilson)

Another late addition to the U-boat war, *UB112* was commissioned on 16th April 1918. She was transferred to the Flanders Flotilla where, under the command of Klt. Wilhelm Rhein she conducted war patrols in the North Sea and English Channel. *UB112* finally accounted for nine ships totalling 9,238 tons. These included the 1,986-ton *Westwood*, and 1,683- ton *Aldebaran*.

UB112 appears in the list of U-boats in British hands on 19th February 1919, when she was moored in Harwich.

No 2/5, UB128

Class: UBIII (UB118 series)	**Built at:** AG Weser - Bremen
Length: 55.85m	**Displacement:** 643t
Date sunk: Unknown	**How sunk:** Blown ashore
Historic Position: Unknown	**Known Position:** Falmouth Bay
Crew losses: None	**Commander:** None

This U-boat was commissioned on 11th May 1918 and was transferred to the Mediterranean theatre of operations. Under her commander Klt. Wilhelm Canaris, she slipped out of Kiel on 1st August and began the patrol that saw her pass Gibraltar and then operate off Sicily and in the Malta Channel. During this patrol, *UB128* sank one ship only. This was the 7,418-ton steamer *Champlain*, which was French-owned and went to the bottom on 21st August.

UB128 set out on her second patrol in company with *U33*. She had been ordered to attack only warships.

A UB-boat being scrapped. (P Gilson)

It was during this patrol that Germany surrendered and *UB128* headed for Kiel. She was decommissioned on 29th November 1918, the day she entered port.

UB128 is the most historically interesting of all of the Falmouth U-boats. This is because her commander later became implicated in the plot to kill Hitler. Canaris remained a Navy man after the war and rose through the ranks to eventually become the head of the Abwehr (German military intelligence). After the 'night of the long knives' he seems to have turned against the Nazis. Initially, he sought to prevent war and latterly to protect Germany from the most excessive of Nazi activities. Of the

A good shot of the stern of a UB-boat. Note the guards around the hydroplanes and rudders. (P Gilson)

many activities Canaris was involved in, his success in turning Hitler's attentions away from invading Spain (thus saving Gibraltar) is worthy of note here.

He had been deposed as chief of the Abwehr by the time of the July 1944 bomb-plot. However, this did not prevent him being hanged by the SS on 9th April 1945 in Flossenburg concentration camp.

Canaris was not the only U-boat officer from World War One who fought against the Nazis. Others included Martin Niemöller, who as Watch Officer on *U73* had laid mines that sank the battleship HMS *Russell* and HMHS *Britannic* in 1916. He became a Lutheran Pastor and an outspoken critic of the Nazi regime.

No 2/6, *UC92*

Class: UCIII (UC90 series)	**Built at:** Blohm & Voss - Hamburg
Length: 56.51m	**Displacement:** 571t
Date sunk: Unknown	**How sunk:** Blown ashore
Historic Position: Unknown	**Known Position:** Falmouth Bay
Crew losses: None	**Commander:** None

Few records for this submarine seem to remain. However, it is likely that she was still working-up at the end of the war, although launched on 19th January 1918. There are certainly no ships reported to have been sunk by her. She was of the latest UCIII-Class and therefore it seems she never saw service.

This class of minelayer was a significant improvement on the UCII-Class and would represent the only example in Channel waters, if she turns out to be one of the submarines that can still be dived.

The records of U-boats in British hands on 19th February 1919 say she was moored in Pembroke on that date.

GERMAN SUBMARINE U.C.95.
One of the Hun Pirates.   Now a prisoner in the Thames.

A propaganda postcard showing one of UC92's sisters. (Author's Collection)

No 2/7, UB118

Class: UBIII (UB118 series)	**Built at:** AG Weser - Bremen
Length: 55.85m	**Displacement:** 643t
Date sunk: 21st November 1920	**How sunk:** Blown ashore
Historic Position: 50 12.30; N04 36W	**Known Position:** 50 11.34N04 46.36W
Crew losses: None	**Commander:** None

Commissioned on 22nd January 1918, *UB118* was to make four patrols before the end of the war. These were to take her to the British east coast, St. George's Channel, and the Orkneys. She sank five ships for 24,000 tons. These included two larger ships, the 6,833-ton *Mesaba* and the 6,545-ton *City of Glasgow*.

The U-boat salvage ship Cyclops. (P Gilson)

The German history of *UB118* states that she surrendered to France on 20th November 1918. However, she appears in the records of U-boats in British hands on 19th February 1919. She was reported as being moored at Harwich. Other stories tell of *UB118* being washed ashore at Hastings on 15th April 1919. The photos of this event seem to reveal the larger *U118* (See Appendix 3), supposedly broken-up where she lay.

UB118 was almost certainly the U-boat that was allocated to Falmouth, but was lost on tow on the way there. It is known that on 21st Nov 1920, *UB118* was being towed from Devonport to Falmouth when the valves in her fore compartment supposedly failed. She became unmanageable and was finally sunk by the fishery patrol vessel *Kennet*.

A submarine was located around 5.5 miles from the given sinking position in 1977. The author dived this wreck during the summer of 2002 and was able to confirm the presence of a UBIII-Class submarine in poor condition, possibly partially salvaged. The visibility in this area is known to be generally poor, as was the case during his investigation of the site.

A UB-boat undergoes salvage – note the radio mast on the deck, a feature of World War One-era U-boats. (P Gilson)

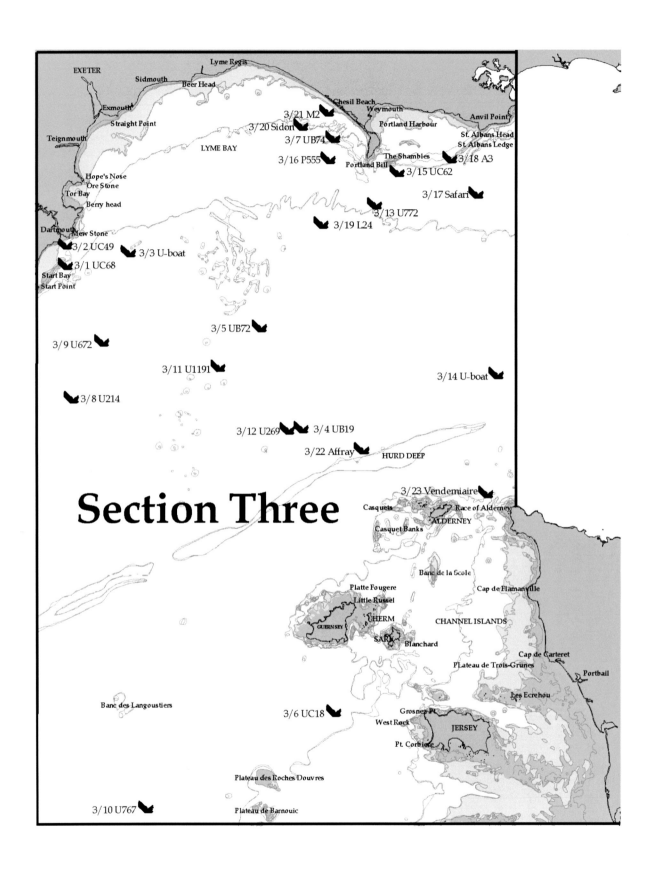

EXETER

Lyme Regis

Sidmouth

Beer Head

Exmouth

Straight Point

Chesil Beach

Weymouth

Portland Harbour

Anvil Point

Teignmouth

3/21 M2

3/20 Sidon

St. Albans Head

St Albans Ledge

LYME BAY

3/7 UB74

3/18 A3

The Shambles

3/16 P555

Hope's Nose

Ore Stone

Tor Bay

Berry head

Portland Bill

3/15 UC62

3/17 Safari

Dartmouth

Mew Stone

3/13 U772

3/2 UC49

3/3 U-boat

3/19 L24

3/1 UC68

Start Bay

Start Point

3/5 UB72

3/9 U672

3/11 U1191

3/14 U-boat

3/8 U214

3/12 U269

3/4 UB19

3/22 Affray

HURD DEEP

Section Three

3/23 Vendemiaire

Casquets

Race of Alderney

ALDERNEY

Casquet Banks

Banc de la Scole

Cap de Flamanville

Platte Fougere

Little Russel

CHANNEL ISLANDS

HERM

GUERNSEY

SARK

Blanchard

Cap de Carteret

PLateau de Trois-Grunes

Portbail

Les Ecrehou

Banc des Langoustiers

3/6 UC18

Grosnez Pt

West Rock

JERSEY

Pt. Corbiere

Plateau des Roches Douvres

3/10 U767

Plateau de Barnouic

Section 3

Submarine Wrecks Around Lyme Bay

The 23 submarines that lie in the waters around Lyme Bay reflect the presence of the Portland Navy Base as the focus point of the area. The largest number of British submarine wrecks in the Channel can be found in this section of the book.

Among them, are three British war-graves HMS *M2*, HMS *Affray* and HMS *L24*. These wrecks all share a common fate; they were lost while exercising in peacetime. Each accident caused a national outpouring of sorrow. The most recent submarine accident occurred just over 50 years ago when HMS *Affray* sank in 1951. She became the last British submarine to be lost at sea. Sadly, the memories of that terrible event were brought back in 2001, when the Russian Navy lost the *Kursk* in an accident.

Aside from the British submarine wrecks, a number of U-boats from both world wars were sunk in these waters. Among them was *UB72*, which was sunk by a British submarine HMS *D4*. Another was *UB19*, which was sunk by the famous British Q-ship, *Penshurst*. Despite a comprehensive search by the author, this wreck has never come to light and awaits discovery in the future.

During World War Two, at least seven U-boats were sunk in this area. Over the last few years, most of them have been located and have been given identities. The process of ensuring these are 100percent accurate continues.

The first of four French submarine wrecks lies in this area. Sharing a similar fate to HMS *L24*, *Vendémiaire* was sunk in an accidental collision with a warship with which she was on exercise. Twenty-four submariners died.

The author would like to express special thanks to Graham Knott for his genuine interest and support in this project. His charter boat has always been a welcome sight when emerging from the deep after another day's successful exploration.

No 3/1, *UC68* - Destroyed While Minelaying

Class: UCII (UC65 series)	**Built at:** Blohm & Voss - Hamburg
Length: 50.35m	**Displacement:** 508t
Date sunk: 13th March 1917	**How sunk:** Own mines
Historic Position: 50 17N; 03 31.5W	**Known Position:** Unknown
Crew losses: 27 (all crew lost)	**Commander:** Olzs. H. Degetau

One of the classic histories of the U-boat war in World War One is R.H. Gibson and Maurice Prendergast's 'The German Submarine War 1914-1918'. It was written shortly after World War One and is based mainly upon the records of the Admiralty. While it is in many ways a fine read, it illustrates the problems associated in attempting to analyse U-boat losses when having possession of only one side of the story.

According to Gibson & Prendergast and other British-based writers of this

UC68 in dry-dock. (U-Boot Archiv)

period, *UC68* was torpedoed and sunk on 5th April by the British submarine HMS *C7* at 51 14; 01 52E – in the North Sea. Yet here we are looking at the history and sinking of this vessel off Start Point. How can this be? The answer lies in the German side of the story. The German records for this period show clearly that the submarine attacked by HMS C7 on 5th April was in fact *UB10*. The torpedo exploded prematurely and *UB10* lived to return to base and relate the tale.

This left the German U-boat command with a problem, because *UC68* was at sea on this date and did not return to base. However, it is known that *UC68* had been ordered to lay mines between Dartmouth and Plymouth. This fits with the heavy underwater explosion witnessed 6 miles northeast of Start Point on 15th April and the subsequent clearing of four German mines from this area.

During this phase of the U-boat war in World War One, at least four UC-boats were lost to their own mines, pointing to the extreme danger of submarine minelaying. During 1917, over half the 63 U-boats lost were UC-boats. These were mostly lost around the British Isles, with their entire crews.

UC68 was on its first patrol when she sank. She had left Zeebrugge on 16th February and had been a commissioned vessel for less than three months.

Perhaps the most interesting element of the analysis of the sinking of *UC68* lies in the fact that her wreck has not been conclusively located, as far as the author is aware. It shows clearly that the role of the Admiralty and later that of the historian cannot be relied upon to always come up with a bona fide sinking position. Divers must play their part in unravelling the final resting-places of so many wartime and peacetime shipwrecks.

There is a U-boat wreck at 50 19.9N;03 30.00W. However, although the evidence suggests that this wreck could be a UC-boat, she could also be *UC49* (see *UC49* wreck No 3/2) which was lost nearby. There is a lot of unexplored wreckage in Start Bay and it may be that *UC68* will be located in the future.

No 3/2, *UC49* - Hunted to Destruction

Class: UCII (UC49 series)	**Built at:** Germaniawerft - Kiel
Length: 52.69m	**Displacement:** 511t
Date sunk: 8th August 1918	**How sunk:** Gunfire and depth charges
Historic Position: 50 20N; 03 26W	**Known Position:** 50.19.9N; 03 30.00W
Crew losses: 31 (all crew lost)	**Commander:** Olzs. H. Kukenthal

On 3rd August 1918, the 7,713-ton passenger-ship *Warilda* was torpedoed and sunk by a U-boat. This ship was an ambulance transport, returning to Southampton from Le Havre. On board her were 614 wounded, a crew of 117 and 70 medical staff. The torpedo entered the space between number four hold and the engine room, exploding and killing 101 patients and some crew. The ship began to sink stern first as the evacuations began. Her two escorts HMS *P39* and HMS *P45* were on hand to take off survivors. As the stern of *Warilda* hit the seabed, she rolled over and sank. In total 123 people were killed.

Often incorrectly labelled a hospital ship, *Warilda* was a legitimate target for the U-boat. This is because she was an ambulance transport. Under the Hague convention, only hospital ships could be employed in that role. To use them for any other purpose was not permitted. Several hospital ships were sunk in the Channel in 1917, including the 6,287-ton *Lanfranc*. The Germans contended that while running to the continent from Britain, hospital ships were being used to bring supplies to the front and deliberately targeted these vessels in 1917. These shocking acts ceased when the hospital ships in the Channel were converted to ambulance transports. Hospital ships were painted white, they were also illuminated at night. This made them easy targets for the U-boats, especially if they were sailing independently.

Paradoxically, when Britain abandoned the use of hospital ships in favour of using ambulance transports, fewer ships were lost and more cargo could be carried to the front on their outward-bound voyages. Ambulance transports could also be armed (like troopships) and be escorted in military convoys. However truthful (or otherwise) Germany's contention as to the real use of hospital ships, it's direct targeting of these vessels proved to be folly.

The *Warilda* was sunk by *UC49* while operating on its 11th and final patrol. She had been commissioned on 2nd December 1916. During her operational career, which was a long one, especially for a UC-boat, she had sunk 23 ships for 63,195 tons. One of her victims had been the British auxiliary cruiser HMS *Patia,* sunk in the Bristol Channel.

On 1st August, *UC49* left Zeebrugge and passed through the Dover barrage to lay mines in the area between Plymouth and Falmouth. By the 8th, *UC49* was finishing its job when it appears that the destroyer HMS *Opossum,* in company with seven motor-launches detected her. They were equipped with hydrophones that were dropped over the side while the vessels drifted with engines off. The hydrophone could detect the sound of a moving submarine. So it was with *UC49* who was heard, making her way underwater. The entire area was liberally plastered with depth charges and the noises ceased. At this point it seems as if the commander, Olzs. H. Kukenthal was lying 'doggo' on the bottom. The British knew that this had become operational procedure during an attack, because hydrophones could not hear a stationary submarine. A game of patience developed, which ended briefly when *UC49* began to crawl away and was depth charged again. Two and a half hours later, after her pursuers dropped some more depth charges and withdrew to wait developments, *UC49* stirred again, presumably thinking she had survived the attack. However, as soon as she surfaced, she was attacked by gunfire and more depth charges. This attack destroyed her. Confirmation was obtained in the form of a glove with the owner's hand still in it and a light bulb made in Vienna.

Today, the wreck of *UC49* is thought to lie at 50 19.9N;03 30.00W. Divers report that she has one stern torpedo tube and is damaged amidships. This could be *UC49*, although other U-boat classes also match this description.

No 3/3, Large Mystery U-Boat

Class: U81 onwards	**Built at:** Unknown
Length: Unknown	**Displacement:** Unknown
Date sunk: Unknown	**How sunk:** Unknown
Historic Position: N/A	**Known Position:** 50 17.97N 03 21.25W
Crew losses: Unknown	**Commander:** Unknown

The location of a large submarine at the location above poses something of a mystery. The author has dived this location, with local diver and charter boat operator, Nick Bright and has video footage of the wreck. It shows a very large World War One era U-boat. From the details gleaned on the video we can limit the possibilities of which boat this may be to a large U-class, following from *U81*.

This is because of the presence of twin stern tubes and four bow tubes, all captured on film. The sheer size of this vessel is hard to determine underwater, but in the author's experience, it is one of the largest submarines that can be dived in the Channel, and it is immense. Interestingly, the deck gun (or guns) has been removed, as have some of the hatches. Also there is substantial damage to the forward end of the wreck, where at least two of the forward torpedo tubes can be seen to have broken away from the front of the pressure hull.

As to the wreck's possible identity? The fact that the wreck has some items missing from it points to two possible conclusions. First, it was partially salvaged before being towed to a breakers yard, or it was commercially salvaged while a wreck. There is simply no way of knowing which may have occurred.

If a war loss, then it could only possibly be *U93*, which was lost in the Channel, position unknown. If a lost tow, then the final identity of this wreck will probably never be known with any satisfaction, because the records for this period are so sparse and many of the companies that operated in this period are no longer in existence. A shipyard stamp on one of the propellers offers the best chance of identification.

No 3/4, *UB19* - Q-ship Victim

Class: UBII (UB18 series)	**Built at:** Blohm & Voss - Hamburg
Length: 36.13m	**Displacement:** 292t
Date sunk: 30th November 1916	**How sunk:** Q-ship HMS *Penshurst*
Historic Position: 49 56N; 02 45W	**Known Position:** Unknown
Crew losses: 8 (from 24)	**Commander:** Olzs. Erich Noodt

Commissioned on 17th December 1917, *UB19* served exclusively with the Flanders Flotilla. During her life she operated in the North Sea and in the Channel. She sank 11,558 tons of allied shipping including the 3,803-ton steamer *San Bernado*, which was sunk by explosives on 10th August 1916 in the North Sea.

Although *UB19* was not a particularly successful U-boat, her place in history was to be sealed by another event altogether - her fate. *UB19* became only the second Q-ship victim of 1916 when she was

engaged in a classic U-boat versus Q-ship encounter south of Portland on 30th November 1916. The Q-ship in question was one of the best, HMS *Penshurst*, commanded by F.H. Grenfell, RN a retired naval officer who had rejoined the Royal Navy at the beginning of World War One. Grenfell, along with Gordon Campbell became the most celebrated Q-ship commanders of the war.

A UBII class U-boat similar to UB19. (U-Boot Archiv)

When compared to the war in the trenches, the exploits of the Q-ships offered a more romanticised view of the conflict and their names became known around the world. *UB19* would become Grenfell's first victim.

On the morning of her destruction, *UB19* was going about her work in the usual manner. She had already boarded the Admiralty vessel *Behrend* and destroyed it with scuttling charges and was on the lookout for another victim, when she spotted an innocent steamer and was in pursuit when an approaching seaplane caused her to crash-dive. A bomb was dropped but *UB19* did not notice this. When *UB19* raised her periscope again, she saw another innocent-looking steamer 5 miles off. The submarine surfaced and began to fire at the steamer, so as to encourage the crew to disembark and allow inspection.

After three rounds had been fired the crew of the merchantman abandoned ship in a very slow and uncoordinated way. *UB19* approached one of the lifeboats to speak to the master and inspect the ship's papers. The submarine was now around 500 yards from the steamer, when suddenly the tables turned alarmingly. Fire poured from the merchant vessel, striking the submarine two or three times as she frantically tried to dive. This took time because several crew members were on deck.

However, once underwater, it was clear that *UB19* was holed and would sink. The command to surface was given and *UB19* once more rose up. Hatches were opened, and under a hail of fire, the crew abandoned ship. The U-boat now proceeded to sink and the survivors were picked up.

UB19 had got careless and had treated the attack on this merchant vessel as a routine exercise in conducting war under the 'prize rules', which were in force at the time. Later in the war, Q-ships could expect long and detailed inspections of every feature of their designs by periscope before a U-boat would surface. Sometimes they would simply disappear, unconvinced by the Q-ship's disguise.

When first spotted, *Penshurst* was actually in the process of hauling the seaplane on board. It had crashed, after landing to liase with the Q-ship as to how best to attack the submarine.

The survivors of *UB19* were quite forthcoming with information when interrogated. They revealed that they had been caught in nets in the Dover Barrage on more than one occasion. When questioned as to HMS *Penshurst's* disguise, one of the crew said 'we take so many risks, we get careless'.

For this textbook destruction of a U-boat, Grenfell was awarded the DSO and the crew received £1,000. In 1919 another bounty award was made. Grenfell and HMS *Penshurst* had waited nearly a year, patiently cruising the waters of the British Isles for their first kill. Its second, *UB37* (see wreck No 4/5) was less than two months away.

The author has devoted some considerable time looking for Grenfell's first victim. However, all the known submarine wrecks in the area surrounding *UB19's* sinking area do not fit her design and can be identified as other types. Undoubtedly, *UB19* is there to be found. She would be a classic U-boat dive, steeped in our bravest of naval traditions; the Q-ships.

No 3/5, *UB72* - Sunk by Submarine

Class: UBIII (UB72 series)	**Built at:** AG Vulcan - Hamburg
Length: 55.52m	**Displacement:** 639t
Date sunk: 12th May 1918	**How sunk:** Torpedoed by HMS *D4*
Historic Position: 50 08N; 02 41W	**Known Position:** 50 06.58N;02.50.58W
Crew losses: 34 (from 37)	**Commander:** Olzs. Friedrich Träger

UB70 seen here under Royal Navy colours at the end of the war was very similar in design to UB72. (U-Boot Archiv)

The sinking of one submarine by another is a rare event in the annals of both world wars. There are only two instances of it occurring in the Channel. In both cases it was Royal Navy submarines that did the sinking. In this instance, it was *UB72* that was destroyed. The other example is *UC65* (see No 5/11), sunk off the Sussex coast.

UB72 was commissioned on 9th September 1917 and was on her fifth patrol when she was sunk. This submarine had amassed 12,578 tons of shipping sunk during her career. This included the 3,463-ton armed boarding steamer, *Tithonus*.

On 12th May 1918, *UB72* was operating in the Channel, having taken the long route around Scotland to reach her area of operation. She had left Kiel on 27th April and by 9th May was off the Isles of Scilly. Throughout this voyage, she had been repeatedly harassed by surface craft and had been depth charged on more than two occasions. It was one of these that had caused a leak in her portside fuel tank that left her constantly trailing oil.

Her patrol area seems to fit in with a pattern given to several U-boats that were ordered into the western Channel in May 1918. It is now known that this formed a plan by U-boat Command to attack the troop convoys coming from America. These plans failed utterly, with *UB72* and *U103* being sunk (see wreck No 1/20) and such a numerous concentration was never tried again.

Although not confirmed by the Admiralty at the time, it seems likely that HM Submarine *D4* was not in the area in which *UB72* was operating, simply by chance. Either way, at 05.30 HMS *D4* sighted a surfaced submarine. Her log records what happened next with the orderly simplicity of a submarine going about her business:

> "5.35 Put on Stbd 20° altered course south, enemy bearing 20°
> 5.43 Stbd 20° altered course 10° enemy course 60° approx speed 6 knots, distance 1200 yards
> 5.50 Fired two bow torpedoes, heard explosion
> 5.53 Surfaced. Rescued 3 seamen, no others of crew or wreckage afloat
> 6.20 Dived to 20ft, periscope watch altered course 270°"

The three survivors of *UB72* were all on their first patrol. Two had been on watch and the other had luckily come up for a breath of fresh air at the fateful moment. He spotted the incoming torpedo and jumped overboard. From the sea, he then watched the submarine sink stern first. It is from the interrogations of these survivors that the story of the numbers of attacks *UB72* had withstood came to light. Interestingly, survivors from *UB72* and *U103* expressed amazement at their rescue. They had been told that the British did not take prisoners, and when they did, the U-boat men were hanged as pirates. This may be one reason why nearly all captured U-boat men seemed willing to talk.

In the summer of 1997, a diving team, including the author, located the wreck of *UB72* at 50 6.58N;02.50.58W. The wreck is now in a very poor state of repair, with bow and stern sections collapsed. Her conning tower hatch is shut and periscopes retracted. Her most interesting feature is the 105mm deck-gun, which has swung about, with the muzzle now resting against the port side of the conning tower. This is consistent with a U-boat of this type sinking stern first. The wreck has a large, heavy trawl net covering her stern, aft of the conning tower. She lies in 70 metres of water.

No 3/6, *UC18* - Q-ship Victim?

Class: UCII (UC16 series)	**Built at:** Blohm & Voss - Hamburg
Length: 49.35m	**Displacement:** 493t
Date sunk: 19th February 1917	**How sunk:** Q-ship HMS *Lady Olive*?
Historic Position: 49 15N; 02 34W	**Known Position:** Unknown
Crew losses: 28 (all crew lost)	**Commander:** Olzs. W. Kiel

UC18 was commissioned on 15th August 1915 and served as part of the Flanders Flotilla. Carrying torpedoes and mines, the small UC-boats were capable of laying their minefields and then operating as commerce raiders, according to the doctrine of U-boat war. *UC18* had accounted for 33,616 tons of allied shipping when she was lost.

UC18 sailed for her operational area of the Bay of Biscay on 16th February 1916, and was never heard from again. Her fate has, over time, become generally accepted to have been due to a fight with the Q-ship HMS *Lady Olive* in a position to the south of Guernsey on 19th February 1917.

HMS *Lady Olive* was steaming west of Jersey in the morning, when a submarine coming up on her from astern attacked her. The 'panic party' was deployed and the submarine closed for a closer look at the stern of the vessel, presumably to read its name. At this point, the Q-ship revealed its true identity by opening fire. The first two shots hit the base of the conning tower and the third swept the deck-gun over the side. At a range of 100 yards, it seems credible that some significant damage could have been done to the submarine, which was seen to submerge bow first.

The Q-ship had, however, received two hits in the engine room when the submarine attacked. She now began to sink and the officers and gun-crews abandoned ship. By 09.30 all were in the boats or on rafts, heading for France. It was 32 hours before rescuers appeared in the shape of the French destroyer *Dunois*. As she closed on the two lifeboats (into which all of *Lady Olive's* crew now huddled), she sighted a 'periscope' and opened fire. This happened twice during the rescue of the lifeboats. The famous maritime writer and historian, Keeble Chatterton, ascribed this incident to being *UC18* following the lifeboats of its last victim, waiting for a rescue ship to sink, which he alleges, was 'a favourite ruse'.

However, this view could be considered to be a slightly biased one, bearing in mind the damage done to the U-boat during the fight. It is just as probable that the French destroyer was being particularly cautious. There does not appear to have been another U-boat operating in this area at the time.

While the mutual destruction of Q-ship and submarine seems to be the plausible fate of *UC18*, this is far from certain. Only the presence of survivors of the sinking U-boat could confirm this, and there were none.

UC18 has been the subject of a search by Jersey-based diver, John Ovenden. However, at time of writing, the elusive *UC18* was still to be located. It is possible that due to its patrol area being further west, *UC18* escaped destruction, only to be lost by some other unknown cause in the Bay of Biscay. However, it seems more likely that she will one day be found in the seas between Guernsey and Jersey.

No 3/7, *UB74* - 'Kamerad, Kamerad'

Class: UBIII (UB72 series)	**Built at:** AG Vulcan - Hamburg
Length: 55.52m	**Displacement:** 639t
Date sunk: 26th May 1918	**How sunk:** Depth charge Yacht *Lorna*
Historic Position: 50 32N; 02 32W	**Known Position:** 50 31.48N;02 33.34W
Crew losses: 35 (all crew lost)	**Commander:** Olzs. E. Steindorff

UB74 was commissioned on 24th October 1917 and served as a front-boat with the Flanders Flotilla from January 1918. She had completed three successful patrols and sunk 19,530 tons of allied shipping before she too was destroyed.

The steam yacht *Lorna* (hired from Lord Hollenden) had been converted for anti-submarine work and had fruitlessly been working from Weymouth for many months. However, on 26th May 1918, knowing that a submarine was in the area, *Lorna*, under the command of Lt. C.L. Tottenham, spied a periscope nearby. The helm was put over and scraping the side of the rapidly descending conning tower, *Lorna* dropped a depth charge, followed by a second 50 yards further on.

1. Lieut.Branscheid, in command of a small S/M in Flanders
2. Lohs   in command of UB 57 in Flanders
3. Walters   1st Officer UC 48, interned in Spain
4. Bieber
5. Ziemer   formerly flag officer in Flanders, now Imperial Navy Office, Berlin
6. Franz Schmitz, jr., in command of a UC boat in Flanders, one
7. Krameyer,   in command of UC 70   of 700.
8. Fürbringer in command of a new UB boat
9. Dobberstein in command of UB 40
10. Steindorf in command of UB 74
11. Stosberg   in command of UB 78
12. Lorenz   in command of UC 48, interned in Spain
13. Hecht +   UB 54
14. Meier (?)
15. v.Rabenau, in command of a new UB boat
16. Wenninger, UB 55 (P/W)

This extraordinary photograph, probably taken from a U-boat survivor, and then used during prisoner interrogations, clearly demonstrates the depth of knowledge that the Admiralty possessed about the German U-boats and their Commanders. UB74's Commander died in the Channel. UB78 (see No 6/16), UB55 (6/14) and UB54 (Appendix 1) were also lost there. Their Commanders feature in this photo. (U-Boot Archiv)

Four objects rose up in a bubble of air as *Lorna* dropped another depth charge and buoyed the spot. The cries 'Kamerad, Kamerad' were heard coming from the water. Of the four U-boat men on the surface, only one was alive. He lived long enough to confirm that the submarine was *UB74* and she had sunk three ships since she left Zeebrugge. However, he was dead within three hours. It seems likely that the concussion of the final depth charge killed his comrades and fatally wounded him. Lt. Tottenham received a DSC for this successful anti-submarine attack.

UB74 was first located by divers in 1918 when a Royal Navy diving team recovered the logbook. It showed that *UB74* had sunk nothing, contradicting the evidence of the survivor, although the log ended on 16th May. It stated that *UB74* had survived a ramming by a steamer off Beachy Head on 13th May.

UB74 had survived just two weeks longer than one of her sisters, sunk in the same area by the British submarine HMS *D4* (see No 3/5).

Today the wreck of *UB74* makes an interesting dive. Local rumour has it that during commercial salvage operations on this wreck in the 1970s, one of *UB74*'s torpedoes exploded, giving the salvage team something of a shock! The wreck was quite broken up when visited by the author in 1999. Although overgrown, the wreck was clearly of UBIII class. Her hull has been blasted right down to the keel in two places and her bow and stern ends have been removed.

Interestingly *UB74*'s conning tower has gone, and lies on the seabed some way from the main wreck. It was a well-used technique for Navy divers to drag off the conning towers of sunken U-boats. This made it a lot easier for divers in standard dress to enter the wrecks. It is likely that this explains why *UB74*'s has been removed.

There is no evidence of the deck-gun, although the ammunition lies scattered on the seabed.

No 3/8, *U214* - A Rare Design

Class: VIID	**Built at:** Germaniawerft AG - Kiel
Length: 76.9m	**Displacement:** 1080t
Date sunk: 26th July 1944	**How sunk:** Depth charges HMS *Cooke*
Historic Position: 49 55N; 03 31W	**Known Position:** Unknown
Crew losses: 48 (all crew lost)	**Commander:** Olzs. Gerhard Conrad

U214 during construction – note the mine chute compartment aft of the conning tower. (U-Boot Archiv)

U214 was of the rare VIID variant, of which only six were ever built. It was based on the workhorse VIIC, but was modified to include a section behind the conning tower with five vertical mine chutes. This adaptation made the submarine longer, heavier and slower to dive. These were successful designs, but suffered heavy casualties in operation, with only *U218* surviving the war to be consigned to the depths during Operation Deadlight.

The new *U214* was commissioned in November 1941 and went on her first operational patrol (from Brest) in April 1942. This makes her one of the longer serving U-boats from World War Two to be lost in the Channel. *U214*'s service history is worthy of note. On her third patrol, she operated off the Azores and off Freetown. Her fourth patrol, which began on 30th November 1942, took her to the eastern Caribbean. Up to this point, *U214* had functioned as a normal VIIC, because the SMA mines for her chutes had not been fully developed.

The next patrol was cut short in the Bay of Biscay by an air attack from a Whitley. This attack severely injured the commander and caused the mission to be curtailed. During May 1943, *U214* laid a minefield off Dakar. In August, she left to lay a minefield in the mouth of the Panama Canal. Having survived an air attack, *U214* laid 15 SMA mines near Colon and turned for home. On 15th August, the US submarine USS *Dorado* is thought to have sunk in this minefield, becoming the only such craft sunk by a U-boat in World War Two. In February 1944 *U214* laid mines off Casablanca.

Before her next patrol, D-Day had commenced and *U214* had been fitted with a schnorchel. Her first attempt to leave Brest was foiled by a Liberator that was shot down, but only after damaging *U214* severely, forcing her back to base. In mid June 1944, she laid a minefield outside Plymouth. It was while attempting the same in July 1944 that *U214*'s lengthy career was cut short.

On 26th June, *U214* was located by the destroyer HMS *Cooke* under the command of Lt. Cmdr. L.C. Hill, which destroyed the submarine with depth charges. There were no survivors, and no concrete evidence of *U214*'s destruction was gathered. However, the Assessment Committee was morally convinced that *U214* was destroyed here.

U214 has yet to be positively located. She lies in a relatively unexplored area off Start Point. In the future, when divers investigate this area, *U214* may well be located. Being of a rare design, she would make an interesting find.

U214's last commander, Gerhard Conrad had been watch officer on *U260*, which was sunk off southern Ireland in March 1945. Her entire crew survived. Such are the twisting fortunes of war.

Her sister, *U218* was dived by the author in 2001 in the waters off Northern Ireland. She is the only located example of the Type VIID anywhere in the world.

No 3/9, *U672* - A Lucky Boat

Class: VIIC	**Built at:** Howaldtswerke - Hamburg
Length: 67.1m	**Displacement:** 871t
Date sunk: 18th July 1944	**How sunk:** Depth charge HMS *Balfour*
Historic Position: 50 03N; 03 25W	**Known Position:** Unknown
Crew losses: None	**Commander:** Olzs. Ulf Lawaetz

U672 became a front boat in October 1943 and made two patrols in the North Atlantic, during which her most dangerous moments came in the form of air attacks, once by a Sunderland and once by a Liberator.

The submarine left St. Nazaire for the Channel on 6th July 1944. For a U-boat it was a very dangerous stretch of water during months following D-Day. *U672* took 12 days to reach the area where she was sunk. Using her schnorchel at night at no more than 5 knots and running submerged at 50 metres at 2 knots during the day, she slowly covered the distance. On 17th July she received orders to proceed to an area south of the Isle of Wight.

However, on 18th June at 18.00, while lying on the bottom at 50 03N;03 25W, the submarine was detected by a group of escorts and was attacked as the ships passed over her. The explosions caused water to enter through the stern glands. Further blasts wrecked the battery panels and caused more leaking. The water was pumped out slowly to correct the trim, but it was realised after some time that the submarine was too badly damaged to be saved. Moreover, the air was becoming very foul.

Ulf Lawaetz with the humorous boat emblem badge (inset) on his cap. (U-Boot Archiv)

The commander, Ulf Lawaetz, ordered the vessel to be readied for possible abandonment, if necessary. Secret papers and equipment were destroyed and with only a small working reserve of high pressure, *U672* attempted to rise. When she finally left the bottom, *U672* ascended at an angle of 70 degrees, bow first. On the surface, the diesel engines could not be started, so the crew took to the life rafts while the chief engineer and commander scuttled the submarine.

On 19th July at 13.30, a squadron of Spitfires sighted the survivors 17 miles southeast of Start Point. A Walrus seaplane was dispatched to collect the commander and surface vessels rescued the rest of the crew. *U672* became the only U-boat to be sunk east of Start Point where the entire crew survived.

U672's helmsman, Horst Hofmann held the Knight's Cross. This was an extremely rare award for a sailor of non-officer rank. He had been a crew member aboard the most successful U-boat of World War Two, *U48*. His experience and calmness during this ordeal undoubtedly contributed to the safe evacuation of the entire crew.

Interestingly, the usual sinking position for *U672*, given in all histories up to now, shows her being sunk at 50.03N;02.30W. This is most likely a typing error and it probably can be traced back to the report made by HMS *Balfour*. The survivors interrogation reports state the position 50.03N;03.25W. This is close to the position where the survivors were located, and is far more likely to be the right one.

In an area rich in shipwrecks, the wreck of *U672* would be a significant find. She is not a war-grave, but lies in a similar area to *U214* (see wreck No 3/8).

Flotilla Commander Karl Emmerman inspects the crew of U672. Her Commander walks behind. (U-Boot Archiv)

No 3/10, *U767* - One Survivor

Class: VIIC	**Built at:** Kriegsmarinewerft - Wilhelmshaven
Length: 67.1m	**Displacement:** 871t
Date sunk: 18th June 1944	**How sunk:** Depth charges 14th Escort Group
Historic Position: 49 03N; 03 13W	**Known Position:** 49 02.4N; 03 13.56W
Crew losses: 48 (from 49)	**Commander:** Olzs. Walter Dankleff

U767 during commissioning – note the heavy anti-aircraft armament on the later-war Type VIIC wintergarden. (U-Boot Archiv)

U767 left the Norwegian base of Marviken on 22nd May 1944 to operate in the Channel. She successfully made the transit and was responsible for the destruction of the frigate HMS *Mourne* off Wolf Rock on 9th June.

However, this success was to be short-lived. It seems that *U767* decided to either enter the Channel by sneaking along the Brittany coast, or was attempting to reach the German-occupied island of Guernsey, where other U-boats had stopped off to fully recharge their batteries in relative safety. Either way, it was not to be. On June 18th, she was detected by the 14th Escort Group made up of the experienced destroyers HMS *Hotspur*, HMS *Icarus*, HMS *Inconstant*, HMS *Havelock* and HMS *Fame*. The ensuing hedgehog attack by HMS *Fame* claimed at least three hits on the U-boat, sending her to the bottom in 75 metres. Once detected on the seabed, the Escort Group depth charged *U767* until they were certain of her destruction.

During the melee' of falling depth charges, one crew member burst to the surface in an air bubble. He was wearing a Dräger escape lung and was plucked from the sea by HMS *Fame*. His name was Walter Schmietenknop and he identified the submarine as *U767*. His escape from 70 metres remains to this day one of the deepest successful submarine escapes ever successfully carried out. Schmietenknop stated that he had been blown out of the submarine in an air bubble.

The Escort Group did not have long to savour their victory, as German shore batteries along the French coast opened fire on them. Under smoke, the destroyers departed.

There was supposed to be a submarine wreck at 49 02.4N;03 13.56W. This is very close to where *U767* was reported sunk. This position was dived by the 'Starfish Enterprise' group of divers in 2002. The video footage, which the author has seen clearly shows a Type VIIC U-boat. The open stern hatch corroborates Schmietenknop's tale of his escape.

No 3/11, *U1191* - Loss Confirmed by Divers

Class: VIIC	**Built at:** F Schichau - Danzig
Length: 67.1m	**Displacement:** 871t
Date sunk: 25th June 1944	**How sunk:** Depth charge HMS *Affleck*
Historic Position: 50 03N; 02 59W	**Known Position:** 50 01.29N; 02 59.67W
Crew losses: 50 (all crew lost)	**Commander:** Olzs. Peter Grau

The case of the sinking of *U1191* is one where the real possibility of finally ending several years of debate over the sinking of this submarine has occurred because of the efforts of divers.

The original sinking assessment, made in 1945, credited the destruction of *U1191* to HMS *Affleck* and HMS *Balfour* at 50 03N;02 59W on 25th June 1944. However, due to the absence of reliable evidence of a sinking, the assessment only received a 'B' grade. This meant that the Assessment Committee morally believed that a submarine had been sunk in this attack, but that it could not be proved (due to thick fog). The assessment was reviewed in the 1990s by Dr. Axel Niestlé and it was decided that, due to the presence of the possible wreck of *U269*, supposedly at 50 01N;02 59W, also sunk on 25th June 1944, that HMS *Affleck* and HMS *Balfour* had depth charged the wreck of *U269*. While this is plausible, there was no new evidence at that time to support either contention.

U1191s officers and crew (U-Boot Archiv)

In the summer of 1999, the author identified a VIIC U-boat at 49 55.86N;02 46.58W. This is probably *U269* (see wreck No 3/12). Later that summer, the author found another VIIC U-boat at the position given in the box above. At first, it was assumed that the second discovery was likely to be *U269*, because of the proximity of the location to where she was supposedly sunk. However, this wreck was extremely intact and afforded the rare opportunity for the diver to identify a wreck by 'Lennart Lindberg'.

Lennart Lindberg was a German historian who worked out a method of identifying U-boats by the patterns of drainage slots cut into the outer hull during their manufacture. Each shipyard used a slightly different pattern. This is an excellent way of identifying U-boat photographs. However, it is also an excellent way of identifying sunken U-boats too! Sadly though, in most cases, the outer hulls of so many U-boat wrecks are now in such poor states of preservation, that this is simply not possible. So imagine the author's surprise when he stumbled across an entire row of slots on the starboard side of the wreck and was able to film them, then, at home that evening, eliminate the possibility that the wreck dived that day could be *U269*! The drainage slots (3-14-4) however, matched *U1191*! Although a full set of slots on either side of the submarine are needed for a perfect match, this was very strong evidence to support the original assessment.

The author has concluded that the wreck dived at this position is probably, though not certainly, (both *U650*, *U441* and *U1055*, could have been sunk in Channel and are also remote candidates) *U1191*. Other evidence to support this comes from the different build qualities of the two wrecks. This one seemed to be of a later period, with a higher degree of steel fittings, where earlier U-boats (such as *U269*) would have had brass ones. This was a very intact wreck and was the first time that the author had ever seen the 'wintergarden' anti-aircraft platform still in place on a U-boat wreck. The Aphrodite system's (anti-radar system which used balloons and strips of aluminium) hydrogen cylinders could be seen underneath it. Interestingly, both the upper and lower conning tower hatches were open, suggesting that an escape attempt may have been made.

U1191 was on her first operational patrol when she was lost. She had been at sea for four weeks since leaving Stavangar. Her commander, Peter Grau, was 24 years old. Shortly after *U269* had been sunk, HMS *Goodson* had been torpedoed in the same area. It was the search for the submarine that had done this that led to the destruction of *U1191*. The culprit, however was *U984*, which survived the encounter and later returned to base.

It is quite likely that this was one of the submarines originally located and dived during the search for HMS *Affray* (see No 3/22) in 1951.

No 3/12, *U269* - Macintyre's Last Kill

Class: VIIC	**Built at:** Vegesacker Werft - Vegesack
Length: 67.1m	**Displacement:** 871t
Date sunk: 25th June 1944	**How sunk:** Depth charges HMS *Bickerton*
Historic Position: 50 01N; 02 59W	**Known Position:** 49 55.86N; 02 46.58W
Crew losses: 12 (from 51)	**Commander:** Olzs. Georg Uhl

Captain Donald Macintyre was one of the most successful U-boat hunters the Royal Navy produced during World War Two. The last U-boat he destroyed was *U269*, on 25th June 1944.

The Asdic team aboard Macintyre's lead ship, HMS *Bickerton*, picked up the contact in question as the ship ran over it. HMS *Bickerton* turned independently to re-inspect the contact and found that it had moved, guaranteeing the presence of a submarine. Macintyre ordered an immediate attack and the ship dropped a pattern of depth charges over the contact. Within minutes, a U-boat came to the surface and the crew opened fire, until it was clear that the Germans were abandoning ship. The U-boat then sank stern first, as HMS *Bickerton* came to rescue the survivors.

In all, 12 of the crew of *U269* did not survive. Two were buried at sea the following day, having died once hauled on board. The commander, Olzs. Georg Uhl, was sucked into HMS *Bickerton's* propellers and was killed. Interestingly, two of the survivors had gone down with the submarine and had made unaided escapes from the conning tower at a depth of 70 metres. As with the survivor from *U767* (see wreck No 3/10) they became members of a very exclusive club. The entire attack had lasted less than ten

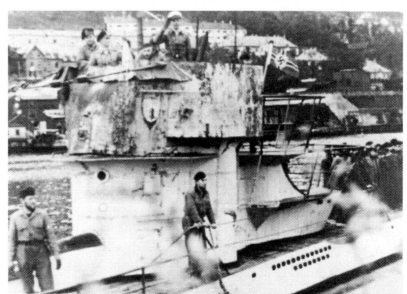

A damaged U269 in Narvik in 1943 (U-Boot Archiv)

minutes. HMS *Bickerton* was on its way to Plymouth when HMS *Goodson* was torpedoed and the hunt for *U1191* began (see wreck No 3/11). Interestingly, Macintyre considered the attack that sunk *U1191* to have 'achieved no success'.

Under interrogation, the survivors of *U269* explained how they had been caught so easily. They had heard the Escort Group pass overhead and had assumed that they had not been detected. The U-boat was ascending to schnorchel depth to air the boat and could not detect the approaching warship against the background noise of the rest of the Escort Group. By the time they realised their folly it was too late. *U269* was on its third major patrol when she was sunk. She had used Guernsey as a staging point to recharge her batteries and was returning there when she was detected.

In the summer of 1999, a diving team led by the author was looking to find the wreck of *UB19*, (see wreck No 3/4) which historically was sunk one mile from the wreck at 49 55.86N;02 46.58W. It was surprising therefore, that the team discovered the wreck of a VIIC U-boat instead, which could be the wreck of *U269*. This is some ten miles from the sinking position reported by HMS *Bickerton*. There is a U-boat much closer to that position (see *U1191* Wreck No 3/11), but it has been ruled out as being *U269*. However, the wreck at this location fits the description of *U269*, being an earlier type VIIC with bronze torpedo tubes and a higher content of non-ferrous metal. The author's video footage clearly shows that both bow and stern are heavily damaged. Also, the two hatches in the conning tower are open, corroborating the story of the two escapees. The wreck is cracked forward of the conning tower, suggesting that she hit the seabed hard. While it cannot be said with the fullest certainty that this is the wreck of *U269*, it seems probable that she is.

Problematically, HMS *Bickerton* was fitted with 'Gee', the early Decca-based system. A positional difference of ten miles from the location of this wreck and the reported sinking position needs to be considered.

This wreck was initially located and dived during the search for HMS *Affray* in 1951 (see No 3/22).

No 3/13, *U772* - 20 Miles From Certainty

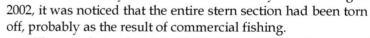

Class: VIIC	**Built at:** Kriegsmarinewerft - Wilhelmshaven
Length: 67.1m	**Displacement:** 871t
Date sunk: 30th December 1944	**How sunk:** Air depth charge from Wellington?
Historic Position: 50 05N; 02 31W	**Known Position:** 50 24 87N; 02 26 20W
Crew losses: 48 (all crew lost)	**Commander:** Klt. Ewald Rademacher

In the summer of 1996 the author first visited a U boat wreck close to the end of Portland Bill. He has returned most years since and watched the wreck steadily deteriorate. Most notably while diving in

2002, it was noticed that the entire stern section had been torn off, probably as the result of commercial fishing.

The wreck is a late World War Two VIIC with some of the features associated with the last of this class to be sent to sea. The four life raft canisters on the bow and the inclusion of advanced radio transmission equipment pointed to a U-boat fresh from Germany, operating in late 1944, or early 1945. This wreck is widely misidentified as *UC62*, (see No 3/15) a World War One minelayer, presumably, because to the inexperienced eye, the life raft canisters resemble mine chutes.

The problem with the identification of this submarine was its location. The most likely (and nearest) candidate for this wreck is *U772*. This sinking fits in some ways, because it occurred on 30th December 1944. The submarine was attacked and sunk while using its schnorchel. The attack periscope on the wreck is extended. It was used when the schnorchel was deployed to see where the boat was heading. Sadly, the damage to the submarine is too great to ascertain, with any certainty, whether the schnorchel was in use when she was

Klt. Ewald. Rademacher (U-Boot Archiv)

sunk. The major problem with accepting this identification is the navigational error involved between the reported attack position and the location of the wreck. This difference is exactly 20 miles. While under normal operational circumstances, such a distance could be accounted for in any number of ways, it raises suspicion. However, in all other respects, the attack report matches the condition of the wreck.

Another piece of evidence that supports the identification of the U-boat, is the proximity of the wreck of the SS *Black Hawk*. This sinking is accredited to *U772* and it was always supposed that *U772* was sunk while moving away from its attack position, having lain 'doggo' until the next day.

However, a recent review of the circumstances relating to the loss of *U772* has shown that HMCS *Calgary* attacked a U-boat contact shortly after the torpedoing of the *Black Hawk*. Oil was seen, but no other evidence of a kill was found. Supporting the success of this attack is the fact it took place exactly where the wreck now lies.

It is unlikely that the attackers that destroyed this U-boat will ever be definitely known. However, it can be presumed with a higher degree of certainty that the wreck is *U772*. There are other U-boats that are thought to be possibly lost in the Channel. *U1055* and *U650* are also possible candidates.

Commissioned a year previously, *U772* was on her second patrol when she was lost. Initially successful, she had sunk three ships prior to being destroyed.

No 3/14, Unidentified VIIC U-boat – (Possibly *U441*)

Class: VIIC	**Built at:** Unknown
Length: 67.1m	**Displacement:** 871t
Date sunk: Unknown	**How sunk:** Unknown
Historic Position: N/A	**Known Position:** 50 02.74N; 02 01.38W
Crew losses: Assume all	**Commander:** Unknown

In 1998, a group of divers from Weymouth reported finding a 'submarine' at the position given above. The following year, the author visited the site and identified the wreck as a VIIC U-boat, schnorchel-equipped, with conning tower hatch open. At first appearance, she seemed quite intact, but towards the end of the dive, a large blast hole was located forward of the conning tower. This allowed the divers to see right through into the control room.

There is a possible ASW attack near to this site that could have caused the sinking. On 11th June 1944, Avenger G of 855 squadron attacked a submerged submarine at 49 59;02 10W. This attack (listed by the Assessment Committee as AUD 1041/44) was recorded as "U-boat present – no damage". If this attack did sink a U-boat, then it is likely that it was *U441*, which would have been passing through here at the time. Other explanations for the loss of this U-boat remain speculative, but there could be many, including unreported ASW attacks, accident and mine.

No 3/15, *UC62* - Lost in a Minefield?

Class: UCII (UC61 series)	**Built at:** AG Weser - Bremen
Length: 51.85m	**Displacement:** 504t
Date sunk: Mid October 1917	**How sunk:** Accident?
Historic Position: Near Portland?	**Known Position:** The Shambles?
Crew losses: 30 (all crew lost)	**Commander:** Olzs. M. Schmitz

UC62 was on a mine-laying mission off the Dorset coast in October 1917 when she disappeared. It was not until World War One was over that cases such as this could be reviewed and a likely explanation for the loss of so many U-boats could be ascertained.

In the case of *UC62*, it is thought that she was responsible for the minefield laid off St. Albans head, which was located and swept. *UC62* was then thought to have been heading toward Portland when she probably hit a British mine, laid in a deep field between St. Albans Head and Portland, apparently in an area just to the south of the Shambles.

From time to time, the wreck of *U772* is reported to be that of *UC62* (see No 3/13), however, this is not correct. Bearing in mind that the area in question has been heavily dived over the last 20 years, it would seem increasingly unlikely that a submarine will be found there. Then again, HMS *A3* (see No 4/18) was located in this area as late as 1989.

Commissioned in January 1917, *UC62* had been responsible for sinking 20,035 tons of shipping before she was lost.

The author has heard unconfirmed reports of a World War One era U-boat near the wreck of *U480* (see wreck No 4/1). *UC62* would be a good candidate, if such a wreck exists.

No 3/16, HMS *P555* - The State Express

Class: Early US 'S' Class	**Built at:** Bethlehem – Quincy, Mass
Length: 219ft 5in	**Displacement:** 1062t
Date sunk: 25th August 1957	**How sunk:** Sunk as Sonar Target
Historic Position: 50 30 87N; 02 33.68W	**Known Position:** 50 30.87N; 02 33.68W
Crew losses: None	**Commander:** None

HMS P555 – originally a US submarine. (Royal Navy Submarine Museum)

HMS *P555* is unique among the submarines that lie on the seabed of the Channel, because she is American. Her original designation was *S24* and she was designed and built to the specifications of the United States Navy during the First World War.

The early US S-class submarine was designed before many of the lessons of submarine warfare from the First World War had been fully realised. This meant that in particular, she was a slow vessel when travelling on the surface. Although several major alterations were made to *S24* and her sisters to remedy this problem, they were never entirely satisfactory and the US Navy quickly began to develop alternative designs.

Although obsolete at the beginning of World War Two, the S-class was pushed into service due to a shortage of better types. Designed primarily for actions in the Atlantic, the S-class did not have the range or endurance to wage submarine war in the vast reaches of the Pacific. However, Britain was short of submarines at this time and S-class boats could be of utility to her.

The lend-lease agreement between the United States and the UK saw several of the S-class submarines transferred to the UK. *P555* was commissioned into the Royal Navy on 10th August 1942 at New London, USA. Her service under the white ensign was primarily one of training vessel for submariners and for anti-submarine forces. She operated primarily from the Clyde bases. However, among all of the six S-class boats lent to the UK during World War Two, *P555* was the only one to become operational as a front-line boat.

P555 became the first ever serving British submarine to have a RNVR commander, Edward Young. Her British crew dubbed *P555* "State Express" after a brand of cigarettes. Her closest scrape came when she was involved in a minor collision in the Clyde.

In May 1944, HMS *P555* was paid-off as being uneconomic to continue to operate. She should have been returned to the US along with her five sisters at the end of the war. However, her fate was to be "intentionally destroyed" as a sonar target in August 1947.

This is excellent news for divers because the *P555* makes a great dive. Standing upright in 44 metres, with her deck at 38 metres, she is still an awesome site. She is totally intact, showing little deterioration for her half century underwater. The author's diving group has visited her and all agreed that this was one of the best submarine dives around Weymouth. One feature that was greatly remarked upon, was the existence of the original teak decking all around the conning tower and bridge areas. Her curiously unique design is not like any other submarine in diving depths around the UK.

No 3/17, HMS *Safari* – Ben Bryant's Boat

Class: S-Class		**Built at:** Vickers Armstrong – Barrow	
Length: 65.7m		**Displacement:** 990t	
Date sunk: 8th January 1946		**How sunk:** Broke tow cable	
Historic Position: 50 24.30N; 02 02.30W		**Known Position:** 50 25.39N; 02 02.55W	
Crew losses: None		**Commander:** None	

HMS *Safari* was one of the most successful submarines to serve in the Royal Navy. She operated in the Mediterranean and from British bases. During her service life she had four commanders. However,

HMS *Safari* will always be best remembered for her association with Cmdr. Ben Bryant.

Bryant commanded HMS *Safari* between May 1942 and April 1943. During this time, the submarine made 10 war patrols. These were conducted primarily off Italy and North Africa. HMS *Safari* accounted for 30,000 tons of enemy shipping during this time. For these successes, Ben Bryant was awarded the DSO with two bars. HMS *Safari* also operated as part of the protective screen for Operation Pedestal, a major supply convoy sent from Gibraltar to Malta.

The famous HMS Safari. (Royal Navy Submarine Museum)

A significant factor in these successes was the use of HMS *Safari's* deck cannon, as an alternative to the torpedo. *Safari's* crack-shot gun crew was also used to shell coastal targets and even trains. During her service life, HMS *Safari* was to fire in excess of 1,000 rounds at enemy targets.

On Bryant's last patrol with HMS *Safari*, he sank six ships and severely damaged a seventh. Among those sunk were a tanker, a liner and two small warships.

With command taken over by Lt. R. B. Lakin, HMS *Safari* went on to claim several more successes and to operate as a landing beacon for Operation Husky, the allied invasion of Sicily. After four patrols, she was ordered back to Britain for a refit. She operated from UK bases for the remainder of the war.

An excellent shot of HMS Safari showing her well-used gun platform. (Dave Saywell)

On a sadder note, HMS *Safari's* Sub-Lt. was John Blackburn. He survived the war and remained in the submarine service afterwards. He was the commander of HMS *Affray* when she disappeared with all hands in 1951 (see No 3/22).

In January 1946, HMS *Safari* was sold for scrap and was on her way to the breakers yard in Newport when her tow cable parted and she made her final dive in the waters off St. Albans Head.

In the summer of 1986, the wreck of HMS *Safari* was located and identified by local diver, Dave Saywell. This proved to be a difficult task, because the wreck was not to be found in the usual lists of wartime losses. Once she was identified, then a two-year paper chase began to try and trace the owners of the wreck. Local diver, Dave Wendes, conducted this. The firm that had originally owned the wreck had been through several hands. Finally in 1988, the salvage rights were obtained from the owners and are now privately owned by Mr Saywell.

Because she was due to be scrapped, the submarine had been totally stripped of munitions and had had its deck cannon and propellers taken off. However, the bronze conning tower proved to be an attractive salvage proposition, and in the summer of 1990, the tower was blasted from the wreck.

Using four one-ton lifting bags and 17 air tanks, it was raised and taken ashore to be weighed-in for scrap. This was not before its key features, binnacle, wheel, telegraph and other items were removed and painstakingly restored.

Today the wreck of HMS *Safari* lies in 42 metres of water on a stone seabed. She lies with the tide and makes a very interesting dive. The submarine lies over to port with her hatches open, giving divers the opportunity to peer into the interior of this historic wreck.

No 3/18, HMS *A3* – Gunnery target

Class: A-Class	**Built at:** Vickers - Barrow
Length: 30.3m	**Displacement:** 180t
Date sunk: 15th May 1912	**How sunk:** Gunnery target
Historic Position: 'Off Portland'	**Known Position:** 50 31.70N; 02 11.42W
Crew losses: None	**Commander:** None

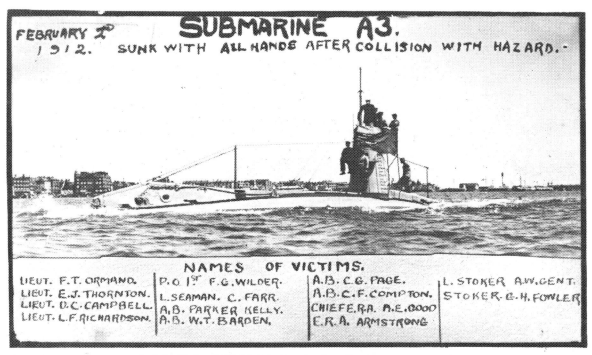

A contemporary postcard of the ill-fated HMS A3. (Author's collection)

HMS *A3* is one of three A-Class submarines that lie on the seabed of the Channel (see also Nos 4/16 and 1/29). Like the other two, her history involves the tragic loss of her crew in a submarine accident.

A3 was one of the first group of A-Class submarines to be built. Like the others, she was primarily used for coastal patrolling and training.

The submarine had been in service for over seven years when disaster struck on 2nd February 1912. At the time, HMS *A3* was under the command of Lt. F. T. Ormond. He was a relatively inexperienced submarine officer at the time and was standing in as a replacement for HMS *A3*'s usual commander, who through illness luckily avoided the sinking.

In concert with several other submarines from Gosport, *A3* was on manoeuvres outside the Solent when she was involved in a collision with the submarine depot ship, HMS *Hazard*. It appears that HMS *Hazard* was functioning as a 'target' vessel at the time and that during the manoeuvres she struck the submerged *A3*. It seems that she was attempting a torpedo attack on HMS *Hazard* at the time.

Although only a glancing blow, it seems as if *A3* passed down the port side of her depot ship and was finally fatally holed by her port propeller and rudder. Both propellers and rudders were later found damaged.

Although located the day after she was lost, Navy salvage teams waited five weeks for the weather to clear so that an attempt to lift HMS *A3* could be made. This was finally successful on 12th March. The bodies of 13 of the 14 dead crewmen were laid to rest nearby their comrades that had died when HMS *A1* (see wreck No 4/15) collided with *SS Berwick*, eight years before.

The damage to HMS *A3* was considered too severe to have her refitted and returned to service. So instead, it was decided to dispose of her as a gunnery practice target. On 15th May 1912, HMS *A3* was towed to a position off St. Albans Head by the tug *Seahorse* and finally sent to the bottom for the last time by 4-inch shells from the battleship HMS *St. Vincent*.

The submarine's small size may have been the main reason why this wreck was not located for 77 years. Simon Bird, who was then captain of the diving vessel *Trio*, found her by chance in the summer of 1989. The nearby wreck of the *Aeolian Sky* had been the day's target. While returning home, Mr Bird ran over an unknown obstruction. With a Decca set and a paper-printing echo sounder, he was able to relocate the position and lay a shot line.

Although well past slack water, two members of Banstead Sub-Aqua Club made the difficult descent to the wreck and identified it as a submarine. Further research by Mr Bird and the divers confirmed that the wreck was a British A-Class, but which one? The answer was reached when the team took their findings to (the late) Mr Gus Britton at the Royal Navy Submarine Museum.

Lying in 39 metres and very close to a rocky ridge, HMS *A3* is not an easy wreck to locate. However, the rewards for the divers that go there are great. This area can be blessed with exceptional visibility, sometimes good enough to see the entire submarine sitting on the rocky seabed.

The author's diving team visited this wreck in 1999 and found it to be a delightful dive. She is upright and mainly intact. Her conning tower hatch and windows seem to be the only items that have been removed. Her torpedo tubes and other features are all in evidence and make interesting items to inspect. This is a small wreck, so ideal for divers who prefer limited bottom times at this sort of depth.

The conning tower hatch from HMS *A3* can be seen on display at Weymouth's shipwreck and diving museum.

No 3/19, HMS *L24* – Collision

Class: L-Class	**Built at:** Vickers - Barrow
Length: 72.3m	**Displacement:** 1089t
Date sunk: 10th January 1924	**How sunk:** Collision with HMS *Resolution*
Historic Position: 11m 217deg Portland	**Known Position:** 50 22.4N;02 37.8W
Crew losses: 43 (all crew lost)	**Commander:** Lt.Cmdr. P. L. Eddis

The minelayer variant of the L-Class design, L24 was tragically lost in a peacetime accident. (Royal Navy Submarine Museum)

The British L-Class was designed to see action during the last two years of World War One. It constituted an improvement in size and performance over the successful E-Class. A total of 34 of the class were built, but only a few were in service before the Armistice.

The L-Class went through a considerable number of design changes during the period over which all of the class was built. Many look quite different from each other. Several were originally designed not to a carry a deck cannon, while others had an elevating 'hidden' gun and others had one built into the conning tower. There were also significant differences in torpedo diameter, number and position of torpedo tubes and beam.

One significant modification to the main features of the L-Class was the development of a minelaying version. HMS L24 was one of only six of these L-Class variants to be built. Apart from the standard armament of four 21-inch torpedo tubes, she also carried 16 mines that were located in vertical chutes on either side of the conning tower area, in replacement of two torpedo tubes.

Launched in 1919 and completed in 1920, HMS L24 was finished too late to see action in the First World War. She spent her four years in service conducting training duties while under three different commanders, her last being Lt.Cmdr. P. L. Eddis, who had taken command the previous August. Eddis

HMS L24 with some of her crew. In the background is HMS M1, also lost tragically in the Channel. (see No 1/26). (Royal Navy Submarine Museum)

was an experienced submariner, having seen considerable combat experience in the First World War. He had been an officer on HMS E13 when she had been stranded in Danish waters and had been shelled by German destroyers, an act which killed half of HMS E13's crew. Eddis's second officer, Lt D. H. Barton was also a veteran of the war, having served on HMS New Zealand during the Battle of Jutland.

On 10th January 1924, HMS L24 was lost on her first trip to sea after a period of Christmas leave. She was involved in 'GA', a naval exercise that pitted submarines against warships. At 11.13, the 25,750-ton Royal Sovereign-Class battleship, HMS Resolution, felt a slight jolt under her keel and noticed a disturbance in the waters around her. Later that day, when HMS L24 failed to return to base, it was realised that she had been sunk.

Quite remarkably, the wreck was located the following day. This was described in the newspapers of the time as being possible because of a secret 'ray' used by the Navy that could detect metal (obviously a simple magnetometer). However, due to bad weather, divers were not able to reach the wreck until the end of the month, although it was known from the damage on the bows of HMS *Resolution*, that there would be no survivors.

When investigated, it was clear by the gash in her stern that HMS *L24* had sunk quickly. Her diving planes were set to hard dive. Sadly, it was noted that the forward hatch was open, suggesting that some of the crew may have attempted an escape from the stricken submarine. The January waters of the Channel would have claimed them quickly.

The wreck of HMS *L24* then remained unnoticed until the summer of 1981, when local diver and charter-boat operator, Andy Smith, took a group of divers from Guildford to examine a fishing snag. To their amazement the divers discovered the wreck of a submarine. Making detailed notes, the team was able to describe the wreck to Mr Gus Britton of the Royal Navy Submarine Museum. During a subsequent visit, the divers identified the wreck from photographs. They had also seen the open forward hatch and the damage to the submarine's stern, confirming the diving reports of 1924.

The author's diving team has visited this wreck on 3 occasions, for no other reason than the fact that she makes a superb dive. Her sheer size marks her out as a British submarine built on the verge of the modern era. She lies with a slight list to port in a general depth of 55 metres. The visibility at the site in the summer can be exceptional. On one visit it was possible to see bow and stern from the top of the conning tower!

The wreck of HMS *L24* has many fascinating features to examine. Notably, divers have often enquired about the strange holes along either side of the pressure hull. These are her mine chutes. Her four bow caps can be seen, along with her periscopes, torpedo loading equipment, rudders and propellers. Also, the features noticed by the divers in 1924 are still evident, including the open fore-hatch, a salutary reminder of the tragic events that happened here over 75 years ago.

No 3/20, HMS *Sidon* – Torpedo Explosion

Class: S-Class	**Built at:** Cammell Laird - Birkenhead
Length: 65.75m	**Displacement:** 990t
Date sunk: 14th June 1957	**How sunk:** Sonar target
Historic Position: 50 32.7N; 02 38.7W	**Known Position:** 50 32.7N;02 38.7W
Crew losses: None	**Commander:** None

HMS *Sidon* is one of three British S-Class submarines that lie in the waters of the Channel (see Nos. 3/17 and 4/17). Unlike the other two, HMS *Sidon* was to see service in the post World War Two Navy.

Commissioned in October 1944, HMS *Sidon* saw little action during the war. She operated on two war patrols; one off Norway, one in the Far East. During her second patrol, HMS *Sidon* rescued a USAAF airman who had been drifting in a dinghy for five days, since the loss of his aircraft. HMS *Sidon* sank no shipping during these patrols.

On return to the UK, HMS *Sidon* was placed on the reserve list and later underwent an extensive refit. She joined the 2nd Submarine Flotilla on 31st August 1950. In April 1951, she was one of the submarines that was employed in the search for HMS *Affray* (See No 3/22).

In June 1951, she hit an underwater rock during an exercise and had to undergo repairs. This was her second accident, she had collided with HMS *Turpin* in January 1945. During her 1951 refit, she had her deck gun removed and was fitted with a snort mast, which was located on the after casing when not in use. She was later fitted with radar as well.

In 1955, HMS *Sidon* was selected to take part in live firing exercises of a new type of torpedo. This new design was derived from a captured German torpedo type. It was powered by hydrogen peroxide, which gave it higher underwater speed. The new propulsion system had been fitted to the British Mark VIII torpedo. Hydrogen peroxide is a tricky material to handle, being explosive. Moreover, it reacted with some of the materials the Mark VIII had been made from. With hindsight, it isn't that surprising that an accident was likely.

Sadly, for the crew of HMS *Sidon*, it occurred on 9th February 1955. While moored alongside her depot ship, a torpedo exploded in one of the forward torpedo tubes. The blast blew off the internal and external torpedo tube doors and the submarine began to sink. This was not initially recognised, and an orderly evacuation of HMS *Sidon* took place. When it was realised that she was going under, the order to abandon ship was given. While most of the survivors of the blast escaped, a Surgeon Lieutenant and 11 crew members perished.

Immediately, attempts were made to raise HMS *Sidon*. These involved the use of 'camels', steel buoyancy devices. Four were attached to her, while flooded. They were then re-pressurised and they brought HMS *Sidon* back to the surface. The submarine re-emerged from the bottom of Portland harbour on the night of 23rd June 1955, under the floodlights erected to help with the lift.

During the next four days, the sad job of removing the dead was carried out and they were duly buried in the local naval cemetery. HMS *Sidon* was paid off a week later.

Used for torpedo experiments, HMS Sidon suffered a fatal accident in port. (Imperial War Museum)

In 1957, HMS *Sidon*'s fate was decided. She was to become a sonar target. In June of that year, she was towed to her present resting site and allowed to sink.

HMS *Sidon* makes an excellent dive. The author visited this wreck in 1999 on a day with exceptional visibility. She lies upright on the bottom and is completely intact. Her most recognisable features include her bow sonar dome, torpedo loading hatch, magnificent bronze conning tower and the snort mast, stowed on the deck, aft of the conning tower.

This is a relatively shallow 33 metre dive, with the top of the wreck in around 27 metres. Unlike the other Channel S-Class wrecks, HMS *Swordfish* and HMS *Safari*, this example of a British S-Class is intact and gives the best opportunity to examine this legendary class of submarine design.

It is probably for this reason, that the wreck of HMS *Sidon* was purchased from the Ministry of Defence in 2000. The company, which bought her, Dorset-based Deepquest Sub Sea, has announced its intentions to raise the wreck. This is to be done via a consortium of various salvage companies. The ultimate purpose behind such an enterprise is unclear. As this book went to press in 2002, the wreck was still firmly attached to the seabed.

No 3/21, HMS *M2* – Aircraft Carrier

Class: M-Class
Length: 89.65m
Date sunk: 26th January 1932
Historic Position: W of Portland
Crew losses: 60 (all crew lost)

Built at: Vickers - Barrow
Displacement: 1946t
How sunk: Diving accident
Known Position: 50 34.57N;02 33.99W
Commander: Lt. Cmdr. John D. de. M. Leathes

HMS M2 awash with the sea perilously close to the hangar doors as she prepares to launch her plane. She sank under similar circumstances. (Royal Navy Submarine Museum)

The three M-Class submarines were built during World War One from the hulls already laid down for the last of the disastrous K-Class. HMS *M2* was originally to have been built as *K19*.

The M-Class was the brainchild of Admiral 'Jackie' Fisher. This freethinking officer had also been the driving force behind the development of the battle cruiser. Fisher's reasoning behind the development of the M-Class was that submarine torpedoes of the time were very inaccurate at anything except extremely short range. Therefore, it would be better to fit a submarine with an extremely high-powered gun as well as torpedoes. The final design of the M-Class incorporated 4 torpedo tubes, a 3-inch foldaway gun and the massive 12-inch gun from an obsolete battleship.

Only HMS *M1* (see No 1/26) was ready to see service during World War One . *M2* was completed on 14th February 1920 and for the first four years of her service life was operated in her original role as 'monitor submarine'.

The 12-inch gun had a flat trajectory at a range of 1200 yards. It was intended that the M-Class submarine should surface, fire the gun and submerge. This could be achieved in around 40 seconds. Its effect on anything, but the largest of ships, can only be imagined. However, it could only be reliably expected to work in the most benign of conditions. This is because of the proximity of the gun to the sea. If water entered the barrel, the gun would be likely to explode. This is known to have happened on at least three occasions on M-Class submarines.

Furthermore, the range to target made it vulnerable to quick-firing, low-calibre weapons aboard the target vessel. In practice, therefore, this class of submarine would have been used essentially as a commerce raider; its range of 4,500 miles being the limiting factor.

For the first four years of her service life HMS *M2* operated from British bases and was used extensively for various trials, including deep diving and resistance to poison gas. In 1923, in a chilling forewarning of the way she was lost, she dived with an open hatch and crashed into the seabed 239 feet below. On that occasion, HMS *M2* was able to surface. However, extensive repairs were needed to bring her back into service. The following year, HMS *M2* drifted helplessly across the Bay of Biscay after her diesel engines failed.

In the same year, 1924, *M2* was placed in reserve and plans began to convert her into an aircraft carrier. Captain Max Horton inspired the design. He considered that aerial reconnaissance at sea could be greatly improved if submarines could be developed to carry aircraft. The cost would be minimal, compared to building surface ships to do the same task. Also, if detected, the submarine could dive to safety.

It took three years to convert HMS *M2* to her now famous role. The George Parnell Company of Bristol built an all stainless-steel framed miniature seaplane for the submarine, the Parnell Peto. The

The Parnell Peto stowed in its hangar. (Royal Navy Submarine Museum)

main gun was removed and an aircraft hangar with a derrick for recovering the seaplane was added. On the foredeck a small catapult was also built to launch the aircraft. Cordite or compressed air would power this.

In operation, the little plane was fitted to a trolley, which carried it over the hangar door (which was hinged on the bottom) and on to the launching ramp. The wings were then unfolded and the launching procedure begun. In all, this took around 5-6 minutes. However, due to the fact that it took nearly 15 minutes for HMS *M2* to become fully buoyant on the surface, the submarine was nearly always close to awash when this procedure was carried out. The stern of the submarine was kept afloat by the aft hydroplanes during launch.

After completion, HMS *M2* was used continuously with submarines and battle squadrons to test Max Horton's theory. These tests were carried out in Gibraltar and in home waters. In 1930, the seaplane went out of control and crashed into the beach at Ryde. It knocked over a beach hut and caused the naked occupant to run for safety! This accident happened because of the weight of the passenger. Aircrew had to be of a specific weight to allow the small plane to fly. The under-powered Peto's operational ceiling was always a cause for concern.

In January 1932, HMS *M2* was operating in manoeuvres based on Portland. She reported that she would be ready to dive at around 10.30a.m. HMS *M2* was never seen in port again. The steamship *Tyneside*, reported that it had seen a submarine (which it thought was HMS *M2*) dive stern first at around 11.30a.m. Although HMS *M2* was the first British submarine to have been equipped with the new DSEA escape equipment, none of the crew was ever found wearing the apparatus.

Using the latest sonar equipment, it took eight days to find the submarine. She was initially investigated by Navy divers and found embedded in the seabed, stern first, with bows pointing upwards. It was decided to go ahead and salvage her.

The recovery operations were placed in the hands of Ernest Cox, the legendary figure of salvage diving in the UK, who had been responsible for raising the German warships in Scapa Flow. The plan was to cement-up the 'holes' in HMS *M2*'s hull and then to fill her with compressed air and refloat her.

It was during these operations that the seaplane was recovered from the hangar and two bodies were also found.

The process of making HMS *M2* ready for lifting was dogged with a number of severe setbacks. These included bad weather and the parting of the lifting 'camels' from the wreck. In fact, a total five different attempts were made to raise HMS *M2* and they all ended in failure. Finally, in December 1932, plans to salvage the wreck were abandoned.

During this time, it was ascertained that the hatches leading from the hangar into the submarine were open. An engine room hatch was also found to be open. It was concluded that the sinking had occurred during the launch of the seaplane. The most likely explanation was that opening the hangar doors too early swamped the submarine. Hydraulic failure may have caused the submarine to begin to subside once the launching procedure had begun.

A great shot of HMS M2 showing the launch catapult on her deck. (Royal Navy Submarine Museum)

For the next 38 years the wreck remained unexplored. Then, on 6th September 1970, in a landmark in the development of British wreck diving, a group of hardy pioneers visited the wreck of HMS *M2*. They reported her being in perfect condition and even still having the spare propeller located on her stern deck. A month later, the first of several fatal diving incidents occurred on the wreck.

During the years since, the wreck of HMS *M2* has become one of the most popular dives on the south coast. On weekends, in the summer months, it is not uncommon to find a dozen or more dive boats over the wreck site.

The author has dived this wreck on several occasions over the years. She is always an impressive dive. Her sheer size is always awe-inspiring. She has many key features, which make for interesting photographic and videographic subjects. Her massive bronze conning tower is so large that two divers can stand in the bridge at the same time. Her foldaway gun makes an interesting feature, as does her massive bow, with its four torpedo tubes.

However, the source of greatest fascination lies in exploring the aircraft hangar and catapult launching system. This is the only site in the world where such technology can be examined. As seen by the salvage divers in 1932, the hangar door is open and now the hangar is full of silt. The catapult is still there and until 1998, the davit, which was used to launch the seaplane, was also in place. It has sadly since, fallen off.

This wreck is showing signs of deterioration. In recent years, a light sheen of diesel oil has been seen over the wreck, as its fuel bunkers slowly corrode. Like many wrecks of its era, the sea is slowly consuming HMS *M2*. As this book was completed, Royal Navy divers were examining the wreck, checking to see if the flow of oil from it could be stemmed.

No 3/22, HMS *Affray* – The Last British Submarine Lost at Sea

Class: A-Class	**Built at:** Cammell Laird - Birkenhead
Length: 85.33m	**Displacement:** 1620t
Date sunk: 16th April 1951	**How sunk:** Diving accident
Historic Position: 67m 228 deg from St. Catherine's Light	**Known Position:** Withheld on request
Crew losses: 75 (all crew lost)	**Commander:** Lt. J. Blackburn DSC

HMS Affray in 1951 - Note the collar aft of the conning tower that held the snort mast when extended. (Royal Navy Submarine Museum)

The British A-Class submarine of World War Two design came into conception as a result of the development of the war in the Far East. The Royal Navy wanted a new design of submarine that could provide a powerful weapon against the forces of Japan.

With this in mind, the A-Class was developed into the most technologically sophisticated submarine built in the UK at that time. HMS *Affray* was one of this class. She benefited from an all-welded hull, which gave a greater diving depth. Operations in the extreme temperatures of the Far East meant that air conditioning and refrigeration were fitted to a British submarine class for the first time. Comfort and habitability for the crew was considered to have reached new heights in the A-Class too. For the first time, each crew member had a bunk, most of which were situated away from sources of noise.

The A-Class carried a considerable punch, with 6 forward torpedo tubes (2 external) and 4 stern tubes (2 external, as well). She also carried a four-inch gun and 20mm anti-aircraft armament.

Of the 46 A-Class boats ordered only 16 were completed and they all were delivered too late to see service during the war. They became important mainstays of the Royal Navy's post war submarine fleet into the 1950s. During this time, HMS *Affray*, along with her sisters, was modified, so that the guns she carried were removed. In their place, a snort mast was fitted. This device was similar to the German schnorchel and was used to allow the diesel engines to be run when the submarine was submerged. On the A-Class it was fitted on the port side of the aft deck and laid flat on the deck when not in use.

In service, HMS *Affray* travelled to all four corners of the world. She sailed extensively throughout the Mediterranean, Far East, South Africa and Europe. She returned to Britain regularly and was in Gosport in January 1951 when she received a refit.

In April 1951, HMS *Affray*, under the command of Lt. J. Blackburn (See No 3/17) prepared to take part in 'Operation Training Spring'. This involved operating as on war patrol in the Channel. Aboard was a party of four Royal Marine Commandos. In addition, there were twenty officer and engineering trainees on board. To make room for the additional numbers, ten of the usual submarine's complement were left at base. HMS *Affray* left Gosport on 16th April 1951 and never returned.

The following morning at 9.00 am, the submarine was expected to make its daily report. When this did not occur, the 'Subsunk' submarine rescue procedure was immediately launched. It developed into the largest peacetime air/sea operation ever carried out in the Channel.

Due to the considerable degree of latitude given to Lt. Blackburn during this exercise, it was far from certain just where the submarine might be. While her diving position was known, it was impossible to know what course she had taken once submerged. However, the search focused on an area 20 miles southeast of Start Point.

During this search, hull tapping was heard. In addition, on the 18th the message 'we are trapped on the bottom' was clearly picked up by her sister, HMS *Ambush*. All attempts to get a cross bearing on the sources of these sounds proved fruitless.

Sadly, by the 19th, the rescue operation was scaled down, because it was considered that there would no longer be any survivors on board. However, the search for HMS *Affray* was still in its infancy. Under the command of Captain W. O. Shelford, the hunt for the wreck of the submarine was to go on for another 56 days.

HMS Affray in Simonstown in 1946. She is sporting her gun platform that was removed in a later refit before her loss. (Royal Navy Submarine Museum)

Based on the Navy salvage vessel HMS *Reclaim*, Shelford conducted a difficult search in a 1,500 square mile area. The seabed is infested with shipwrecks. Although a squadron of frigates was available and equipped with the best sonar equipment around at the time, the identification of any wreck had to be made by divers. This was a time consuming process because only a limited amount of time (slack water) could be used in any one day. For the divers, the depths and endurance of the dives were major challenges. On one occasion, a diver was lucky to escape from serious injury when he blew up to the surface, feet-first.

After several weeks of using divers, the Royal Navy employed a remotely operated camera for the first time. It comprised a television camera mounted in a large steel housing. Not confined to searching during slack water, the search for HMS *Affray* was greatly accelerated. In fact, within 2 weeks of the camera being employed, HMS *Affray* was located. The camera was lowered to a wreck and the letters on her conning tower were beamed to the salvage team above. The date was 14th June 1951.

There followed a detailed inspection of the wreck site. It was during this that it was discovered that HMS *Affray* had been operating at periscope depth. Her radar aerial was extended, as was one periscope. A little later it was noticed that the snort mast (which had been in use), had snapped off a couple of feet above the actuator mounted on the aft deck. Importantly, it was noticed that all of HMS *Affray*'s hatches were closed. This showed that there had been no attempt by the crew to escape from the submarine.

One puzzle, which was not immediately answered, is why HMS *Affray*'s indicator buoy had not been released. However, it was later found out that it had a tendency to come loose and had, therefore, been wired in place; a fatal measure.

Further examination of the entirety of the submarine showed that the telegraphs read 'stop' and that the hydroplanes were all set to 'hard arise'. It was clear from this that an attempt to arrest the sinking had been made at the time.

The Navy took the snort mast away for examination and concluded that while the welding was not up to standard, the mast should have worked properly in normal use. An extraordinary shock would have been needed to cause it to break. It seems that the breaking of the mast probably flooded the submarine, but what had caused it to fail?

Ultimately, no certain answer could be given. However, it was suspected that either a battery explosion had occurred (this was not entirely uncommon in A-Class boats), causing the mast to break off; or alternatively the mast had broken off when the submarine impacted with the seabed, due to some unknown cause. The real answer for why HMS *Affray* sank will never be known for certain.

A benevolent fund, set up for the widows and children of the bereaved, reached £250,000 through public subscription. A memorial service was held and slowly the story of HMS *Affray*, the last British submarine lost at sea, faded from public memory.

Just over 47 years later, the author and some friends set out to search for and make a dive on HMS *Affray*. We found her in 83 metres of water, near Hurd Deep. This was one of the most difficult dives many of the team had undertaken up to that time. HMS *Affray* is a long way down and a long way from shore. However, in the safe hands of Andy Smith and his charter vessel *Skin Deep*, two safe dives were conducted.

The diving team found her to be exactly as described by the Navy diving team in 1951. She has a slight list to port, all hatches are shut and the base of the snort mast was clearly visible. The colour video footage taken at the time has subsequently been made into a film. Like other deep wrecks that contain the remains of so many who died tragically, the site of HMS *Affray* is a quiet and lonely place with a poignancy which is unique.

The voyage to HMS *Affray* turned out to be far more than just a dive. The author has made contact with many of

The recovery of Affray's broken snort mast. (Royal Navy Submarine Museum)

the families and other individuals involved in the *Affray* story and has found a deeper understanding of the personal dimensions that exist with tragedies such as this one. In April 2001, a memorial service commemorating the fiftieth anniversary of the sinking was held in Gosport. So many years after the event, such a tragedy still stirs powerful emotions amongst all involved at the time.

In October 2001, the wreck was made a controlled site under the Protection of Military Remains Act, 1986. This means it is illegal to visit the wreck site without a licence from the Ministry of Defence.

HMS *Affray* was the last British submarine to be lost at sea. However, she was not to be the last to sink. Two others sank in Channel ports after 1951 (see Nos 3/20 and Appendix 3). One of these was also an A-Class submarine. After the loss of HMS *Affray*, three other 'Subsunk' operations were launched in subsequent years. They were all aimed at finding A-Class submarines. Fortunately, in each case, the submarines involved were found on the surface.

No 3/23, *Vendémiaire* – Collision

Class: Emeraude – 1904	**Built at:** Unknown
Length: 55.0m	**Displacement:** 550t
Date sunk: 8th June 1912	**How sunk:** Collision – warship *St. Louis*
Historic Position: Off Raz Blanchard	**Known Position:** Raz Blanchard
Crew losses: 24 (All crew lost)	**Commander:** Lt. de V. Audic

A rare photo of the ill-starred Vendémiaire. (Marius Bar)

The pioneering days of submarines in the French Navy were as perilous as they were in the Royal Navy. Five French submarines were lost at sea before the outbreak of World War One. *Vendémiaire*'s collision with a friendly vessel during exercises happened only six months after a similar incident claimed the British submarine HMS *A3* (see No 3/18). She was on exercise in the waters between Cap de La Hague and Alderney when she was rammed and apparently sliced in two by the French warship *St. Louis*, which was supposed to be the target of practice torpedo attacks by the submarine.

However, for some reason, the *Vendémiaire* got out of position and suddenly appeared in front of the *St. Louis*. Nothing could be done to avoid a collision and although the submarine was diving hard and the warship took evasive action, the two vessels came into contact. In all cases of this nature, it is the fragile submarine that ends up being sent to the bottom. This case was no different and the entire crew of 24 including the *Vendémiaire*'s commander, Lt. de V. Audic, lost their lives.

The wreck of this submarine would be an interesting find. She is the oldest of the three French submarines that still lie in the waters of the Channel. To date, the author has not confirmed that this particular submarine has been located. A vague French report suggests that she was found in 1982. However, Jersey-based diver, John Ovenden, believes that the wreck of this submarine is still there to be found by an adventurous group of divers. There still remains the possibility that this wreck was raised by the French authorities, although the author has found no information to suggest this happened.

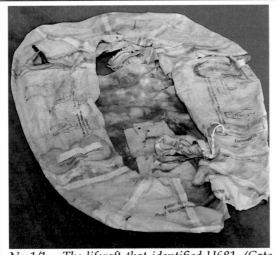

No 1/1 – The liferaft that identified U681. (Cate Groom)

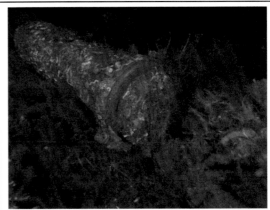

No 1/22 – A dry ready-use ammunition container on UC51. (Innes McCartney)

No 1/25 – HMS M1's forward hatch is found open. Did the crew attempt an escape? (Innes McCartney)

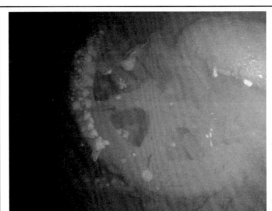

No 2/7 - One of UB118's radio mast elevators. (Innes McCartney)

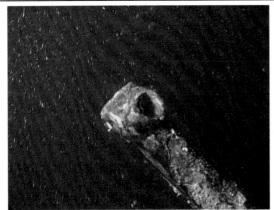

No 3/3 – The best use for a diver's knife – cleaning up periscopes! This one on the mystery U-Cruiser was covered in marine growth. (Innes McCartney)

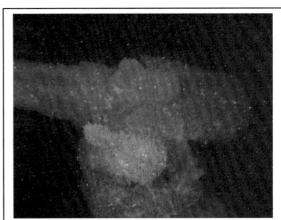

No 3/5 - UB72's upgraded 105mm deck-gun. (Innes McCartney)

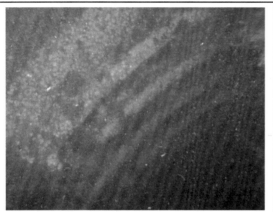

No 3/7 - The ribs inside UB74's pressure hull. (Innes McCartney)

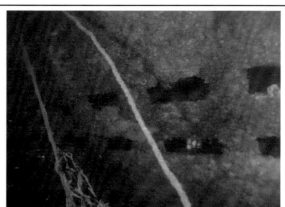

No 3/11 - The complete set of drainage slots on the bow of U1191 which helped identify her. (Innes McCartney)

No 3/11 – The hydrogen gas cylinders of U1191's Aphrodite rader-decoy system. (Innes McCartney)

No 3/12 – The blast hole that sank U269. (Innes McCartney)

No 3/13 – U772's conning tower seen from above, with its periscopes, H/F loop and opened hatch. (Innes McCartney)

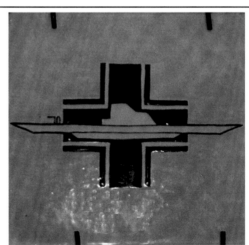

No 3/13 - U772's emblem on a ceramic tile in the U-Boot Archiv. (Innes McCartney)

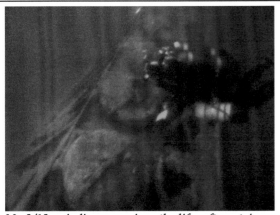

No 3/13 – A diver examines the life raft containers on the bows of U772. (Innes McCartney)

No 3/14 - The H/F loop on the wreck of an unidentified Type VIIC U-boat – possibly U441. (Innes McCartney)

No 3/16 - Teak decking on HMS P555. (Innes McCartney)

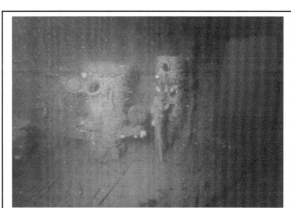

No 3/17 - Inside HMS Safari's conning tower, the compass binnacle. (Dave Saywell)

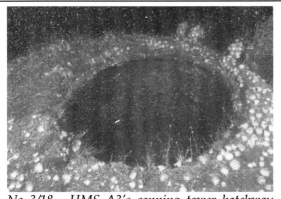

No 3/18 - HMS A3's conning tower hatchway. (Innes McCartney)

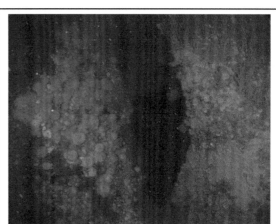

No 3/19 – The knife-shaped hole in L24's hull caused by her fatal collision with a battleship. (Innes McCartney)

No 3/19 – The rare design of mine chute fitted to the sides of HMSL24. (Innes McCartney)

No 3/21 - HMS M2's plane catapult. (Innes McCartney)

No 3/21 - The plane cradle on HMS M2. (Innes McCartney)

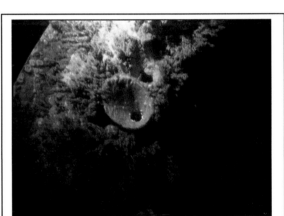

No 3/22 - A speaking tube in the bridge of HMS Affray. (Innes McCartney)

No 3/22 – The base of HMS Affray's snort mast at the point where it broke off. (Innes McCartney)

No 3/22 – The broken end of HMS Affray's snort mast, a perfect match to the base it parted from shown in the previous picture. (Innes McCartney)

A mine of the type laid all over the Channel by the UC-boats. (Innes McCartney)

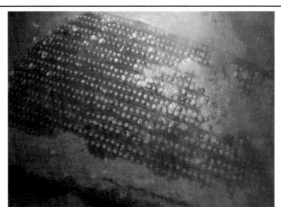

No 4/1 – The rubber "Alberich" coating which identified the wreck of U480 off Dorset. (Innes McCartney)

No 4/1 – U480's port side propeller hangs clear of the stern that was blown off by a mine. (Innes McCartney)

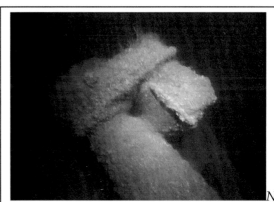

No 4/1 – U480's schnorchel head with ball float in place. (Innes McCartney)

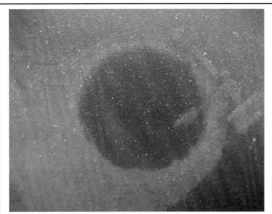

No 4/2 – The forward torpedo-loading hatch on U1195. (Innes McCartney)

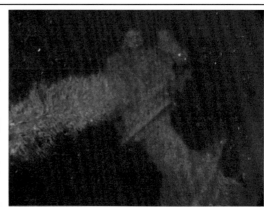

No 4/5 – UB37's 88mm deck-gun was in action shortly before she was destroyed. (Innes McCartney)

No 4/5 - Spent shell cases next to UB37's gun, clearly showing that she had been involved in a gun action before sinking. (Innes McCartney)

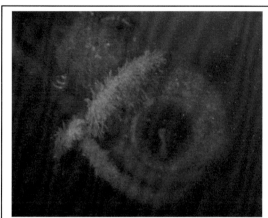

No 4/5 – UB37's lower bow cap is open, suggesting that HMS Penshurst may have been about to receive a torpedo when she opened fire. (Innes McCartney)

No 4/13 - UB81's deck-gun that has now fallen off the wreck. (John Hammond)

No 4/14 – U90's periscope in the Bembridge Shipwreck Museum. (Innes McCartney)

No 4/13 – UB81's horn on display at the Bembridge Shipwreck Museum. (Innes McCartney)

No 4/15 – This beautiful signal lamp was recovered from HMS A1 by Martin Woodward. (Innes McCartney)

No 4/16 – The helm wheel on HMS Swordfish. (Martin Woodward)

No 4/16 - How HMS Swordfish was identified; the brass "W" is on display in the Bembridge Shipwreck Museum. (Innes McCartney)

No 5/1 - U678's conning tower hatch lies in a heap of twisted wreckage now mostly buried under the sand of the Channel. (Innes McCartney)

No 5/1 – One of U678's external torpedo doors. (Innes McCartney)

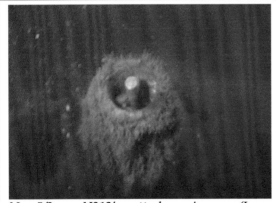

No 5/2 – U212's attack periscope. (Innes McCartney)

No 5/4 – A conger eel guards one of U413's hatchways. (Innes McCartney)

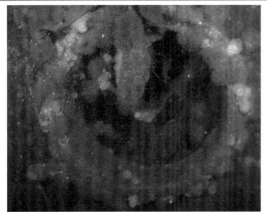

No 5/4 – U413 was blown in half forward of the conning tower – this shot shows the bulkhead hatch that leads into the control room. (Innes McCartney)

No 5/5 – The bronze torpedo tubes of U671. (Innes McCartney)

No 5/5 - U671's conning tower. (Innes McCartney)

No 5/6 – A crab now lives in U741's periscope housing. (Innes McCartney)

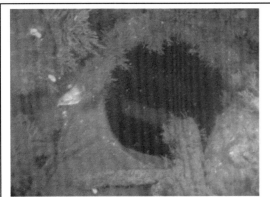

No 5/7 – The open stern loading hatch of one of the Baie de Seines unidentified Type VIIC U-boats. (Innes McCartney)

No 5/8 – The bridge compass from the second unidentified Baie de Seine U-boats. (Innes McCartney)

No 5/10 – The conning tower of the mystery UBIII-Class U-boat off Brighton. (Innes McCartney)

No 5/11 – The tampion in the muzzle of UC65's deck gun. (Innes McCartney)

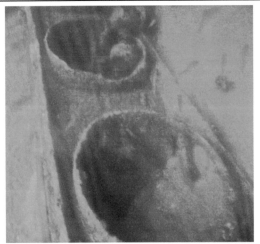

No 5/11 – Mine chutes on the bows of UC65, empty as this submarine was returning to base when sunk. (Innes McCartney)

No 5/12 – An open doorway on the murky wreck of UB130. (Innes McCartney)

No 5/12 – One of UB130's propellers. (Innes McCartney)

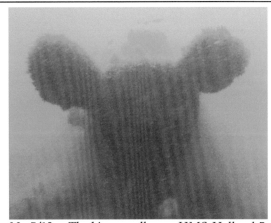

No 5/13 – The big propeller on HMS Holland 5. The guard has fallen away. (Innes McCartney)

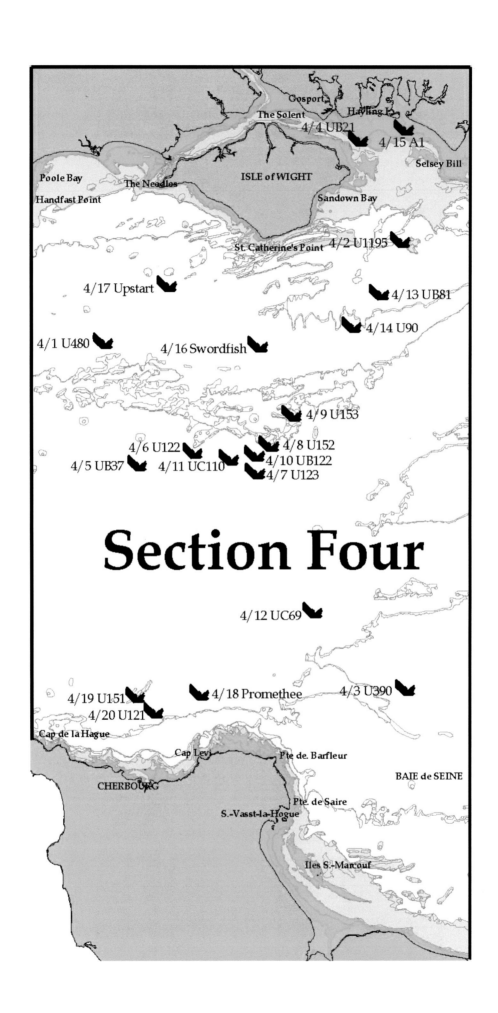

Section Four

Gosport
The Solent
Hayling I.
4/4 UB21
4/15 A1
Selsey Bill
ISLE of WIGHT
Poole Bay
The Needles
Handfast Point
Sandown Bay
St. Catherine's Point
4/2 U1195
4/17 Upstart
4/13 UB81
4/14 U90
4/1 U480
4/16 Swordfish
4/9 U153
4/6 U122
4/8 U152
4/5 UB37
4/11 UC110
4/10 UB122
4/7 U123
4/12 UC69
4/19 U151
4/18 Promethee
4/3 U390
4/20 U121
Cap de la Hague
Cap Levi
Pte. de. Barfleur
BAIE de SEINE
CHERBOURG
Pte. de Saire
S.-Vasst-la-Hogue
Iles S.-Marcouf

Section 4

Submarine Wrecks Around the Isle of Wight

Of the 20 submarine wrecks around the Isle of Wight, several are worthy of historical note. The first British-designed submarine commissioned into the Royal Navy lies in the waters of the Solent. HMS *A1* is a protected wreck site now, thanks to the work of Martin Woodward.

In World War One, Germany was to lose one of its greatest submarine commanders, when Reinhold Saltzwedel was killed while in command of *UB81*. *UB37* became the second victim of F.H. Grenfell's Q-ship *Penshurst* and *UC69* became the only German submarine known to have sunk in an accident in the Channel.

Between the wars, the French submarine, *Prométhée* was sunk with the loss of 61 lives in a diving accident. In 1921, navies of France and Britain disposed of eight surrendered U-boats in waters south of the Isle of Wight. Among them were three examples of the Deutschland-Class, the only submarines purposely built to operate as merchant vessels!

During World War Two, one British (HMS *Swordfish*) and one German (*U480*) submarine were lost to mines in this area. Interestingly, divers made both of these discoveries. Both were lost with their entire crews. Their discovery and identification by sports divers shows clearly the role divers can play in amending the historical record.

No 4/1, *U480* - Divers Write History

Class: VIIC	**Built at:** Deutsche Werft - Kiel
Length: 67.1m	**Displacement:** 871t
Date sunk: Around 24th Feb 1945	**How sunk:** Minefield Brazier D2
Historic Position: 49 55N; 06 08W	**Known Position:** 50 22 14N;01 44 11W
Crew losses: 48 (all crew lost)	**Commander:** Olzs. Hans-Joachim Förster

In the waters of the Potomac River near Washington DC, USA, lies a protected wreck site, the first to be designated in the State of Maryland. The wreck in question is *U1105* – the Black Panther. She was sunk there during explosive tests in 1949 and was forgotten about, until 1985, when a group of U-boat enthusiasts, led by Uwe Lovas, located her. *U1105* is extremely rare, because she was one of the first operational submarines to have been coated in rubber, a standard practice today.

The rubber coating in question was called 'Alberich', after the dwarf with the helmet of invisibility in Wagner's Ring Cycle. *U1105*'s black appearance was responsible for her nickname. In total, only nine Type VIIC

Some of U480's crew enjoy a breather on deck. Note the black Alberich-coated conning tower and the collar for the schnorchel mast to the right. (U-boot Archiv)

U-boats received Alberich. The thin two-ply rubber coating oscillated slightly as the submarine moved through the water, confusing sonar impulses. It worked best at shallow depths.

The first operational U-boat to use Alberich on patrol was *U480*. On her first cruise, she operated in the Channel and was successful, particularly so, considering the period of the war in which she was operating. During that time, Olzs. Hans-Joachim Förster sank four ships, including HMCS *Alberni*, a corvette - the U-boats natural enemy. Upon return, Förster was decorated with the Knight's Cross. He repeatedly claimed that the Alberich coating had saved him from destruction.

Certainly, it seems that the U-boat command took Alberich seriously and believed that it was the answer to Asdic location. However, it took several thousand hours to glue and rivet Alberich to the hulls of U-boats and there had been problems with the bonding process. Although committed to Alberich, U-boat command could not afford to wait for boats to be so treated. This was coupled with shortages of synthetic rubber, therefore only a few U-boats were given Alberich.

On 24th February 1945, a depth charge attack by HMS *Duckworth* and HMS *Rowley* was attributed with sinking a U-boat at 49 55;06 08W (see wreck No 1/3) and the U-boat in question was denoted as *U480* by the Admiralty assessors. This was done, in part, due to the report that fragments of a 'plastic substance' had been seen on the surface, the assumption being that this was

U480's commissioning ceremony is celebrated in simplicity under camouflage nets. The young Commander, Förster, is on the right. (U-boot Archiv)

Alberich.

If *U480* had been present at that attack, or others over the previous two days, she escaped, with her Alberich serving her well. How do we know this?

In the summer of 1998, the author's submarine diving team went to visit the reported site of a U-boat wreck off Poole, at 50 22 14N;01 44 11W. The wreckage was instantly recognisable as a VIIC U-boat, schnorchel-equipped, with the stern outer casing blown off and lying behind the wreck. Most surprisingly (and a clue that many other divers who had been to this wreck since she was located in 1992, had missed) she was coated in Alberich, - a stunning find.

The question now was, which Alberich boat could she be? The author's research narrowed down the options of the other Alberich Type VII boats to two, *U480*, or *U1107*. At this point, the Naval Historical Branch became involved and working together, the wreck was identified as *U480* and the official record of U-boat losses was reassessed to reflect this fact. The key pieces of information lay in the fact that, not one month before, a deep anti-submarine minefield had been laid around the area where the wreck was located, of which Förster would have had no knowledge. This corresponded well with the damage to the U-boat, which looked like she had been mined. Also, when *U1107* was sunk off Brest, there was known to have been survivors. The one thing that Alberich could not protect *U480* from was the mine, and in the end, that was to be her fate.

U480 was on its third operational patrol. A relative newcomer to submarines, Förster was a few days past his 24th birthday when he and his crew perished in the service of their country.

The story of the final identification of the submarine *U480* is, in the author's opinion, one of his finest achievements in diving. It shows clearly how recreational divers can use their access to wreck sites to make a difference to maritime and naval history. A little over 50 years after the event, the final resting place of 48 brave souls had finally been located. In the process, the Alberich technology was perhaps shown to be a little more successful than originally thought.

No 4/2, *U1195* - Sunk After Sinking a Liner

Class: VIIC

Length: 67.10m

Date sunk: 6th April 1945

Historic Position: 50 33N; 00 55W

Crew losses: 31 (from 49)

Built at: Schichau - Danzig

Displacement: 871t

How sunk: Hedgehog HMS *Watchman*

Known Position: 50 33.17N;00 56.09W

Commander: Klt. Ernst Cordes

A rare photo of U1195 at Kristiansand in 1945. (U-Boot Archiv)

The U-boat crews who operated in the Channel during 1944-45 had to tolerate conditions that were new, even to the most experienced submariners. There was almost continuous noise surrounding the submarines. It came from the noise boxes towed by enemy ships, from sonar, depth charges, propellers and bombs. It was difficult for the crews to determine the distance of any noise source. Loud sources of noise could cover over much quieter sounds that were potentially deadly. U-boat crews could never be certain whether any noise source was a developing attack, or not. It was not unusual to find a warship suddenly on top of the U-boat, with death raining down from above (see No 3/9).

The constant presence of surface vessels made ventilating the U-boats far too dangerous. Aside from the poisonous atmosphere inside the U-boat, position fixing became difficult (see No 1/18). Klt Ernst Cordes experienced perhaps the most extraordinary example of this, when on

SS Cuba, the largest U-boat victim of 1945. (U-boot Archiv)

7th July 1944, after being submerged for 30 hours, *U763* drifted into Spithead! By dead reckoning, Cordes believed he was 20-30 miles from Cherbourg. Risking stranding by the tide, Cordes was able to affect his escape by night.

Whether this experience made him confident of being able to operate in the shallows around the Wight, or not, he chose to return to the entrance to the Solent in April 1945 with his newer command, *U1195*. On 6th April, while bottomed, Convoy No VWP16 was located by hydrophone as it headed for Southampton. Cordes approached at periscope depth, selected two vessels including a large troopship, fired two torpedoes and turned away.

U1195s Commander, Klt. Ernst Cordes. (U-boot Archiv)

One torpedo struck the liner *Cuba*. She sank becoming the biggest U-boat victim of 1945. The hunt was now on for the audacious U-boat. *Cuba's* six escorts searched into the 30 metre deep waters for Cordes, as he tried creeping away. However, in that depth of water, with a number of ships hunting her, time was running out.

One hour after the *Cuba* sunk, *U1195* was located by HMS *Watchman;* hedgehogs were fired, which brought up diesel oil and bubbles. However, it was determined that the target might have been a wreck, so it was buoyed and the search for the U-boat continued. Fifty minutes later, FS *L'Escarmouche* was sweeping past the buoy when she spotted men in the water. One was clinging to the buoy. *U1195* had been destroyed.

The survivors reported that a large hole had been blown into the submarine on the port side forward of the control room and she had begun to rapidly fill with water.

Escape from a damaged submarine has always been hazardous. The eight surviving crew members in the control room escaped through the conning tower hatch. However, the list the boat had taken made escape from the aft torpedo room more difficult. The first man panicked and drowned, others began to panic too, but the experienced first watch officer pushed them out in turn, before escaping himself. In all 18 survived from a crew of 49. Ernst Cordes was not among them.

Today *U1195* lies to the south of the Nab tower in 30 metres. The conning tower hatch is still open and the terrible damage to her is clearly visible. The submarine is blown almost in half, forward of the conning tower and has other holes in her structure too. In recent times, visibility on this wreck has improved as the nearby spoil ground is now closed.

Local diver Martin Woodward carried out much research into *U1195*. In 1988, two of the survivors from *U1195* returned to the wreck site with Mr Woodward, who placed a wreath on the wreck on the survivor's behalf. Not surprisingly, this was a deeply emotional event for all involved. Quiet now, the wreck of *U1195* is a serene reminder of the desperate struggle that was the war at sea, 1939-45.

Fanciful rumours persist of another submarine wreck in the very near vicinity. However the author has been unable to substantiate this. The changing conditions on the site may explain why some divers have reported that the submarine wreck they just dived is totally different from that they dived the week before in the same position!

Veterans return to lay a wreath on the site of U1195's wreck. (Royal Navy Submarine Museum)

No 4/3, *U390* - Sole Survivor

Class: VIIC	**Built at:** Howaldtswerke - Kiel
Length: 67.10m	**Displacement:** 871t
Date sunk: 5th July 1944	**How sunk:** HM Ships *Wanderer* & *Tavy*
Historic Position: 49 52N; 00 48W	**Known Position:** 49 49 53N;00 55.94W
Crew losses: 47 (from 48)	**Commander:** Olzs. Heinz Giessler

U390 sailed for the Baie de Seine on 27th June 1944, after an aborted attempt to re-supply the German defences in Cherbourg with ammunition. She is known to have arrived in her area of operations and to have sunk the ASW Trawler *Ganilly* and badly damaged the 7,900-ton American ship *Sea Porpoise*.

However, *U390* was not to escape. She was located and attacked by HMS *Tavy*, which sent her to the bottom with a well-placed hedgehog attack. There has been some confusion as to whether *U390* attempted a counter-attack by T5 torpedo during HMS *Tavy's* initial approach. Ian Bailey, who was serving in HMS *Tavy* as gunnery officer, witnessed the proceedings from HMS *Tavy's* bridge, from where he took the astonishing photographs seen here for the first time in print. He related to the author that *U390* made the first attack with two T5 acoustic-homing torpedoes. One passed on and disappeared and the other exploded prematurely, as HMS *Tavy* was turning into its tracks. It was at this point that contact with the U-boat was made by hydrophone effect. Shortly thereafter, the decisive hedgehog attack was made.

Minutes later, HMS *Wanderer* joined in and both vessels plastered the wreck. The end result was the certain destruction of *U390*. The anti-submarine summary issued at the time stated that the sinking of *U390* was carried out entirely by hedgehogs. Depth charges were used only to open up the wreckage to ensure identification and destruction.

This was confirmed when one survivor was picked-up from the sea by HMS *Wanderer*. Throwing him a float before she attacked with depth charges, (See No 3/7) surely saved his life. He was the Chief Engineer, Erich Tein. The commander of HMS *Wanderer* formed a low opinion of his prisoner describing him as a 'sour, bad-mannered man, very much a Nazi. He did not even thank us for helping him.' Perhaps this is not too surprising under the circumstances.

The wreck is reported to be located at the position given above. The author has not verified

U390's crew are reviewed by flotilla Commander Karl Emmerman. (U-Boot Archiv)

Depth charges explode over U390. (Ian Bailey)

An air bubble marks the end of U390 – note the one-man liferaft to the right. (Ian Bailey)

this. Reports suggest the wreck lies on its starboard side in 47 metres. It is quite possible that the sinking position given by HMS *Wanderer* was accurate, because it is known that she had been fitted with the latest electronic position-fixing equipment.

No 4/4, *UB21* - Hashagan's Little Fighter

Class: UBII (*UB*20 series)	**Built at:** Blohm & Voss – Hamburg
Length: 36.3m	**Displacement:** 292t
Date sunk: 1920	**How sunk:** Parted tow
Historic Position: 50 44.28N; 01 1.6W	**Known Position:** 50 44.28N; 01 1.6W
Crew losses: None	**Commander:** None

UB21 at sea. (U-Boot Archiv)

Ernest Hashagen was a U-boat commander who embodied much of the charm, cunning and guile associated with the naval officers of Imperial Germany. From February to November 1916, he commanded the little UBII class boat, *UB21*. During this time he sank 7 ships for 2,500 tons. Hashagen survived the First World War and became a wealthy businessman. He also wrote an autobiography about his time as a U-boat commander and even toured the UK, lecturing about his experiences.

However, Hashagen's most famous exploit while in command of *UB21* was undoubtedly the "*Fritzoe*" incident. This audacious, if somewhat humorous event, has gone down in the annals of submarine warfare as a unique success against shipping. During the autumn of 1916, the U-boat service was operating under prize-rules and was prohibited from sinking non-military vessels without warning. More importantly, ships could not be sunk if the crews could not be saved. Upon stopping the Norwegian steamer *Fritzoe*, Hashagen noticed that the ship's lifeboats were in no state to be used. To sink the ship would have meant a watery grave for the crew. Ever resourceful, Hashagen ordered *Fritzoe* to steam for Cuxhaven as a war-prize. He falsely told the ship's captain that he would be watching the steamer and that she would be torpedoed if she strayed off course. They parted, and Hashagen resumed his patrol, not giving the incident a second thought. He could not have sunk the ship anyhow. Four days later when *UB21*'s patrol ended in Cuxhaven, there was the *Fritzoe* waiting for her!

Some of Hashagen's charisma must have rubbed off on the little submarine as she went on to have three other commanders and to survive the war. During this time she had several close scrapes including hitting a mine which failed to detonate. At the Armistice, she was surrendered to the Royal Navy. Put onto the 'For Sale' list, she was intended to go the way of many of her compatriots – broken up for scrap. However, it is as if UB21, which had been through so much, had other plans. Early in 1920, she was on tow to Cherbourg to be scrapped, when she slipped her lines and ran aground under the Seven Sisters. In so doing she ran into a ship that was already aground there, (the Oushla) destroying a ship while unmanned! UB21 was partially scrapped where she lay, but most of her was then towed toward another scrap yard, when again, she slipped her tow and foundered in the Solent, where she became a shipping hazard again. In 1921, she was reduced by the use of explosives.

UB21 aground next to SS Oushla. (Seaford Museum)

She was a dived wreck for many years and was sold to a private firm in 1970 and was still being dived into the 1980s. However, in 1998 a diving team from Gosport went looking for UB21 and reported that the last traces of her had finally disappeared under the mud of the Solent. A worthy resting place, for a vessel that resisted destruction for so long.

No 4/5, *UB37* - Q-Ship Victim

Class: UBII (UB30 series)	**Built at:** Blohm & Voss - Hamburg
Length: 36.9m	**Displacement:** 303t
Date sunk: 14th January 1917	**How sunk:** Q-ship *Penshurst*
Historic Position: 50 07N; 01 47W	**Known Position:** 50 10.20N; 01 38.40W
Crew losses: 21 (all crew lost)	**Commander:** Olzs. Paul Gunther

As previously related in this book, the Q-ship HMS *Penshurst* had sunk *UB19* in the Channel in December 1916 (see No 3/4). For a Q-ship to even sight a submarine during its career was a rare event. However, the incredible HMS *Penshurst* fought 11 anti-U-boat actions. During this time, she sank two. *UB37* was the second.

On 14th January 1917, *Penshurst* was travelling between the Isle of Wight and Alderney when a U-boat was spotted approaching. When it opened fire, the usual 'panic party' was set on its way, as the shells rained in. Grenfell then ordered HMS *Penshurst's* engines to be stopped to draw the submarine in on her. At around 700 yards, the U-boat turned to inspect the lifeboat with the 'crew' in it. However, she then stopped and began to rain a fierce torrent of shot into HMS *Penshurst*. On board nerves were frayed as the bridge was hit repeatedly, killing the hidden 6-pounder's gun-layer and wounding others. It seemed as if the U-boat was content to sink the ship from that range with gunfire, so Grenfell had no option but to open fire.

The British aiming was superb and shells quickly overwhelmed the U-boat that soon sank. HMS *Penshurst* passed over the wreck and dropped a depth charge. So ended the career of *UB37*. She was sunk on her 10th patrol, having claimed over 20,000 tons of allied shipping. *Penshurst* went on to duel with other U-boats, but was sunk by *U110* within the year. She went down in the Bristol Channel, her crew luckily survived.

In 1999, the author discovered the wreck of *UB37* at the position given above. She lies, virtually completely intact, with a list to starboard. Her two bow caps are, surprisingly, open, suggesting that HMS *Penshurst* may well have been about to receive a torpedo. On her foredeck, her little 88mm short-barrelled cannon was found to be in excellent condition. She makes a very rare submarine dive. A completely intact UBII-Class U-boat is a not an everyday dive.

No 4/6, *U122* – Unwanted Prize

Class: U122 (U117 minelayer series)	**Built at:** Blohm & Voss - Hamburg
Length: 82.0m	**Displacement:** 1468t
Date sunk: 1st July 1921	**How sunk:** Dumped
Historic Position: 50 11.30N; 01 24.0W	**Known Position:** 50 12.25N; 01 26.36W?
Crew losses: None	**Commander:** None

The large ocean-going U122. (U-Boot Archiv)

Wreck numbers 4/6 to 4/11 form the largest portion of the surrendered U-boats of World War One that were disposed of in the Channel. These submarines were dumped in a group during the period 28th June to 1st July 1921. Two others were dumped further west, (see Nos 1/23 and 1/24) and one broke its tow and fell short of the dumping ground (see No 5/9). It seems that this was done to comply with one of the stipulations of the Versailles Treaty. The French also did the same with *U121* and *U151* (see Nos 4/20 and 4/21).

These wrecks fall into two distinct categories. Submarines still under development and working up at the end of the war, and the large ex-Deutschland-Class U-cruisers. *U122* was of the first of these.

This class was designed for a long-range war against shipping, being equipped with torpedoes, mines and two deck guns. *U122* was the only one of this class to make a war patrol. Under Olzs. Korte, she sank one ship of 278 tons. However, there can be no doubt that these larger and more powerful U-boats would have been a major shipping threat, if they had been in service in 1918.

A survey of the area where these submarines were sunk, points to *U122* being at the position given above. As far as is known, this has not been confirmed.

No 4/7, *U123* – Unwanted Prize

Class: U122 (U117 minelayer series)	**Built at:** Blohm & Voss - Hamburg
Length: 82.0m	**Displacement:** 1468t
Date sunk: 28th June 1921	**How sunk:** Dumped
Historic Position: 50 11.10N; 01 18.50W	**Known Position:** 50 11.16N; 01 18.32W?
Crew losses: None	**Commander:** None

U123 was sister ship to *U122* (see No 4/6) having been built at the same yard and launched within one month of her. However, unlike *U122*, *U123* was not operational at the end of the war. She was commissioned on 20th July and surrendered on 22nd November 1918. Curiously, her date of transfer to the UK is unknown. However, on 28th June 1921, she was towed out and sunk. Along with the others sunk during this operation, it is clear that they could either not be sold, or simply were of no more use to the Admiralty.

A recent survey of the area located a wreck at the position given above. It is thought that this is *U123*, although this is yet to be confirmed.

No 4/8, *U152* - Unwanted Prize

Class: U151 (ex-Deutschland series)	**Built at:** Hull by Reiherstieg – Hamburg
	Finished by Germaniawerft - Kiel
Length: 65m	**Displacement:** 1875t
Date sunk: 30th June 1921	**How sunk:** Dumped
Historic Position: 50 13N; 01 17.45W	**Known Position:** near 50 14.50; 01 12.05W?
Crew losses: None	**Commander:** None

The very heavily gunned U-cruiser U152. (U-Boot Archiv)

The wrecks of *U151* (No 4/20) *U152* and *U153* (see No 4/9) represent, perhaps, the most unique examples of U-boat design. These three wrecks are very rare examples of the Deutschland–Class U-boat. They are by any standards increasingly important historical wrecks.

They are intriguing because they were originally built as merchant vessels. They could slip under the British blockade of Germany and travel to the US and garner urgently needed supplies for the German war-effort. The first of this class was named *Deutschland*. She sailed for the US on 14th June 1916 and arrived in Baltimore on 9th July. She carried $1.4m worth of goods that were used to purchase valuable commodities, such as rubber. There was great interest and not a little sympathy with the merchant U-boat, with its merchant captain, Paul König. America had yet to be turned against Germany. The *Deutschland* returned to Germany in triumph and despite the mysterious loss of its sister ship *Bremen*, six more merchant U-boats were ordered.

However, during the construction of the next six of the class, relationships with the US turned sour. *Deutschland's* second voyage to America was neither as successful nor as popular as the first. This was because the U-boat war had come to American shores. *U53*, under the command of Hans Rose, had been sinking British ships off the American coast, and had caused a growing revulsion in the US for the practice of sinking unescorted merchant ships. Therefore, when *Deutschland* reached New London in November, America was a different place and her arrival was greeted with ambivalence.

As a result, the seven Deutschland-Class U-boats were converted for military purposes, with the *Deutschland* herself, becoming *U155*. However, these converted merchant submarines were not designed for war. Their extremely large cargo-carrying capacity was gained at the expense of power. The 800hp diesel engines they were fitted with could only propel them at a maximum of 12 knots. In reality, this was much too slow to allow the U-boat to overhaul surface ships. Moreover, their underwater endurance was extremely limited too and their diving time was dangerously slow. However, their size gave them one advantage. They were good gun platforms for submarines and, therefore, were fitted with very powerful surface armament. This included two 150mm and two 88mm guns. This was the most formidable firepower ever mounted on a U-boat, up to that time.

U152 was launched on 20th May 1917 and commissioned in October. She sailed on three war patrols, under three separate commanders. She was a successful U-boat, accounting for some 20 ships of 37,726 tons. The most interesting aspect of her anti-shipping activities was the way that she relied almost entirely on gunfire to sink ships. Although equipped with two torpedo tubes, this did not give her enough underwater firepower to tackle a convoy with any certain degree of success. Also, her limited underwater speed hindered her ability to get into a favourable attack position.

This reliance on her deck armament was rare in 1917-18. Most U-boat commanders had opted for the use of the torpedo by then, because most cargo vessels were now escorted by warships and were also armed in their own right. Despite this, *U152* was able to perform her duties with some degree of success, although by the standards of the time, this tactic was extremely dangerous. The most extreme example of the potential danger was during a gunnery duel with the American troopship *USS Ticonderoga*. This was a close-run fight, with the U-boat's gun-crews suffering casualties. *U152* only needed to be hit once to suffer potentially fatal damage. The troopship fought hard, and almost escaped when *U152* had to dive to avoid a cruiser which briefly entered the proceedings.

U152 survived to be turned over to the allies. She was disposed of, at sea on 30th June 1921, in the dumping area behind the Isle of Wight.

No 4/9, *U153* – Unwanted Prize

Class: U151 (ex-Deutschland series)	**Built at:** Hull by Reiherstieg – Hamburg, Finished by Germaniawerft - Kiel
Length: 65m	**Displacement:** 1875t
Date sunk: 30th June 1921	**How sunk:** Dumped
Historic Position: 50 13N; 01 17.45W	**Known Position:** 50 14.50; 01 12.05W?
Crew losses: None	**Commander:** None

U153 was originally built as part of the Deutschland-Class of merchant U-boats (see No 4/8 and 4/20) and was converted for military purposes when that program was abandoned in 1917. *U153* was launched on 19th July 1917 and commissioned on 17th November. Under the command of Klt. Gernot Goetting, *U153* conducted one war patrol only. This was done in harness with her sister ship, *U154*. The patrol was conducted off Dakar. During the course of this patrol, the pair of submarines destroyed the British Q-ship, *Bombala*. They also tore up underwater cables and sank several other vessels. One of these was the British *Santa Isabel* of 2,023 tons, which was destroyed by gunfire on 14th April.

On the return journey, *U154* was sunk by the British submarine HMS *E35* off Cape St. Vincent. She was the first 'U-cruiser' to have been sunk in the war. In view of this, the Admiralty took the unprecedented step of publishing the news of the sinking. The incidence of submarine sinking submarine was comparatively rare in both world wars.

U153 sailed once more only, to surrender to the Royal Navy after the Armistice. However, her activities in Kiel, after the return from patrol, are obscure. This is because her records were

This photo of U153 during gunnery trials shows the large proportions of the Deutchland-Class U-cruisers (U-Boot Archiv)

destroyed by fire after the sailors uprising at the end of the war.

U153 is listed as being in the UK on 22nd February 1919. Clearly unsold and unallocated to another country, *U153* suffered the ignominious fate of being dumped at sea. She is supposed to lie at the position given above, near to her sister, *U152* (see wreck No 4/8) although this has not been confirmed. She would be an important find, as one of the rare merchant U-boats.

No 4/10, *UB122* – Unwanted Prize

Class: UBIII (UB118 series)	**Built at:** AG Weser - Bremen
Length: 55.85m	**Displacement:** 643t
Date sunk: 30th June 1921	**How sunk:** Dumped
Historic Position: 50 11.53N; 01 18.0W	**Known Position:** 50 12.20N; 01 18.32W?
Crew losses: None	**Commander:** None

One of the later UBIII Class, *UB122* was built just in time to see action in the dying months of World War One. She was launched on 2nd February 1918 and commissioned on 4th March; an unbelievably short period of time.

Under the command of Olzs. Alexander Magnus, *UB122* made 2 patrols. The first, which ran from 17th July 1918 to 6th August, took her to the east coast of Britain. The second, which ran from 6th September 1918 to 4th October, took her along the west coast during which, one ship of 3,150 tons was sunk.

UB122 was in Kiel when the war ended and surrendered to the allies. She was listed as being in Portsmouth by February 1919. There she remained until 30th June 1921 when she was dumped at sea.

The late-war UBIII-Class UB122 at sea. (Imperial War Museum)

The known position given above has not been confirmed by diving. However, it is in the right area for the wreck to be located. There are at least another five dumped U-boats in this area (Nos 4/6 – 4/11), so the process of identifying each one would require a significant degree of diving activity.

No 4/11, *UC110* – Last of the Minelayers

Class: UCIII (UC90 series)	**Built at:** Blohm & Voss - Hamburg
Length: 56.51m	**Displacement:** 571t
Date sunk: 1st July 1921	**How sunk:** Dumped
Historic Position: 50 11.30N; 01 24.0W	**Known Position:** 50 11.33N; 01 22.77W?
Crew losses: None	**Commander:** None

The way the remains of *UC110* have come to lie on the bottom of the English Channel must be one of the more unique U-boat stories of World War One. *UC110* was of the UCIII-Class, which were the last of the UCs to be designed. They were the largest of the class to be built and were intended for use on the high seas. They were better sea-boats and could have posed a major threat outside more remote ports, where minefields would not have been expected.

UC110 was launched on 6th July 1918, close to the end of the war. She was incomplete when Germany surrendered. However, it was decided to continue to build and fit her out, to become part of Germany's war reparations. So *UC110* became one of the only U-boats to be commissioned in 1919, after her engines and torpedo tubes had been fitted. The same was done to the rest of the UC106-UC114 series. These submarines were then sent to the UK, although the author has been unable to ascertain dates of their arrival.

However, *UC110* was in Portsmouth when the time to dispose of all the unsold and unallocated U-boats arrived. Therefore on 1st July 1921, she was towed out and sunk in the dumping ground with five other sister U-boats.

The known position given is not yet confirmed by diving.

No 4/12, *UC69* - Collision

Class: UCII (UC65 series)	**Built at:** Blohm & Voss - Hamburg
Length: 50.35m	**Displacement:** 508t
Date sunk: 6th December 1917	**How sunk:** Collision with *U96*
Historic Position: 49 57N; 01 10W	**Known Position:** 49 56.90N; 01 10.09W
Crew losses: 11 (from 29)	**Commander:** Olzs H. Thielmann

UC69 was of the UCII-Class of minelaying U-boat. This class operated extensively in the Channel. What makes the story of *UC69* so unique is that another U-boat sank her.

She was launched on 7th Aug 1916 and commissioned on 23rd December and had been built with the intention of being transferred to the Austro-Hungarian Navy as *U69*. However, this did not occur and *UC69* became a Flanders-based U-boat. During 1917, under two commanders, she sank an incredible 50 ships for 88,138 tons. Even by the standards of World War One, this is an exceptional record for a coastal-going U-boat. Not many UC-boats bettered this during the war.

However, *UC69* is better remembered for the way she was sunk. Operating in the same area as *U96*, the two U-boats had been ordered to cruise off Barfleur. Operating in pairs runs the risk of collision. The German U-boat command regularly took this chance and got away with it most of the time. However, on 6th December 1917, luck ran out and it was the crew of *UC69* that paid dearly. During the night, *U96* was proceeding on the surface when she ran into *UC69*. All the lights went out and the engines stopped. The crew scrambled out on deck and there they saw the horrifying site of a U-boat almost cut in two. *UC69*'s commander was not on the bridge, so the commander of *U96* gave them the order to abandon. Engines restarted, *U96* managed to keep her bows embedded in the wound in *UC69*'s side, to stop her sinking. This enabled over half of the crew to escape before the stern collapsed and the U-boat sank. Only 18 of *UC69*'s crew were saved.

This incident can only really be put down to poor watch keeping. It is surprising that the U-boats seemed to occasionally be fairly lax at this. Another example is the sinking of *UB72* (No 3/5).

U96 radioed an accident report shortly after it happened. It seems, however, that the British did not decipher it. This is because in the House of Commons on 7th August 1918, Lloyd George listed the U-boats destroyed up to that date. Among the omissions was *UC69*. However, the author came across a document in the Public Records Office that shows that under interrogation, one of the survivors of *UB109* admitted that he had served on *UC69* and that she had been sunk in a collision. The note is dated August 1918. So before the end of the war, at least, the Admiralty knew of the loss of this U-boat.

The known position given for this wreck is unconfirmed by divers, as far as the author is aware.

No 4/13, *UB81* – The Death of Reinhold Saltzwedel

Class: UBIII (UB80 series)	**Built at:** AG Weser - Bremen
Length: 55.85m	**Displacement:** 647t
Date sunk: 2nd December 1917	**How sunk:** Mine and collision
Historic Position: 50 27N; 00 53W	**Known Position:** 50 29 22N; 00 58.12W
Crew losses: 29 (from 35)	**Commander:** Klt. Reinhold Saltzwedel

One of the greatest and most respected of the World War One U-boat aces was Reinhold Saltzwedel. The American journalist, Lowell Thomas described him in the following words:

"the fair-haired boy of the Flanders base, young Reinhold Saltzwedel. He was an upstanding chap, blond and blue-eyed, with a fine wide brow, a firm chin, a humorous mouth and a proud carriage of head – a gallant, laughing, frank-eyed boy, as far from the popular conception of the barbarous Hun. He was the favourite of the base, and when he was lost…..' (Raiders of the Deep)

UB82 (in front) and UB89 were two of UB81's sisters (U-Boot Archiv)

Saltzwedel is credited as being the 11th most successful U-boat commander of World War One. He sank an incredible 150,000 tons of shipping. This was achieved over 12 patrols. For this degree of success, he was awarded the 'Pour le Mérite', Germany's highest military honour.

The measure of the prowess of this superb exponent of undersea warfare can be judged by his fight with the Q-ship, HMS *Dunraven*. Britain's greatest Q-ship commander commanded this vessel. He was Gordon Campbell VC. He had sunk three U-boats, the highest number any Q-ship commander reached. He became a national hero for his bravery and his brilliant exploits in the cruel war at sea. However, in *UC71*, commanded then by Saltzwedel, he met an entirely different quality of opponent.

The date was 8th August 1918 and HMS *Dunraven* was cruising in the Bay of Biscay and on the lookout for marauding U-boats. The Q-ship was well prepared for a fight. Since the Germans had learned of the existence of these secret ships, fooling the U-boat commanders had become far more difficult. They would only come within close range when absolutely certain that the 'merchant' was a safe target. Therefore, deception had to be perfect. To assist with this, HMS *Dunraven* had been filled with timber to keep her afloat, even if torpedoed. She had also been armed with depth charges and torpedoes. Another innovation was the fitting of a steam pipe from the engine room, which was designed to give the impression that a boiler had exploded, and giving the Q-ship the opportunity to stop dead if necessary, to aid in closing range with the target. She was also fitted with a 2.5 pounder stern gun to give the impression of being 'armed', like the other tramp steamers.

The two great captains, Campbell and Saltzwedel joined in battle at 11.00, when the U-boat sighted *Dunraven*. After inspection, the artillery 'duel' began at a range of 5,000 yards. *UC71* was taking no chances and continued to pour shells into HMS *Dunraven*, as the range closed to 3,000 yards. HMS *Dunraven* slowly 'lost speed' and sent out dummy wireless messages. Campbell ensured that the stern gun was shooting short and was operated in a most amateur fashion. After an hour, Saltzwedel was satisfied that the merchant ship seemed to offer little danger and closed to 1,000 yards and opened fire again. The U-boat's fall of shot became more accurate and eventually one fell near enough to the engine room for the steam ejector to be used. Campbell then ordered the 'abandon ship' routine to be played out.

At this juncture, HMS *Dunraven* stopped. However, *UC71* kept up the shelling, presumably because she did not realise this at once. This was the break of luck that can change any engagement. As the U-boat closed to the point where HMS *Dunraven* would open fire with all of her hidden artillery, a shell from the U-boat exploded a depth charge hidden under the poop deck. A massive explosion shortly followed as fire gripped the stern of the ship and the rest of the depth charges exploded. The entire 4-inch gun was blown into the air with its crew. The gun landed on the foredeck and the crew in the sea. The ruse had failed. Saltzwedel crash-dived, realising he was confronted with a U-boat trap.

Campbell had no choice but to raise the white ensign and open fire with the remaining guns. The gunners thought they struck *UC71* as she submerged. However, *Dunraven* was now in a very difficult position. *UC71* would inevitably fire a torpedo next. But Campbell decided to sit tight. He knew that the timber might still keep him afloat, although most of his ship was now an inferno. The decks were red-hot and the gun crews were holding the ammunition in their arms to stop it exploding.

Saltzwedel had the initiative and fired a torpedo from short range. The aim was true and it hit HMS *Dunraven* amidships. The explosion wrecked the bulkhead aft of the engine room and effectively doomed the ship. Now Campbell ordered the second 'abandon ship' routine, thinking that this would fool Saltzwedel into believing the ship had finally been left to the sea. Still 34 men remained on board, manning two guns and the torpedo tubes.

The submarine now surfaced and began to shell the burning ship. Campbell sat tight throughout. The submarine then submerged again, presumably thinking that this brave vessel would now sink. In a desperate last move, Campbell attempted to fire his torpedoes at the periscope of the U-boat. Both were fired, but missed. Saltzwedel clearly heard them, because *UC71* disappeared entirely. What Campbell could not have known is that Saltzwedel was out of torpedoes, although by now that was immaterial, as HMS *Dunraven* was a blazing inferno. Finally, Campbell radioed for rescue and evacuated HMS *Dunraven*. Although taken in tow, she sank. Saltzwedel had long since made for Flanders. So ended the greatest and most famous fight between a Q-ship and U-boat. An action that considerably increased the fame of both of the commanders involved.

Later that year, Reinhold Saltzwedel took command of the new UBIII-Class *UB81* and it was during his second patrol in this vessel that disaster struck.

In December 1917, *UB81* was operating off the Owers light vessel, near Portsmouth. As night closed in, a sudden and violent explosion shook the submarine. While none of the crew had been hurt in the blast, the submarine was critically damaged and sinking stern-first. The only option was to blow all the compressed air into the ballast tanks to make her rise. At the angle of 53 degrees, the bows of *UB81* burst through the surface into the night air. The highest torpedo tube was opened and the crew began to climb out onto the casing. The weather was worsening and only seven crew members could safely stand on the bows. The rest waited nervously below.

The patrol boat, HMS *P32* arrived on the scene, attracted by the German's emergency flares. What happened next has been the cause of controversy ever since. One way or the other, HMS *P32* sank the stranded U-boat by making contact with her. British accounts claim this was an accident, caused by the worsening weather. Even the most recent German histories say *UB81* was rammed. Either way, *UB81* sank immediately as the sea poured down the open torpedo tube, drowning the crew trapped inside. Only the seven crew members on the outside were saved, twenty-nine others perished. Saltzwedel was one of the dead.

Today, *UB81* makes an excellent dive. Her deck gun, conning tower and hatch, and torpedo tubes make excellent photographic subjects. At some point in the past, this vessel has received the attentions of commercial salvage. The bow, stern and conning tower have been blown off. This gives the diver a glimpse into the interior of the World War One U-boat. At 30 metres depth, she makes an excellent wreck for sports divers. Her wreck is the grave of one of the noblest sea-warriors of World War One, the "fair-haired boy of the Flanders base".

No 4/14, *U90* – Last Surrendered U-boat

Class: U81 (U87 series)	**Built at:** Kaiserliche Werft - Danzig
Length: 65.8m	**Displacement:** 988t
Date sunk: 1921?	**How sunk:** Broke tow?
Historic Position: 50 26.00N; 01 04.00W	**Known Position:** Withheld on request
Crew losses: None	**Commander:** None

The U81-Class of ocean-going U-boat was the most common of the World War One U-boats. 50 of this type were launched, although not all saw active service. Built in Danzig, *U90* was launched on 12th January 1917 and commissioned on 2nd August 1917. It didn't take long for her to sink her first ship. The tunny boat *Union Republicaine* became the first of *U90*'s 35. The amount of shipping she deprived the allies of totalled 104,509 tons by the end of the war.

U90 in port – note her two deck guns. (U-Boot Archiv)

The most noteworthy incident in the career of this submarine was the sinking of the SS *President Lincoln* (18,168 tons) on 31st May 1918. She was a troopship, which thankfully was on its return journey to the US and was empty, apart from its regular crew. The commander at the time, Klt. Walter Remy, put three torpedoes into her and she sank by the stern. Upon surfacing Remy approached the lifeboats and took four of the most senior crew prisoner, returning one junior seaman he had picked up from the wreckage. He informed the survivors that destroyers were on the way to rescue the men in the lifeboats.

The four taken prisoners included Lt. Edward Izac. He was determined to escape, because for the nine days he had been aboard the U-boat, he reckoned that he had learned much that would be of use to the allies. Passing the coast of Denmark, he prepared to jump from the submarine and swim for it. Reading his mind, Remy put his hand on his shoulder and said 'don't be a damn fool, you'll never make it'. Izac took the advice. However, once in Germany, he determined to escape again. In the next attempt, he jumped through the window of a moving train, luckily not killing himself in the process. He was recaptured. However, Izac later tried again when in POW camp. He and four others cut through the wire and made it to Switzerland, living on raw vegetables on the way. The Red Cross returned Izac to the US, where he was awarded the Congressional Medal of Honour for his bravery.

The crew of U90. (U-Boot Archiv)

U90 surrendered to the allies at the end of the war and was sailed to the UK. She is listed as being in Pembroke during February 1919. Admiralty records bizarrely show she was sold in 1965!! Sometime after that date, it appears that she was lost on tow in the Channel. In 1988, after a search, local diver, Martin Woodward, located her east of St. Catherine's Point. Once he had established whom the wreck belonged to, he purchased her and now guards her position closely. He does this to keep her pristine condition. She is in a remarkable state of preservation, from the video footage the author has seen. Martin Woodward has several interesting items from this U-boat on display in his wreck museum on the Isle of Wight.

There is a strong possibility that this may turn out to be the wreck of *U86* (see No 5/9), because the likelihood of *U90* being around to be sold in 1965 would seem to be very slim.

No 4/15, HMS *A1* – The First 'British' Submarine

Class: A-Class
Length: 30.3m
Date sunk: August 1911
Historic Position: Near Selsey Bill
Crew losses: None

Built at: Vickers - Barrow
Displacement: 180t
How sunk: Explosive testing
Known Position: Withheld on request
Commander: None

HMS A1 undergoing sea trials. (Royal Navy Submarine Museum)

The Holland-Class may have been the first class of submarines commissioned into the Royal Navy (see Appendix 3 and No 5/13), but HMS *A1* is, in some way, just as historically important in the fact that she was the first British-designed submarine.

Originally HMS *A1* was laid down as Holland 6. However this was soon changed to the A-Class design, as the Navy quickly absorbed the lessons of the Hollands. The A-Class was larger, faster and had better endurance than the Holland-Class. This was the first A-Class, as opposed to the second series developed in the 1940s (see No 3/22).

After launching and trials, HMS *A1* was transferred to the submarine flotilla in Gosport and began to operate with the Holland submarines. Clearly, more performance was expected of the A-Class than the Hollands. Probably more was expected of them than they were able to deliver. Certainly, it became obvious quite quickly that the A-Class did not have sufficient reserve buoyancy, among other problems. Moreover, they handled poorly in rough seas. Although given a larger conning tower than that originally fitted to the Hollands, it too proved to be too small for rough weather.

In contrast to the Holland-Class, the A-Class proved to be dangerous submarines to operate. No less than 58 submariners were killed in A-Class submarines in peacetime. Three A-Class wrecks lie on the bottom of the Channel and all had, at some point, been involved in fatal accidents (see Nos 4/18 and 1/29).

In the case of HMS *A1*, the poor seaworthiness of the A-Class and the danger of using petrol engines in confined spaces would both be contributors to the accidents she suffered. The first occurred on 18th March 1904. She had been on exercise with the submarine flotilla and was returning to Gosport when she collided with the SS *Berwick Castle*. She was struck in the conning tower and sunk immediately, killing all 11 on board. The pressure hull was untouched. A month later HMS *A1* was raised, the bodies buried, and the submarine re-commissioned. As a result of the accident, British submarines were fitted with a second hatch at the bottom of the conning tower. Those that died in this accident were the first British submariners to be killed. Like so many others that were to lose their lives in the Channel, a peacetime accident was the cause.

Although obsolete within a few years of building, HMS *A1* remained in service until 1911. She was used primarily for harbour defence and training. So it was then, on 6th August 1910, HMS *A1* had another mishap. She was being prepared for diving when petrol fumes inside the submarine ignited. The resultant explosion severely burned seven crew men. One was blown out of the conning tower into Haslar Creek. The electrical system was found to be the cause.

By 1911, HMS *A1* was reduced to a test bed for explosives testing. In similar experiments to those conducted on *Holland 5* (see No 5/13), HMS *A1* was suspended in shallow depths and subjected to varying explosive charges at varying distances underwater. In August of that year, her pressure hull finally broke under the tests and she sank near Selsey Bill. A mechanism designed to fill her ballast tanks failed to keep her off the bottom.

A Selsey fisherman trawled into the wreck of HMS *A1* in 1988. She was found to be in an amazing state of preservation. The explosive testing was carried out on *A1* as if she had been a fully equipped operational submarine. Therefore, a totally intact submarine was found which was not a grave – a rare find indeed. The divers who first found her invited Martin Woodward to help identify the wreck. He now owns her, and has subsequently successfully lobbied to have the wreck designated as an historical wreck site and a buoy now marks her position. Diving is not permitted without the permission of Martin Woodward and DCMS.

No 4/16, HMS *Swordfish* – Mined

Class: S-Class	**Built at:** HM Dockyard - Chatham
Length: 61.36m	**Displacement:** 927t
Date sunk: 7th November 1940	**How sunk:** Mined (probably)
Historic Position: unknown	**Known Position:** Withheld on request
Crew losses: 42 (all crew lost)	**Commander:** Lt. M. A. Langley DSC

Of the 20 British submarines that lie on the seabed of the English Channel, only two were lost in wartime. HMS *Swordfish* was the only one lost during World War Two and her tale, like so many others is a sad reminder of the nature of submarine warfare. For 53 years she was believed to have sunk over 200 miles from where she was found, and in an unknown location. For the families of those lost, there was nowhere to go to pay their respects, and nowhere to even see on a map to show where their loved ones were lost. Submarines, by their very nature are stealthy craft, but when they are lost in circumstances like this one, the friends and relatives of the deceased have nowhere to grieve.

HMS *Swordfish* was one of the first of the S-Class of British submarines to be built. The S-Class was the most widely used class of submarines ever operated by the Royal Navy, with 62 launched by the end of World War Two. Three of these lie in the waters of the English Channel (see also Nos 3/17 and 3/20). The medium size S-Class was designed by the Navy out of a need to have a submarine that was suitable for operations in the European theatre. After much trial and error with HMS *Swordfish* and the three others initially ordered (at a cost of £230,000 each), the S-Class was perfected into a fine fighting machine.

The war career of HMS *Swordfish* was, tragically, to be a short one. Highlights of her operational career show that she operated in the North Sea, Channel and Bay of Biscay. On 14th September 1939, when the war was but a few days old, she was almost sunk by her sister HMS *Sturgeon*. Fortunately, the torpedo missed. On 1st October 1940, *Swordfish* took on a German convoy north of Barfleur and claimed

HMS Swordfish at sea – note the guards added to protect her forward hydroplanes. (Royal Navy Submarine Museum)

a hit. Later that year she attacked another convoy with similar results. The identity of the two vessels so struck has never been satisfactorily established.

HMS *Swordfish* sailed on her last patrol on 7th November 1940. She had been ordered to replace HMS *Usk* on patrol in the Bay of Biscay. Nothing more was ever heard from her. Analysis at the time, and after the war, seemed to suggest that she was either mined in the Bay or possibly fell victim to one of the German destroyer groups that operated there. No credible claim was ever made for her sinking, so her loss was always subject to some degree of scepticism.

After the war had ended and time passed, the story of HMS *Swordfish*, like many of her contemporaries, faded into history, only remembered by close friends and relatives and among that tightest of all groups of war veterans, the ex-submariners.

However, the story of HMS *Swordfish* was far from over. In 1983, while looking for a World War One-era steamship, local diver, Martin Woodward, located a British submarine wreck in 48 metres, south of the Isle of Wight. Mr Woodward has described to the author that this was probably one of the greatest days of his long and successful diving career, for it is not every day that one finds one of HM Submarines.

The submarine was found blown into two halves, forward of the conning tower. Her telegraphs were pointed to 'slow ahead'. Everything one would expect to see on a submarine wreck was there, proving that the wreck had not previously been located. Sadly, the stern hatch was found to be open, pointing to the fact that after the explosion, some of the crew had survived and probably tried to escape from her. The damage to the pressure hull seemed to point to an external force being responsible for her destruction. The most likely candidate being a drifting mine.

Clearly a British submarine, Mr Woodward had a job on his hands to work out which one she may be. Her six forward torpedo tubes, deck gun and overall layout pointed to an S-Class submarine. With the assistance of the late Gus Britton from the Royal Navy Submarine Museum, the most likely candidate was narrowed down to HMS *Swordfish*.

The identity of the wreck was confirmed when on a subsequent dive, the brass letter 'W' was found on the sand near the conning tower. The wreck was also extensively photographed, giving submarine experts the ability to support Mr Woodward's findings.

The discovery of HMS *Swordfish* caused a stir in the national newspapers and on television. During this time, a memorial service was held at HMS Dolphin and near the site of the wreck, so that the Navy and the relatives of the dead could finally pay their respects to the fallen with the full knowledge of what had happened to them. On display in Martin Woodward's museum on the Isle of Wight is the letter 'W' and a few other items recovered (at the request of the Royal Navy Submarine Museum for identification purposes) from the wreck. Once a year, the relatives gather there to remember their loved ones.

Martin Woodward has never divulged the position of the wreck to any party. He believes that this wreck, as a war grave, should now be left as it was when he found her, because nothing more can be learned from the wreck being re-visited by other divers.

No 4/17, HMS *Upstart* – Sonar Target

Class: U-Class	**Built at:** Vickers – Barrow-in-Furness
Length: 59.6m	**Displacement:** 740t
Date sunk: 29th July 1957	**How sunk:** As sonar target
Historic Position: 50 30.37N; 01 32.75W	**Known Position:** 50 30.37N; 01 32.75W
Crew losses: None	**Commander:** None

A great photo of HMS Upstart, her crew and Jolly Roger. (Royal Navy Submarine Museum)

The British U-Class was developed in the 1930s essentially as a training platform. However, during the Second World War, the U-Class became the backbone of the British submarine effort in the Mediterranean up to 1943. In total 60 of the U-Class were built and 21 were lost during the war.

Originally named as HMS *P65*, HMS *Upstart* was renamed in accordance with the wishes of Winston Churchill, who on hearing that many British submarines had not been named, immediately insisted that all should be.

HMS *Upstart* was launched on 24th November 1942 and commissioned under the command of Lt. Paul Chapman. It was he who designed the submarines logo, the mythical upstart, Ixion, who had seduced Juno and been sent to Hades.

Under Chapman's command, HMS *Upstart* made nine patrols in the Mediterranean. During the course of these, Chapman was awarded the DSO. Her operational cruises, saw her involved in convoy actions and in the bombardment of shore installations.

A popular commander, Chapman allowed the submarine to keep a collection of pet mascots. Over time, these came to include Percy the Goat, Pancho the Dog and a carrier pigeon.

As operations wound down in the Mediterranean in 1943, HMS *Upstart*'s future became less certain. Ultimately, she was transferred to the Greek Navy where she became *Amfitriti*. She was originally transferred to the Greek Navy with HMS *Untiring* (see No 1/27) and both were returned to the UK in 1957. At that time it was decided that both vessels should be sunk as sonar targets. HMS *Upstart* made her last dive on 29th July 1957.

Today, HMS *Upstart* is a popular dive around the Isle of Wight. Divers originally located her in 1975. She lies in 35 metres of water on a shingle bottom in an area where there can be excellent visibility in the summer months. Since her discovery, she has been subject to commercial salvage and her conning tower, which was made of bronze, has been removed, so that only the lower conning tower hatch can be seen.

No 4/18, *Prométhée* – Sunk on Trial

Class: 1928-9	**Built at:** Cherbourg
Length: 92.3m	**Displacement:** 2084t
Date sunk: 7th July 1932	**How sunk:** Diving accident
Historic Position: N of Cap Lévi	**Known Position:** Cap Lévi
Crew losses: 61 (from 68)	**Commander:** Lt. de V. A. Couespel du Mesnil

Prométhée during trials – she was lost shortly afterwards. (Marius Bar)

Some of the most testing times in the history of any submarine, are the few times it first puts to sea for trials. Britain has witnessed tragedy when brand new submarines have sunk while fitting-out and working-up. For example, HMS *K13* sank during acceptance trials and HMS *Thetis* sank the first time she put to sea, killing 99. The French were not to escape such tragedies either. In Channel waters, the brand new submarine *Prométhée* sank on excursion from the dockyard, on 7th July 1932.

She left Cherbourg at 09.00 to undergo routine testing of her engines and motors. On board were several personnel from the shipyard that built her, including the director of engineering. Initially, all went well and the electric motors were found to be working perfectly. However, problems immediately occurred when it was decided to test the diesel engines. *Prométhée* had been fitted with a brand-new design of hydraulic control system, which had not been used before. When this was employed to engage the clutch to the diesel engines, the vents opened instead, and the submarine immediately began to dive out of control.

The crew on the bridge jumped for their lives, and the commander, Lt. de V. A. Couespel du Mesnil, ran up the ladder from the control room and saw that he had no option but to jump off too. The *Prométhée* was then seen to rear-up and descend stern-first. The survivors were in the sea for over an hour before being picked up by a passing fishing boat. It was only then that the alarm was raised.

The submarine was located the following day, because the indicator buoy was found on the surface. However, there was no one alive on board to answer the telephone link. Neither did any of the searchers' surface vessels pick up any underwater wireless telegraphy or any other sounds emanating from the wreck. It was, therefore, assumed that the 61 on board had already succumbed to the sea. Among the dead were several dockyard personnel who had built the submarine at Cherbourg.

A deep diving specialist was called upon to investigate the wreck, which lay in the challenging depth of 80 metres. However, the French Navy and the legendary Italian salvage company, Sorima quickly realised that the depth in which *Prométhée* lay would make salvage extremely difficult. This was the same conclusion reached by the Royal Navy, 19 years later when HMS *Affray* sank in similar depths (see No 3/22).

With a submerged displacement of 2,084 tons, the *Prométhée* is the largest submarine wreck in the Channel. Lying in over 80 metres of water to the north of Cherbourg, it seems as if this wreck, too, is a target waiting for the right group of technical divers to locate and attempt to dive. Her sheer size, coupled with her dramatic history would make for a superb piece of exploration.

No 4/19, *U151* – The *Oldenburg*

Class: U151 (ex-Deutschland series)
Built at: Built at Flensburger Schiffsbau. Finished at Germaniawerft - Kiel
Length: 65m   **Displacement:** 1875t
Date sunk: 7th June 1921   **How sunk:** Gunnery target
Historic Position: Off Cherbourg   **Known Position:** Off Cherbourg
Crew losses: None   **Commander:** None

The historic U151. (U-Boot Archiv)

U151 was one of the ex-Deutschland-Class U-cruisers (see Nos. 4/8 and 4/9). She was originally named *Oldenburg* and was never used in the merchant ship role for which she was built. In 1917 she was converted to operate as a long-range commerce raider.

In this guise she operated off Gibraltar and North Africa, but she will always be associated with the now notorious attacks on the East Coast of the United States during May 1918. Although not the first U-boat to operate off the shores of America, *U151*'s patrol sank several large ships, including the 5,093-ton *Carolina* (recently located by US wreck-hunter John Chatterton) and the 8,173-ton British troopship *Dwinsk*. One of *Dwinsk's* lifeboats with 22 on board was never seen again. *U151* also laid mines in Delaware Bay and cut international telephone cables, gaining much notoriety. This cruise is brilliantly described in Lowell Thomas' classic "Raiders of the Deep".

U151 was easily the most successful of the Deutschland-Class. Under two commanders, Kophamel and Von Nostitz, this raider sank 51 ships in total for 138,284 tons – an impressive record for such a lumbering giant.

At the end of the war, she was transferred to the French Navy and was sunk as a gunnery target on 7th June 1921 'off Cherbourg', presumably in the same location as *U121* (see No 4/21)

U151 is a historically important submarine wreck and her location by divers would be of considerable interest to researchers and historians. *U151* was one of the most successful submarines ever to menace the East Coast of the United States.

No 4/20, *U121* – Gunnery Target

Class: U117 (U117 minelayer series)	**Built at:** Vulcan - Hamburg
Length: 81.52m	**Displacement:** 1512t
Date sunk: 1st July 1921	**How sunk:** Gunnery target
Historic Position: Off Cherbourg	**Known Position:** Off Cherbourg
Crew losses: None	**Commander:** None

U121 was of the late-war class of U-cruiser/minelayers (see No 4/6). She was launched on 20th September 1918 and did not see war service. This submarine was to be sent to the Mediterranean to be operated by the Austro-Hungarian Navy.

However, she was still in Germany at the end of the war. This new submarine was transferred to the French Navy. In accordance with the Treaty of Versailles, she was disposed of as a gunnery target on 1st July 1921.

The only positional data the author has been able to locate states that sinking took place 'off Cherbourg'. As with the wreck of *U151* (see No 4/20) she would make an exciting discovery.

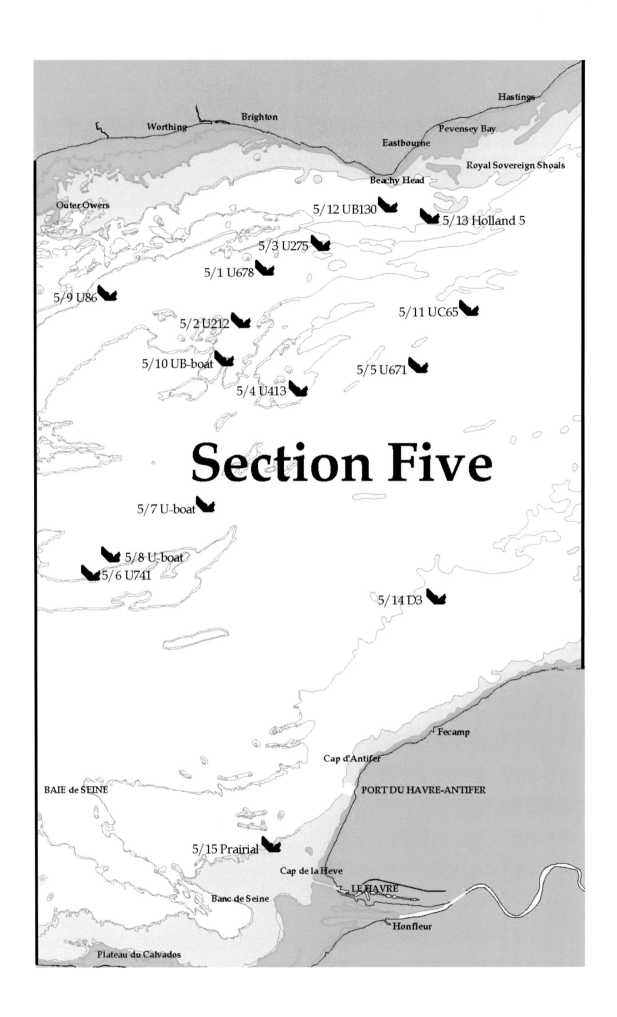

Hastings
Brighton
Worthing
Pevensey Bay
Eastbourne
Royal Sovereign Shoals
Beachy Head
Outer Owers
5/12 UB130
5/13 Holland 5
5/3 U275
5/1 U678
5/9 U86
5/11 UC65
5/2 U212
5/10 UB-boat
5/5 U671
5/4 U413

Section Five

5/7 U-boat
5/8 U-boat
5/6 U741
5/14 D3
Fecamp
Cap d'Antifer
PORT DU HAVRE-ANTIFER
BAIE de SEINE
5/15 Prairial
Cap de la Heve
Banc de Seine
LE HAVRE
Honfleur
Plateau du Calvados

Section 5

Submarine Wrecks off Sussex

The submarine wrecks in the Brighton area are dominated by U-boats lost attempting to stop shipping reaching France after D-Day. No less than eight were destroyed in this area. However, the most interesting aspect of these wrecks for the historian is the fact that the loss register states that there should only be six!

Divers found the two additional ones. When the author visited these sites and identified the wrecks as late war Type VIICs, a major task was begun to work out which U-boats they could possibly be. This work is ongoing and only very tentative identities are given here. The discovery of these two wrecks yet again shows how the recreational diver can add to our knowledge of our maritime past.

The considerable degree of success shown by the Canadian ASW ships operating in this area was, in no small part, down to the extremely efficient tactics they employed. In particular, it should be noted here that they buoyed every known wreck between Britain and France in this sector, so as to avoid depth charging wreckage when hunting U-boats.

Among the other submarine wrecks in this area is HMS *D3*, sunk in a regrettable friendly-fire incident with a French airship. Also *U86* was dumped in these waters in 1921. She holds the dubious distinction of being the submarine involved in one of the worst atrocities in submarine history. Also, one of the wiliest of the World War One U-boat commanders, Claus Lafrenz was captured off Eastbourne, when his minelaying *UC65* was torpedoed by a British submarine in 1917.

During World War One, the French submarine, *Prairial* was lost in a collision off Le Havre. She holds the distinction of being the only steam-powered submarine wreck in this book.

Special thanks should be given to Tim Bonetto and Ivan Warren for supporting this project. The discoveries made in this section are in no small part down to their knowledge and experience as wreck researchers and charter boat operators.

No 5/1, *U678* - Identified by a Scrap of Paper

Class: VIIC
Length: 67.10m
Date sunk: 6th July 1944

Historic Position: 50 32N; 00 23W
Crew losses: 52 (all crew lost)

Built at: Howaldtswerke - Hamburg
Displacement: 871t
How sunk: Hedgehog & D/Cs *HMCS Ottowa,* HMCS *Kootenay* and HMS *Statice*
Known Position: 50 33 50N; 00 04.50W
Commander: Olzs. Guido Hyronimus

U678 was part of the first wave of U-boats sent into the Channel from Norway as a response to the D-Day landings. She had sailed from Marviken on 8th June 1944 and arrived in the invasion area just over three weeks later.

On 5th July, she attempted to attack a convoy south of Brighton. The attack was

The scrap of paper that identified U678. (U-Boot Archiv)

unsuccessful, but it brought *U678* to the attention of the convoy's escorts who began to hunt for her. One escort, HMS *Statice,* located a number of targets and made several attacks throughout the night. In the morning, elements from the powerful Canadian Escort Group 11 arrived on the scene. After HMCS

U678's Commander when watch officer on U461. (U-Boot Archiv)

Ottawa had located a good target, attacks by HMCS *Kootenay* and HMS *Statice* caused the target to bottom. It is fairly certain that the hedgehog attack from HMS *Statice* destroyed the U-boat, as much debris surfaced after the attack. However, the absence of human remains, led HMCS *Kootenay* and HMCS *Ottawa* to plaster the position for a further ten hours. During the course of these further attacks a scrap of paper bearing *U678's* identity was picked from the water.

U678's commander, Olzs. Guido Hyronimus was lost with his entire crew, having found it impossible to escape from the hunting vessels

above. Hyronimus had lost his first command, *U670,* in a collision during training in Danzig Bay in which 21 of his crew had been killed.

In 2000 the author discovered the wreck of *U678* at the position given above. It was considered to be a difficult target to locate, due to the amount of damage the wreck was likely to have sustained. At a depth of 70 metres, the conning tower hatch cover was seen sticking out of the sand. Only her bow section, with its torpedo tubes is clearly visible, with the rest of the U-boat now covered by a large sand drift, a fitting burial for its hapless crew.

There is some small possibility that this could be the wreck of *U275* (see No 5/3) or *U212* (see No 5/2). There is a considerable difference between the reported sinking position and the location of this wreck, possibly explained by the length of the hunt for the U-boat.

No 5/2, *U212* – Lost on her 13th Patrol

Class: VIIC
Length: 67.10m
Date sunk: 21st July 1944
Historic Position: 50 27N; 00 13W
Crew losses: 49 (all crew lost)

Built at: Germaniawerft - Kiel
Displacement: 871t
How sunk: D/C HMS *Curzon* and HMS *Ekins*
Known Position: 50 29 00N; 00 10 62W
Commander: Klt. Helmut Volger

The veteran U-boat, *U212* was one of the oldest to have operated in the Channel. By the time she was sunk, she was on her 13th patrol. While she never sank a ship, some of her exploits are worthy of note. For instance in June 1943 she landed a commando party on Bear Island, which destroyed an abandoned allied weather station. In July 1943, she laid mines in the Pechora Sea. On 6th June 1944, she was almost sunk by two 57mm cannon-equipped Mosquitoes, outside Brest.

On her final patrol, *U212* departed Brest on 5th July 1944. Little else is known as to what exactly happened to her; however, it is clear now that she reached her operational area on about 13th July. Her destruction has been attributed to the frigates, HMS *Curzon* and HMS *Ekins.* They saw a U-boat using

U212 at sea earlier in the war - commissioned in 1942, she had originally been fitted with a deck gun, which had been removed by the time she was lost (U-Boot Archiv)

U212's elaborate conning tower emblem. (U-Boot Archiv)

her schnorchel and attacked with depth charges and hedgehogs. At the time the attack was reported, it was classified 'U-boat probably sunk' and was fully attributed after the end of the war.

In 1998, the author visited a wreck, thought to be a submarine, at the position given above. The diving was conducted from Ivan Warren's *Michelle Mary*. Ivan Warren is extremely knowledgeable of the wrecks around Littlehampton. The wreck, lying in over 60 metres, turned out to be a VIIC U-boat. It was in a very poor state of repair, with most of its outer cladding missing and a major blast hole on the port side, forward of the conning tower. The stern was totally blown off the wreck, with the aft tube lying 10 metres behind it.

It is possible that this could be the wreck of *U678* (see No 5/1), or possibly *U275* (see below).

No 5/3, *U275* - Mine Victim

Class: VIIC	**Built at:** Vegesacker Werft - Vegesack
Length: 67.10m	**Displacement:** 871t
Date sunk: 10th March 1945	**How sunk:** Mined
Historic Position: 50 36N; 00.04W	**Known Position:** 50 36.311N; 00 03.049W
Crew losses: 48 (all crew lost)	**Commander:** Olzs. Helmut Wehrkamp

The veteran U-boat *U275* was ordered to operate in the eastern Channel and left St. Nazaire on 25th February 1945. It is known that she reached her patrol area and was active there from at least 8th March. For it was on that date that the 4,934-ton *Lornaston* was torpedoed and sunk. With *U275* being the only U-boat known to have been operating in this area, she was credited with the destruction of this vessel.

Two days later, a massive explosion was heard to emanate from the position given above.

U275 coming alongside – note the air radar warning receiver built onto the conning tower shroud. (U-Boot Archiv)

Several warships investigated this over the next 24 hours and the conclusion drawn was that a U-boat had been mined in the locale. There was a fair degree of evidence to support this contention. Much diesel oil was smelt (at night) and seen the following morning in the area. A potential U-boat wreck was located and 'tin opening' commenced. Among the items that came to the surface were leather trousers, wooden doors, first aid kits and (notably) scraps of paper in German.

The author's diving team visited the wreck considered most likely to be *U275*, in the summer of 2001. It was confirmed as a heavily damaged Type VII submarine.

The commander of *U275*, Olzs. Helmut Wehrkamp was just 23 years old when he was lost with his entire crew just a few weeks before the end of the war.

No 5/4, *U413* - Sole Survivor

Class: VIIC	**Built at:** Danziger Werft - Danzig
Length: 67.10m	**Displacement:** 871t
Date sunk: 20th August 1944	**How sunk:** D/Cs and hedgehogs HMS *Vidette*, HMS *Forester* and HMS *Wensleydale*
Historic Position: 50 21N; 00 01W	**Known Position:** 50 21.5N; 00 00.5W
Crew losses: 45 (from 46)	**Commander:** Olzs. Dietrich Schase

U413 was by far the most successful World War Two U-boat to have been sunk in the Channel. Commissioned in June 1942, *U413* survived seven patrols before destruction. Some of the highlights of these include the sinking of the 20,107-ton troopship *Warwick Castle* off Gibraltar in September 1942. This was the 13th largest ship sunk by U-boats during the war. Two more cargo vessels were sunk on her next patrol. In January 1944 *U413*, in a strange co-incidence, sank the destroyer HMS *Warwick* off Trevose Head, North Cornwall.

U413 earlier in the war, before her conning tower was extended to accommodate further AAA. (U-Boot Archiv)

Up to this point in her career, Klt. Gustav Poel had been in command. In March 1944, Poel received the Knight's Cross and was posted to an instructor position. His successor was Olzs. Dietrich Schase.

U413 left Brest for her last patrol on 2nd August 1944. She was ordered to patrol in the eastern part of the Channel. She arrived there some time before the 19th and on that day torpedoed and sank the 2,306-ton steamer *Saint Egonat*. This was to be *U413*'s last success. Although she succeeded in giving the escorts the slip on the 19th, a powerful and experienced group of submarine hunters continued to search for her.

The following day, HMS *Vidette*, HMS *Forester* and HMS *Wensleydale* located and destroyed *U413*. HMS *Forester's* original depth charge attack fell wide, but HMS *Vidette's* hedgehog attack wrecked the U-boat, which sank to the seabed. A few moments later, HMS *Wensleydale* picked up a survivor. He was Karl Hütterer, the Chief Engineer, who was the only crew member to make a successful escape from the stricken submarine. Wood and scraps of paper were also collected from the sea.

It seems as if the attackers (now without any ammunition) were not certain that the submarine had been destroyed and suspected that the survivor may have been sent to the surface to fool them. However, the three ships were credited with the destruction of the U-boat.

In the summer of 1999, the author visited the most likely sinking position for *U413* and discovered a rocky reef with an old scallop drag on top of it in 64 metres! Later in that year the author was diving with a group of friends from the BSAC High Wycombe Branch, on an 'unknown wreck' in the same area when *U413* was discovered. The author returned to the site in 2000 and made a thorough exploration of the wreckage. *U413* is blown nearly clean in half, just forward of the conning tower. The wreck lies in an area of poor visibility and is quite heavily netted.

The major area of damage clearly shows that the wreck was subjected to further attacks after the survivor had been plucked from the sea.

No 5/5, *U671* - Sunk on its First Patrol

Class: VIIC	**Built at:** Howaldtswerke - Hamburg
Length: 67.10m	**Displacement:** 871t
Date sunk: 5th August 1944	**How sunk:** Hedgehogs and D/Cs HMS *Stayner* and HMS *Wensleydale*
Historic Position: 50 23N; 00 06E	**Known Position:** 50 23.50N; 00 19.00E
Crew losses: 47 (from 52)	**Commander:** Klt. Wolfgang Hegewald

U671 was one of the first wave of U-boats sent from Norway to intercept the D-Day landings. She had left Bergen on 28th May for the North Atlantic, but had been diverted to the Channel after the landings took place. *U671* arrived in the landing area on 25th June. So intense was the anti-submarine activity during this period that *U671* was thwarted each time she attempted to attack the mass of shipping crossing the Channel.

Although *U671* fired at least three torpedoes during this time, she achieved no successes and was detected and attacked at least twice. An attack on 2nd July nearly sank the U-boat, which then, badly damaged, made for Boulogne, reaching safety on 5th July. On arrival, her battery was completely flat! Boulogne was not a submarine repair centre and the technical expertise there to make good the damage she had sustained was not available. Therefore, U-boat command sent 30 technicians from St. Nazaire to effect the necessary repairs to *U671*.

U671 sailed again on 26th July for operations off the Isle of Wight. However, the schnorchel malfunctioned, forcing her back to Boulogne. On 1st August, she went to sea for the final time. Again the schnorchel mast malfunctioned and *U671* had no option but to turn for Boulogne once again.

However, HMS *Stayner* detected *U671* on the evening of 4th August. The frigate was on her way to an anti-E-boat patrol and did not have hedgehogs loaded. She, therefore, attacked with depth charges three times before her hedgehog was readied.

U671's commander, Klt. Wolfgang Hegewald had been skilfully making last minute turns in

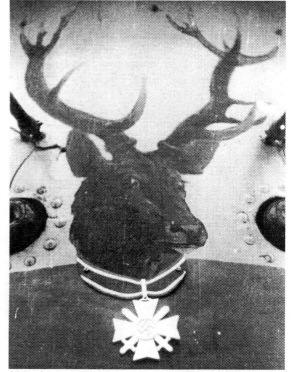

U671's conning tower emblem. (U-Boot Archiv)

direction as the depth charges were dropped. However, the switch to hedgehogs fooled him and the forward-firing projectiles found their mark. HMS *Wensleydale* now arrived on the scene and made further attacks. While passing over the wreck, survivors were seen struggling in the water. Six were rescued, although one later died.

Under interrogation, the survivors stated that the fatal damage had been done by the first hedgehog attack. Hegewald had unsuccessfully tried to raise the U-boat at that time. Bulkhead doors had been closed and escape attempted. The survivors all came out through the conning tower hatch, although there had been 20 men (including the captain) in that section.

In early summer 1999, the author located the wreck of *U671* at the position given above. Local divers had discovered the wreck earlier in the year. *U671*'s conning tower hatch is open, as is the lower hatch into the control room, supporting the escapee's story. Her bronze torpedo tubes can be seen, where the plating has rotted on her bows. However, the major damage to the U-boat is a massive blast hole in the port side of the forward torpedo room. This is clearly the damage that sank her. Aft of the conning tower, the galley hatch is also open, with a ladder next to it, pointing to the possibility of the crew in the stern making an unsuccessful attempt to escape too.

No 5/6, *U741* - Unlucky Patrol

Class: VIIC	**Built at:** F Schichau - Danzig
Length: 67.10m	**Displacement:** 871t
Date sunk: 15th August 1944	**How sunk:** D/Cs and Hedgehogs HMS *Orchis*
Historic Position: 50 02N; 00 36W	**Known Position:** 50 02.00N; 00 35.00W
Crew losses: 48 (from 49)	**Commander:** Olzs. Gerhard Palmgren

U741 was commissioned on 10th April 1943. She was on her fourth and final patrol when she was sunk. Up to that point, her only success had been the shooting down of a Wellington from 407 Squadron on 10th March 1944.

She had left Brest for operations in the Channel on 5th July 1944. From the outset, this patrol was dogged by bad luck. Within a few hours of departure, she was attacked and suffered damage to her sky observation (search) periscope. *U741* pressed on and on 12th July collided with a minesweeper's deployed gear. This caused the antenna cables to break, which then snagged one of her propellers. That

U741's officers during her commissioning; her Commander is third from the left. (U-Boot Archiv)

evening, *U741* bravely surfaced to free the propeller. This done, the submarine reverted to schnorchel as she progressed toward its patrol area. In the darkness, the submarine collided with a surface vessel, which wrecked the other periscope and damaged the schnorchel. Olzs. Gerhard Palmgren had no choice but to make for Le Havre, the nearest port of safety, duly arriving on 15th July.

The repairs to *U741* took more than three weeks to make good and the U-boat sailed again on 8th August to operate near the Isle of Wight. However, on 15th August, Palmgren sighted convoy FTM69 and put two torpedoes into *LST404*, which miraculously survived to be towed to safety. As *U741* made its escape, the corvette, HMS *Orchis*, which was escorting a nearby convoy, detected her. *U741* was located lying 'doggo' on the bottom. Two depth charge attacks and two hedgehog attacks followed. The second hedgehog attack caused a large explosion and much debris came to the surface.

The survivors of this attack were all in the stern section of *U741*. Only two managed to reach the surface by using the aft torpedo-loading hatch. The only survivor, Leo Leuwer, escaped from there and was picked up. HMS *Orchis* then buoyed the wreck.

In the summer of 2000, the author located the remains of *U741*. The major damage to her is a blast hole in the port side, forward of the conning tower, supporting the survivor's report that he escaped from the stern section. The conning tower hatch was closed and the schnorchel was in its retracted position.

No 5/7, Unidentified VIIC – (Possibly *U988*)

Class: VIIC	**Built at:** Unknown
Length: 67.1m	**Displacement:** 871t
Date sunk: Unknown	**How sunk:** Unknown
Historic Position: Unknown	**Known Position:** 50 09.5N; 00 15.00W
Crew losses: Assume all	**Commander:** Unknown

A submarine wreck was located at this position in 1995. The author visited the site in 1999 and confirmed the presence of a VIIC U-boat. The H/F loop is partially extended and heavily netted. Much of the outer cladding has fallen away from the pressure hull. The bow section has broken, just forward of the pressure hull bulkhead. The hatches are open all along the wreck, with only the conning tower hatch closed. However, it is the stern section that has clearly suffered the most damage, being flattened and partially collapsed into the sand. The schnorchel is in the retracted position, although the head has fallen off.

The identity of this wreck may never be known, without a very detailed diving survey. However, there is one possibility as to when she may have been sunk. From this, a tentative identity can be given to the wreck, challenging the official history of U-boat losses.

The proceeds of the assessment committee for 1944-45 show one reported and analysed ASW attack at this position. It took place on 3rd-6th July 1944 and was recorded as AUD1172/44, AUD1198/44 and M07743/44. Essentially, this was a combined attack by six vessels, HMS *Brissenden*, HMS *Onslaught*, HMS *Oribi*, HMS *Seymour*, HMS *Wensleydale* and HMS *Talybont*. The target located on the 3rd was soon stopped on the bottom and was repeatedly attacked for the next two days. The evidence that came to the surface was diesel oil, white-painted wood and some 'diving suits'.

The assessment committee decided that the target was not a U-boat, due to the white wood and the diving suits, which were not recognised when shown to U-boat POWs. However, the position of these attacks (50 10; 00 15W) is simply too close to this wreck to be discounted now.

Several U-boats were operating in the Channel at this time. Most have been located, or have viable sinking assessments associated with them. Only after much research and deliberations by the author and the eminent U-boat loss historian, Axel Niestlé did one plausible solution emerge.

It is quite likely that this wreck is *U988* (see No 1/14) because the date of the sinking points to the fact that *U988* was known to have been operating in the area at this time. *U988* did not return from patrol and is thought to have been sunk while exiting the Channel. If there is a U-boat wreck at the sinking position generally given to *U988*, this could well be where *U441* was destroyed.

No 5/8, Unidentified VIIC – (Possibly *U984*)

Class: VIIC	**Built at:** Unknown
Length: 67.1m	**Displacement:** 871t
Date sunk: Unknown	**How sunk:** Unknown
Historic Position: Unknown	**Known Position:** 50 04.00N; 00 32.2W
Crew losses: Assume all	**Commander:** Unknown

In 2000, the author learned of a submarine wreck at the position given above. Upon investigation, it turned out to be another VIIC U-boat wreck in an unexpected location. This wreck is in generally good condition. There is a large net covering the bow section. The damage that sank her is easy to see. There is a major blast hole in the starboard section, just aft of the conning tower. It is so large one can peer into the control room. The schnorchel is retracted and the hatches are closed.

The presence of another unidentified VIIC wreck in a location so close to the wreck of *U741* causes significant problems when attempting to work out its possible identity. There are no assessed ASW attacks near to this position, apart from the one that accounted for *U741* (see No 5/6). The nearest report is at 49 59;00 37W which occurred on 17th February 1945 (it is logged as attack No AUD 326/45).

It is far more likely, however, that the reported attack that destroyed this U-boat was never fully assessed, being immediately dismissed as an attack on the wreck of *U741*. Not every ASW attack made in 1944-45 was fully evaluated.

Dr Axel Niestlé and the author have carefully considered which U-boat wreck this may be. At present, the best identification, which can be alloted to the wreck, is *U984*. This submarine was supposedly destroyed off Brest on its return from the D-Day landing area in August 1944. The attack that supposedly sank it was originally assessed as a 'B' grade attack. It seems however, that it was sunk here, not five days after *U741*, with an attack on the wreck of *U741* being considered the most likely reason why the loss of another U-boat in this area was discounted in 1944.

If this is *U984*, then she is a rare find. The commander, Olzs. Heinz Sieder, held the coveted Knight's Cross. He would be only the second Knight's Cross holder to have been lost in Channel waters. The other was Förster in *U480* (see No 4/1).

No 5/9, *U86* – War Crimes

Class: U81 (U81 series)	**Built at:** Germaniawerft - Kiel
Length: 70.06m	**Displacement:** 946t
Date sunk: 30th June 1921	**How sunk:** Dumped
Historic Position: 50 28.50N; 00 34.30W	**Known Position:** 50 31.10N; 00 33.90W
Crew losses: None	**Commander:** None

U86 whilst under British Command. (Imperial War Museum)

U86 was one of the first of the popular U81 series of ocean-going U-boats built. She was commissioned on 30th November 1918, three weeks after launch. The impressive tonnage sunk during her career (33 ships for 125,580 tons) is not the reason that this U-boat is remembered. There is a darker side to her operational history. This is made all the more appalling because of its general rarity during World War One.

The hospital ships operated by the allies were permitted by international law, to sail independently and were according to the rules, safe from enemy attack. However, the German government had on several occasions made assumptions about the use of these ships as subterfuge troop and supply transports. Several hospital ships were sunk during World War One. Each case, such as that of the *Lanfranc* in the Channel, caused international revulsion. While the allies abandoned the use of hospital ships in the Channel during 1917 (in favour of armed 'ambulance transports'), their use on the Atlantic run still continued, with Bristol being the centre of operations in Britain.

Any U-boat commander, who deliberately sank a hospital ship, was taking a very grave chance of being labelled a butcher. Only absolute proof (never established) that the ship was in contravention of the rules could possibly excuse an attack. The case of *U86* under the command of Conrad Patzig went even further than this. Not only did Patzig sink a hospital ship, but also when he realised his fatal error, he tried to cover it up by murdering the survivors.

It was 27th June 1918, 116 miles from Fastnet Rock, when *U86*, having followed her for four hours, torpedoed and sank the hospital ship *Llandovery Castle*. Fortunately, there were no wounded on board, but there were 80 medical staff, 14 nurses and 164 crew members. As the ship sank, the survivors took to the lifeboats. Then, *U86* surfaced and inspected the survivors. When Patzig realised the enormity of his folly; that there were only innocent medical staff on board, he resolved to remove any evidence of his actions from the pages of history. Along with one gunner and two officers, Boldt and Ditmar, *U86* shelled the surviving lifeboats, destroying all except one, which had 24 survivors in it. They miraculously survived being located and sunk. This lifeboat was found, drifting 50 miles from Fastnet Rock and the story of the atrocity got out.

After the war, in the face of mounting international demands for justice, Patzig, Boldt and Ditmar were arraigned for a war crimes trial in Leipzig. Patzig fled and was never prosecuted. Boldt and Ditmar pleaded that they had been following orders, but were found guilty on the grounds that they knew they were acting illegally. Both received four-year sentences, but in the climate of the times, only served a few months. Although 17 U-boat commanders were listed as war criminals, only Patzig's case never came to trial. In 1945, the allies, probably remembering this incident prosecuted the commander of *U852* for a similar act. He was executed by firing squad. Patzig lived the rest of his life a free man.

Unlike most of her counterparts, *U86* was actually commissioned into the Royal Navy for a short spell. From September 1919 until March 1920 she was used to test the overall design of this class of U-boat and to make comparisons with later designs.

After decommissioning, *U86* remained unsold and unallocated. Therefore, like several other U-boats she was dumped at sea at the end of June 1921. Her historic position, several miles from the main dumping ground suggests that the tow parted, although the remaining records from this period have not substantiated this. The known position given above has not been confirmed by diving, as far as the author is aware, but marks the most likely charted wreck. There is a strong possibility that the wreck of *U86* is in fact the wreck owned by Martin Woodward, currently designated *U90*.

No 5/10, Unidentified UBIII Class

Class: UBIII	**Built at:** Unknown
Length: 56m approx.	**Displacement:** 670t approx.
Date sunk: Unknown	**How sunk:** Unknown
Historic Position: Unknown	**Known Position:** 50 25.00N; 00 12.30W
Crew losses: Unknown (assume all)	**Commander:** Unknown

In 1998, the author's submarine diving team went to investigate the reported wreck of a submarine located in the position given above. From the official histories of U-boat losses, the team was certain that it would uncover one of the several World War Two VIIC U-boats destroyed in this area. However, what the team found was totally unexpected.

There on the sand lay the wreck of a World War One UBIII-Class U-boat. It was in good condition and easily identifiable as this class from its features, general size and layout. The outer hull at bow and stern has collapsed revealing the four forward and one aft torpedo tube associated with the UBIII-Class. The 88mm deck-gun now points skyward, probably as a result of being snared by a fishing vessel at some time in the past. All hatches on the wreck are closed. Located in the sides of the conning tower are the familiar recesses associated with U-boats of this era. Interestingly, surrounding the deck gun was a large amount of expended ammunition. This points to the wreck being an operational U-boat, which had already seen action before sinking. There is no evidence of any catastrophic damage to the wreck in any location.

The presence of a UBIII-Class U-boat in this location was a major surprise. The best histories of U-boat losses from World War One do not list a UBIII class sunk anywhere in the entire area of this chapter. Clearly a review of the UBIII loss register is needed. This could be carried out with further sympathetic diving to help identify this wreck. In the meantime, she should be regarded as a war grave.

Although far from certain, one possible candidate could be *UB54*, which according to French reports (dismissed at the time) was attacked by a French patrol vessel south of this point. Her possible loss in the Dover Straits remains unconfirmed (see No 6/15). This wreck does not appear to be either *UB104* or *UB113* (both unexplained UBIII losses) because of the presence of the 88mm gun. Both the former were retrofitted with a 105mm and both were expected to return to base via the Scotland route.

There is also the possibility that this could be the wreck of *UB63* (see Appendix 2).

No 5/11, *UC65* – Submarine v Submarine

Class: UCII (UC65 series)	**Built at:** Blohm & Voss - Hamburg
Length: 50.35m	**Displacement:** 508t
Date sunk: 3rd November 1917	**How sunk:** HM Submarine *C15*
Historic Position: 50 28N; 00 17E	**Known Position:** 50 30.25N; 00 28.37E
Crew losses: 22 (from 27)	**Commander:** Klt. Claus Lafrenz

UC65 is one of the most remarkable of the World War One U-boats lost in the Channel. She stands out for a number of reasons. She was the fourth most successful UC-boat ever built, she was commanded by two of the most capable U-boat commanders of the war, she sank a British cruiser and became the rare victim of an enemy submarine.

The successful UC65 in harbour. (U-Boot Archiv)

UC65 was built in Hamburg and commissioned on 10th November 1916. She operated with the Flanders Flotilla and as such, came to be commanded in the first instance by the remarkable Otto Steinbrink. He was one of the finest submarine commanders of all time, whose prowess to this day inspires awe in all who learn of his exploits. Apart from single-handedly destroying around 210,000 tons of allied shipping, Steinbrink is remembered for another remarkable exploit. On a patrol in the North Sea aboard *UB18,* Steinbrink took on four British submarines, sank one (HMS *E22*) and stopped to pick up the survivors before evading the other three to escape. No wonder the Admiralty dreaded him!

Near to the wreck of *UC65,* lies one of its more notable victims. Under the command of Steinbrink, the UC-boat despatched the cruiser HMS *Ariadne* off Beachy Head. In total, *UC65* was responsible for the destruction of 103 ships! This remarkable number added up 112,859 tons of allied shipping.

Her last commander was Klt. Claus Lafrenz. He was one of a clutch of genuinely capable submarine commanders possessed by the Flanders Flotilla. Nicknamed 'Lala', he was highly thought of by his contemporaries and had already been decorated with the House Order of Hohenzollern. This was awarded for being the first U-boat commander to photograph a British Q-ship. The Kaiser was apparently impressed with this exploit and kept a copy of the photo.

On 3rd November 1917, Lafrenz was on the return leg of his second patrol in *UC65.* Off Beachy Head, he was on the bridge with four

Claus "Lala" Lafrenz the first U-boat Commander to photograph a Q-ship. (U-Boot Archiv)

others. Ahead lay the British submarine HMS *C15,* under the command of Lt. E.H. Dolphin. Both submarines saw each other at the same time. While Dolphin flooded his torpedo tubes, Lafrenz opted to continue on course for home. He could see HMS *C15's* periscope and remarked to those on the bridge that if a torpedo was fired at him, he would use the manoeuvrability of *UC65* to evade it. Shortly thereafter, a torpedo was spotted streaking toward *UC65.* Lafrenz put the helm over and evaded it. Seconds later *UC65* exploded and sank. Dolphin had fired two torpedoes, close spread. In so doing, Lafrenz paid for his overconfidence, because he could not have evaded both. The five men in the bridge were blown into the air. Coming down in the sea, they were the only survivors from *UC65.* In being sunk in this manner, the minelayer became one of only two U-boats in the Channel sunk by HM Submarines. The other was *UB72* (see No 3/5). For once, Lala had met his match.

As with all other survivors of U-boats, the five men were interrogated at the Admiralty. Much useful information was usually gathered from these sessions, even if the German sailors thought they were being evasive. Lafrenz's interrogation report makes interesting reading, for he was particularly helpful. From him, the allies learned how the U-boats were evading the Dover Barrage - priceless information indeed!

The German high command had no idea what had happened to *UC65* for several months. This was at the time when many of the old hands of the Flanders Flotilla were being killed. Indeed, when Werner Fürbringer was sunk in *UB110* in July 1918, he was amazed to be told by his interrogators that Lala was alive. He was even more surprised by the extensive knowledge the Admiralty seemed to possess of all operational aspects of the Flanders Flotilla, which he assumed had come from Belgian spies.

Today the wreck of *UC65* lies at the position given above. It is a great dive, being a comparatively rare UC-Class. It is easy to see the damage done to her, because the wreck lies in two halves around 20 metres apart. The empty mine chutes can be seen in the bow section along with most of the features of this class. The stern section is also interesting, especially so, because the break is exactly at the point of the engine room entrance, allowing for a rare inspection of a pair of 1916-era MAN diesel engines. The short-barrelled 88mm deck-gun is also an interesting item to examine.

No 5/12, *UB130* (or *UB131*?)

Class: UBIII (UB118 series)	**Built at:** AG Weser - Bremen
Length: 55.85m	**Displacement:** 643t
Date sunk: Unknown	**How sunk:** Unknown
Historic Position: Hastings?	**Known Position:** 50 40.54N; 00 15.21E
Crew losses: None	**Commander:** None

UB130 was one of the last of the UBIII Class to be commissioned into the U-boat service before the end of World War One. She was originally intended for allocation to the Austro-Hungarian Navy, but instead remained in Germany. During her brief career, the aristocratic-sounding Heinrich XXXVII Prinz Reuss commanded her. *UB130* made only one brief excursion into the North Sea during her career.

At the end of the war, she sailed to Harwich to surrender. This is where story of *UB130* becomes confusing. Most German histories state that she was allocated to the French Navy and used for explosive tests in Toulon in 1921. So the location of a UBIII Class U-boat with at least one propeller clearly stamped *UB130* in the waters off Beachy Head came as a surprise to historians and divers.

More confusing is the fact that during January 1921, *UB131* was supposedly washed ashore at Hastings, having broken tow from the government tug *Woonda*. This was reported in the Lloyds weekly casualty reports and at least one photo depicting a late-war UBIII ashore there exists. She was supposedly broken up in situ, by a local salvage concern.

Both *UB130* and *UB131* were in Harwich awaiting disposal in February 1919. It is possible that they both came to grief in 1921, quite close together. It is also possible that the wreck located could be the same as the one on the beach at Hastings. Both submarines were made at the same yard, within a month of each other. Shortages were crippling German shipbuilding at the time. It is possible (although seemingly unlikely) that for some reason *UB131* ended up with a propeller meant for *UB130*. However, on balance it seems that the confusion between these two submarines has been caused simply by the proximity of their respective losses.

The wreck of *UB130*, is now very broken. The author's diving team inspected the site in 2000 and found that it was in at least three pieces, with only the central section being recognisable as a U-boat. The reports that this wreck has been heavily salvaged have been confirmed by what the divers found. This fits in with the discovery by the author of a propeller from the wreck, salvaged in the 1980s in a garden on the Isle of Wight.

There are also unconfirmed reports of another submarine wreck in the area close to this wreck. Sometimes referred to as *U40*, this is probably an error. *U40* was sunk off Calais (see No 6/3).

No 5/13, HMS *Holland 5* – Lost on Tow

Class: Holland	**Built at:** Vickers - Barrow
Length: 39.3m	**Displacement:** 150t
Date sunk: 8th August 1912	**How sunk:** Broken tow line
Historic Position: Off Beachy Head	**Known Position:** Withheld on request
Crew losses: None	**Commander:** None

The Holland-Class were first the submarines to be commissioned into the Royal Navy. From this perspective, the Hollands represent the beginnings of our submarine service and the starting point upon which all else developed.

The Irish-American inventor, John Philip Holland, designed the Holland-Class. He was born in Ireland in 1841 and was there to see first-hand the effects of the famine, a period of terrible suffering for the people of Ireland. Under British rule, Ireland was left to starve after several disastrous potato crop failures. Much of the social and political issues that still confront us today can be traced to these years.

Holland 5 – the first British submarine completed for service. (Royal Navy Submarine Museum)

In 1873, John Philip Holland moved to America with ideas of developing a small submersible craft, which could be used to exact revenge on the British Navy. The Fenian Brotherhood funded his initial research and development; the same organisation being dedicated to throwing Britain out of Ireland. John Philip Holland built his first submersible in 1878 and continued developing designs over the next two decades.

In 1893, he incorporated the business that was to become the Electric Boat Company, the builder of US submarines to this day. The Holland design as adopted by the Royal Navy was completed in 1897, by which time, Holland's views seemed to have mellowed, as he saw no difficulties in licensing his design to the once hated British.

Although several other individuals were also working on submarine designs over the same period, it was Holland who seemed to consistently produce the most innovative and revolutionary designs. It is not an understatement to say that he is the father of the modern submarine. When he died in 1914, World War One was about to begin, and the potency of his wonder weapon was about to be shockingly displayed to the world.

The Holland-Class was a tiny, one-compartment vessel, powered by a 160-horse power petrol engine on the surface and a small 120-volt electric motor when submerged. Originally it had no periscopes, but Cmdr. Bacon, the father of the British Submarine Service, devised an upright telescope arrangement for it. Looking at one of these vessels today, one is struck by their 'Heath Robinson' appearance, which makes one all the more admiring of the pioneers who took these vessels to sea and demonstrated the potentially devastating capability of undersea warfare.

The British built five Holland-Class submersibles under licence at Vickers and Maxim Sons. After some teething problems, the little submarines were to provide a wake-up call to Their Lordships. These little vessels proved themselves to be potent weapons of war on exercises, continually sneaking up on dreadnoughts and torpedoing them. It became obvious to the Royal Navy that submarines simply could not be ignored as the weapon of 'the weaker power'.

Holland 5 was built at the cost of £35,000 and launched on 10th June 1902. Along with *Holland 3*, she became the first of the class to be completed. The sheer pace of submarine development meant that she was very quickly obsolete. Thirteen A-Class submarines were already ordered before she was launched. However, in the 1904 manoeuvres, the Holland-Class proved their worth by 'torpedoing' two battleships without being detected.

Holland 5, along with her sisters, was reduced to the role of training and harbour defence shortly thereafter. In 1910, *Holland 5* ran aground outside Fort Blockhouse. By 1912, the Hollands were of no further use to the Navy. *Hollands 1, 2* and *3* were sold for scrap. *Holland 1*, broke its tow cable and sank near the Eddystone Lighthouse (see Appendix 3). *Hollands 4* and *5* were retained for explosive testing. *Holland 4* was disposed of as a target, and to this day has not been located, to the author's knowledge.

Holland 5 would have faced the same fate, however, on 8th August 1912 while being towed to the Navy base at Sheerness, she parted her tow cable and sank 'near Beachy Head'. There she remained until 1995, when local diver Gerry Dowd passed over a 'lump' on the seabed which when dived revealed the perfectly intact wreck of *Holland 5*.

In 2000, Mr Dowd kindly allowed the author's diving team to visit the wreck, by giving the author her exact position. She is by all measures a unique diving experience. A perfectly intact example of Britain's first submarine lay on white sand in spectacular visibility. Her little conning tower was shut, with the glass deadlight in place. All her key features were there, including her little propeller and hydroplanes. In the excellent conditions it was possible to see the entire submarine sitting there, a wonderful sight. To make this dive as rewarding as possible, the author visited the Royal Navy Submarine Museum first and toured *Holland 1*, which is on display there. This gave a thorough grounding on all the aspects of the *Holland 5* wreck.

In 2001, the little wreck was protected as an historic site under the 1973 Act and can now only be dived with a permit from DCMS and permission from its owners, The Ministry of Defence.

No 5/14, HMS *D3* – Victim of Friendly Fire

Class: D-Class	**Built at:** Vickers - Barrow
Length: 49.1m	**Displacement:** 620t
Date sunk: 12th March 1918	**How sunk:** Bombed by French airship A.T.O.
Historic Position: 12nm N of Fécamp	**Known Position:** 12nm N of Fécamp
Crew losses: 29 (all crew lost)	**Commander:** Lt. W. Maitland-Dougall

Of the 21 British submarine wrecks that litter the seabed of the Channel, only two were lost in wartime, HMS *Swordfish* (see No. 4/17) and HMS *D3* - one in each world war.

HMS *D3* was one of the first class of British submarines designed for operations overseas. Whereas the predecessors of the D-Class (the Holland, A, B and C-Classes) were all designed for coastal and harbour protection, advances in several technologies during the first decade of the 20th Century enabled certain radical advances in submarine design to be made just prior to World War One. The key innovations which were pioneered in the D-Class design, included the adoption of a double-hull (external ballast tanks), the introduction of twin screw propulsion, coupled with diesel engines, the significant increase of battery capacity, inclusion of a stern torpedo tube, adoption of wireless radio, and the installation of a deck gun. In all of these features, the British D-Class signifies the basic technological blueprint that shaped the design of HM Submarines for the next five decades.

HMS D3 at sea (Royal Navy Submarine Museum)

As early as 1910, the potential of this 'long range' design was realised when HMS *D1* was able to patrol from Portsmouth to Scotland and back. Due to the general success of the D-Class, the Navy went ahead to develop the most successful class of British submarine of World War One - the E-Class. In all 10 D-Class submarines were built. They were based in the UK and operated in the North Sea and Channel. As with the E-Class, 50 percent of those built were sunk in World War One. However, in the case of the E-Class, 28 were tragically lost.

HMS *D3*'s service career is interesting in that she had two Canadian captains, the second of whom was in command when HMS *D3* was sunk. During her career she fired torpedoes at two other submarines, missing both. In the first case this was a fortunate event, because the target in question turned out to be the British submarine HMS *E48*, which survived, in part, due to its excellent watch keeping. The second target turned out to be *UC66*, which was lost in the Channel a few months later (see No 1/17).

During the war, HMS *D3* operated from bases in Scotland, Ireland and finally at Gosport. She departed for her final patrol on 7th March 1918. She was to rendezvous with a patrol vessel off St. Helens (Isle of Wight) and then head for her patrol area, which was the southeast area of the Channel. On her return, she was to pick up an escort vessel off Brighton on the 14th March.

On the morning of 12th March, the French airship, A.T.O. was patrolling the waters north of Dieppe, as the day drew on, she meandered to the west. In the early afternoon, the airship spotted a submarine on the surface 12 miles north of Fécamp. With the sun behind her, the airship headed toward the submarine and attempted to identify her. There was no one on the bridge and the airship's French crew saw no identifiable markings on the submarine.

As A.T.O. drew closer, the submarine was seen to fire rockets from an area astern of its conning tower. These came perilously close to the airship. The dirigible's captain thought that these were aimed at destroying him and closed to attack. Machine gun fire was opened and the first of six bombs was dropped. This caused the submarine to crash-dive. However, around five minutes later, the submarine broke the surface and men were seen attempting to abandon ship. The submarine then sank from sight.

The unlucky crew of HMS D3. (Royal Navy Submarine Museum)

Convinced that he had sunk a U-boat, the French commander brought his airship close to the sea and saw four crewmen struggling in the water. As he drew close to them he heard one shout, "You have got us". Suddenly realising that he may have inadvertently sunk a British submarine, Lt. Saint-Rémy did all he could to try and rescue the survivors. However, his radio calls for assistance proved futile and none of the crew of HMS *D3* was ever seen again.

It seems that the recognition symbol carried by HMS *D3* on her bow had either been lost or could not be distinguished by the airship. Certainly the rockets fired by HMS *D3* were the recognition signals used by the British and she seems to have been sending these up to an airship she had recognised as allied. Sadly, the records for this incident, which can be viewed at the Public Records Office, show that the French were not familiar with this form of recognition signal. The French required a smoke signal. Although *D3* would have known this, it is possible that since A.T.O was originally a British airship, the grenade signal had been given instead. In any case, once attacked HMS *D3* had no option but to dive. The bombs that destroyed her mark the only 'success' a French aircraft had against a submarine in World

HM Submarines D3 and D4. HMS D4 sank UB72 (wreck No 3/5) in the Channel. (Royal Navy Submarine Museum)

War One and HMS *D3* can be considered to have been extremely unfortunate in being sunk.

There were similar incidences during World War One involving Zeppelins and U-boats, although in the cases known to the author, the U-boats always survived the attacks.

Lt. Saint-Rémy was absolved of any blame for this incident in the following court of inquiry. It was noted that under the circumstances, the airship had taken appropriate action.

The loss of HMS *D3* marks one of the sadder episodes of the war at sea 1914-18. She remains the last British submarine in the Channel that has not been located, as far as the author is aware. Bearing in mind her likely position and depth, it is possible that French divers may have found her by now.

No 5/15, *Prairial* – Collision

Class: Labeuf 1905 Program	**Built at:** Cherbourg
Length: 51.1m	**Displacement:** 550t
Date sunk: 29th April 1918	**How sunk:** Collision SS *Tropic*
Historic Position: off Le Havre	**Known Position:** 49 32.82N; 00 05.30W
Crew losses: 19 (from 25)	**Commander:** Lt. de V. Latron

The French submarine *Prairial* is unique among the submarines lost in the Channel, because she was powered by steam! Britain's experiments with steam-powered submarines led to the development of the disastrous K-Class, in which many submariners were tragically killed. The loss of the *Prairial* is also a tragic tale of the potential misfortunes that awaited all submariners of this era. In French, she was called a 'sous-marin à vapeur'. She was ordered as part of the 1905 building programme, and built and completed in Cherbourg.

Her commander, Lt. de V. Latron commented that the low-pressure steam engines were not powerful enough to give her a surface speed of more than 12 knots. Her submerged speed was also slow for the times. He recommended that the steam engines in this class of submarine should be fitted with condensers to give the submarine a faster top speed.

During her career, *Prairial* operated from Le Havre and from Cherbourg. Her role would have been one of coastal defence, looking out for U-boats especially. She was conducting such a patrol, in concert with the destroyer, *Chasseur II,* on the early morning of 29th April 1918. The weather was poor that night and surface visibility was bad.

At around 4.00am, the 8,262-ton British steam ship, SS *Tropic*, collided with the submarine. It is not

The steam-propelled Prairial. (Marius Bar)

clear whether she was awash or fully buoyant at the time. However, seven men managed to escape from her before she sank. The collision was hardly felt aboard *Tropic*, and she had no idea that she had accidentally killed 25 allied submariners.

SS *Tropic* was under government service when involved in this accident. The White Star Line owned her. She was not the only White Star liner to sink a submarine in World War One. The SS *Olympic* sank a U-boat (see No 1/20).

French divers have, apparently, located the wreck of the *Prairial*. She lies well over on one side and has a large hole in her stern. She lies in a general depth of only 19 metres.

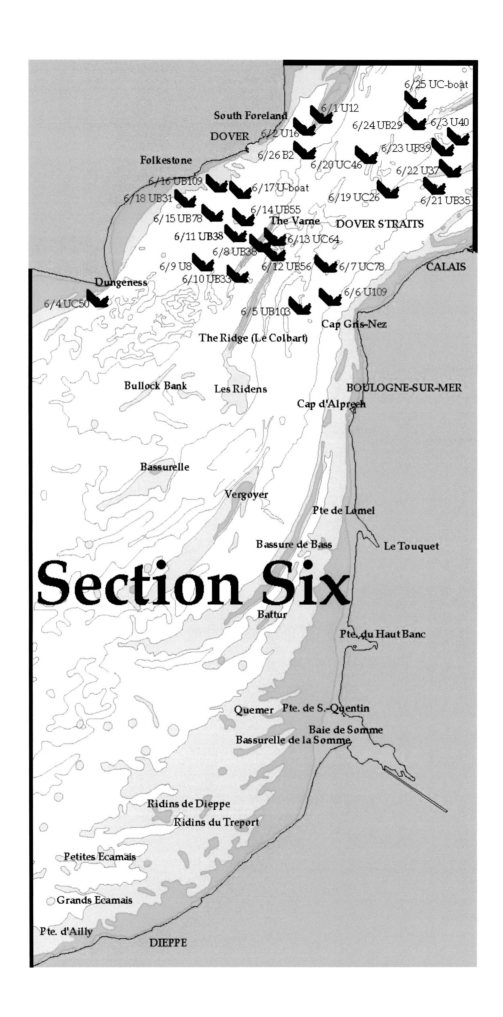

Section Six

Section 6

Submarine Wrecks of the Dover Straits

This chapter is characterised by the activities of the Dover Patrol, which in World War One sank an estimated 20-22 U-boats in the waters in and around Dover. Divers are still confirming this figure. The story of The Dover Patrol's development and ultimate victory over Germany's submarines is one of the greatest naval tales of the twentieth century.

Initially, under the command of Admiral Bacon and later under the tireless Admiral Keyes, the Dover Patrol was constantly developed and upgraded throughout the war. The patrol itself was made up of minefields, warships and other smaller vessels, which were staffed, in part, by the local populace of Dover.

The first sinking of a submarine in this area, sadly happened in 1912, when the British submarine HMS *B2* was lost in a collision with a liner. Divers have found this wreck.

Aside from HMS *B2*, all the other submarine wrecks in this area are U-boats. The first was the petrol driven *U8*, sunk in March 1915. Thereafter, the minefields, destroyers and drifters claimed many others. As the minefield became more sophisticated U-boat losses increased. Finally, in 1918, the Dover Straits were as good as closed to U-boats.

A most interesting feature of the U-boat wrecks of the Dover Straits is the diving activity carried out on them by Navy divers. The wrecks were routinely located and then penetrated by divers, looking to recover secret material and identify the wrecks. In command of the divers was Cmdr. Damant. Twelve U-boats were dived by his team. The records of the Navy salvage department, Sir Roger Keyes autobiography and R. M. Grant's "U-Boat Intelligence" describe much of their fascinating activities and to a large part did the job of this author over 80 years ago!

The blockage of the eastern end of the Channel was attempted again in World War Two. In this instance, it was achieved in a few months. Three U-boats were lost in Dover waters in 1939. (They are the only examples of the Type II and Type IX Classes in this book.) Thereafter, no further U-boats were ordered to use the Dover Straits.

No 6/1, *U12* - First Channel Loss of WW2

Class: IIB	**Built at:** Krupp Germaniawerft - Kiel
Length: 42.7m	**Displacement:** 328t
Date sunk: 8th October 1939	**How sunk:** Mine
Historic Position: 51.10N; 01.30E	**Known Position:** Unknown
Crew losses: 27 (all crew lost)	**Commander:** Klt. Dietrich von der Ropp

All three World War Two U-boats lost in this section of the book were sunk in 1939 (see also Nos 6/2 and 6/3). Their losses effectively caused U-boat Command to cease using the Dover Straits as a transit route for the U-boats. Importantly, they constitute nearly half of the U-boats sunk in 1939.

U12 had been ordered into the Channel to attack troopships heading for France. This was a throwback to World War One, where such operations were commonplace, especially in 1918. Many U-boat operations, in the opening months of World War Two, seemed to be based on successful tactics from the previous war. Moreover, it was believed by the Germans, that the Dover Straits had not been mined yet. This was a serious miscalculation.

First Channel loss of World War Two – U12. (U-Boot Archiv)

The British had immediately begun to mine the straits as soon as war was declared. By the end of September 1939, over 7,500 mines had been laid in this area. *U12* was the minefield's first U-boat victim, although another also had to be destroyed before the Germans realised just how dangerous the Dover Straits had become.

On 23rd September, *U12* left Kiel and nothing more was heard from her. However, she almost certainly hit a mine in the Dover Straits on 8th October, although there was no way the Germans could have known this. Von der Ropp's body was found ashore near Dunkirk on 29th October.

At present, the location of this wreck is unknown. The position given can be considered to be vague, as no further information regarding this U-boat is available.

However, this did not prevent the Ministry of Defence from designating *U12* a 'protected place' under the 1986 Protection of Military Remains Act in 2002. In the event she is ever found, she is to be treated as a war-grave. This was done as a token gesture to the German authorities, which have registered concern over the looting of several U-boat wreck sites around the British Isles in recent years.

No 6/2, *U16* - Last to Use the Dover Straits

Class: IIB	**Built at:** Deutsche Werke - Kiel
Length: 42.7m	**Displacement:** 328t
Date sunk: 25th October 1939	**How sunk:** D/Cs HMS *Puffin*, and HMS *Cayton Wyke*
Historic Position: 51 09N; 01 28E	**Known Position:** Unknown
Crew losses: 28 (all crew lost)	**Commander:** Klt. Hannes-Horst Wellner

Of similar design to *U12* (see No 6/1), *U16* was of the Type-II class of U-boat. These small craft operated on short patrols in coastal waters, laying mines and attacking ships. Their limited range and endurance meant that they were later reduced to the role of training boats, although some fought in the Black Sea, having been transported there by railway. Type IIs make comparatively rare U-boat wrecks.

U16 was on its third patrol when she was sunk. She had left Kiel on 18th October 1939 to lay mines on the south coast of England. It is believed that she laid her mines off Dungeness and was returning when she was sunk.

On 24th October, she was detected by the St Margaret's Bay monitoring loop and HMS *Puffin* and HMS *Cayton Wyke* were ordered to investigate. They dropped depth charges. Damaged, *U16* radioed that she was going to scuttle. However, it seems that she ran into the Goodwin

The last U-boat to risk the Straits of Dover. (U-Boot Archiv)

Sands and was lost, possibly by hitting a mine, because there were no survivors to indicate that a successful scuttling had been carried out.

This was corroborated the following day when the wreck of *U16* was found aground on the Goodwins. It was discovered that she had been extensively damaged forward, which could have been the result of hitting a mine. An attempt was made to try to salvage *U16*, but due to the poor weather at the time, this was abandoned and the wreck of *U16* was slowly sinking deeper into the sands. In the weeks that followed, several German submariners' bodies, wearing escape lungs were washed ashore near Hythe. These could be from *U16*, or possibly *U40* (see No. 6/3).

U16 became the last U-boat to be lost in the Dover Barrage. Shortly after her loss was confirmed, U-boat Command decided the straits were too dangerous for U-boat transits. This afforded the Channel a significant degree of protection from U-boat operations. However, in the opening months of 1940, U-boats were being sent into the Channel to lay mines. At great risk, *U48* laid mines off Weymouth in January and *U28* laid mines off Portsmouth in February 1940. Thereafter, U-boat Command focused all its attentions on the North Atlantic. It was not until D-Day that a major U-boat offensive was mounted in the Channel.

The position of the wreck of *U16* should be considered to be fairly accurate, because of the salvage attempts made on her in 1939. One report even suggests that this wreck has been subjected to commercial salvage.

However, Bob Peacock, a local diver and archaeologist, has dived this position and reports that the wreck is most likely an upside-down trawler with the stern blown off.

No 6/3, *U40* - Echoes of World War One

Class: IXA	**Built at:** Deutsche Shiff und Maschinenbau - Bremen
Length: 76.5m	**Displacement:** 1153t
Date sunk: 13th October 1939	**How sunk:** Mine
Historic Position: Dover Straits	**Known Position:** 51 07.5N; 01 48.00E
Crew losses: 38 (from 42)	**Commander:** Klt. Wolfgang Barten

The only Type IX ocean-going U-boat lost in the Channel, *U40* is the largest World War Two submarine wreck covered in this book. Her loss in October 1939 is very reminiscent of the U-boat losses in the Dover Straits in World War One.

U40 was designed to carry the submarine war into far-off waters, having the greatest endurance of all of the main classes of U-boat

The large U40 – mined in the Straits. (U-Boot Archiv)

built up to that time. On her first patrol, *U40* had operated off Gibraltar. However, when she left Wilhelmshaven on 10th October, she had been ordered to join up with the first 'wolfpack' U-boat formation of World War Two, which was to form up in the Western Approaches.

Being five days behind the other U-boats, *U40* was ordered to proceed via the Dover Straits in order to catch them up, since they had taken the safer northern passage around Scotland. In the early morning of 13th October, *U40* approached the Dover Straits and attempted to traverse the area on the surface. High water had passed three and half hours earlier and *U40* was fighting a 1.5-knot current.

Almost inevitably, *U40* struck a mine and went straight to the bottom, instantly killing most of the crew.

However, the aft bulkhead door was closed, saving the lives of the nine crew members in that compartment. The depth gauge read 35 metres. The U-boat had landed on the seabed with a heavy starboard list. Before attempting to 'flood-up' and escape, the survivors ate a meal of biscuits, then donned their escape lungs. The aft hatch was opened and the nine emerged into the icy waters of the Channel, becoming the first to make an escape from a World War Two U-boat. Their ordeal had just begun.

One of the survivors, Otto Winkler, saw the Calais lighthouse in the distance and attempted to swim toward it. In so doing, he became separated from the others. Swimming toward a 'small boat', Winkler almost swam into a mine and shortly afterwards he lost consciousness in the cold water. Some nine hours after escaping from the sunken *U40*, British destroyers plucked Winkler and two others from the sea. They were wearing escape lungs inscribed '*U40*'. Theirs had been a miraculous escape.

The Admiralty remarked later that the lessons of World War One had not been learned by Klt. Wolfgang Barten. His predecessors would have only dared cross the minefield at maximum high water, when the mines would be well covered by the tide. However, this is crediting the Germans with more knowledge of the extent of the minefield in the Dover Straits, than they actually possessed.

In recent years, the wreck of *U40* has been located and examined by local diver and archaeologist, Bob Peacock. He reports that the wreck is in generally good condition, showing the effects of the mine that sank her, because the bows are damaged, forward of the hydroplanes. Interestingly, he also reports that the submarine has a very high proportion of non-ferrous metal in its overall construction. Most notably of all are the external spare torpedo containers, which seem to be made of stainless steel. *U40* was built in peacetime and this explains why so much care was given to her build quality. The later World War Two wrecks in the Channel are of extremely poor construction, by comparison.

Mr Peacock also reports that the stern hatch on this wreck is open. This is entirely supportive of the survivors' tale of their escape.

For at least twenty years, rumours have persisted that *U40* lies in the waters off Newhaven. The author has been unable to fully ascertain where this piece of misinformation was originally born. There are U-boat wrecks off Newhaven (see *UB130* No 5/12); however, *U40* is definitely not one of them.

No 6/4, *UC50* - Mine Victim

Class: UCII (UC49 series)	**Built at:** Germaniawerft - Kiel
Length: 52.69m	**Displacement:** 511t
Date sunk: 4th February 1918	**How sunk:** D/C HMS *Zubian*
Historic Position: 50 50N; 01 26E	**Known Position:** 50 52.800N; 00 57.13E
Crew losses: 29 (all crew lost)	**Commander:** Klt. Rudolf Seuffer

Another of the Flanders Flotilla's UCII minelayers, *UC50* was a successful submarine. She was commissioned in December 1916 and conducted operations around the British coast and in the Bay of Biscay. Under the command of Klt. Rudolf Seuffer, *UC50* sank 29 ships for 45,822 tons. This included a 2,557-ton steamer.

On her last patrol, *UC50* had been ordered to lay mines in the Bay of Biscay. She left Bruges on 7th January 1918 and was never heard of again. The most cited fate given for the loss of this vessel occurred on the night of 4th February. It is stated that she was rammed and sunk by the British destroyer HMS *Zubian*. A U-boat was seen flying the German Naval flag (very similar in looks to the British), a common ruse. However, HMS *Zubian* was not fooled and rammed the diving U-boat. Oil was seen to escape as HMS *Zubian* dropped a pattern of depth charges over the spot where the submarine dived.

The destroyer was actually constructed from the bow and sterns of two damaged destroyers, HMS *Nubian* and HMS *Zulu*. The destruction of *UC50* by this composite ship adds a certain moral justification to the process of her rebuilding from two damaged destroyers.

What is interesting about this attack is that scholars have discounted it in the past. It has always been asserted that the U-boat attacked was in fact *UC79*, which survived over 30 depth charges to escape and tell the tale upon arrival at base. Moreover, *UC50* was expected to be on patrol for three weeks only, making the sinking date too late (by seven days) for it to have been her. It is in cases like this, that divers have made the difference.

A UC-Class submarine wreck has been located at the position given above. It can only be *UC50*, as comparatively few ASW attacks took place in this area. This wreck has suffered extensive damage in her middle section, clearly illustrating why there were no survivors.

A survey in the 1970s around HMS *Zubain's* attack position found no wreckage. This is because the wreck lies slightly to the north of the reported sinking position. Interestingly, Cmdr. Damant's

UC55 very similar to UC50. (U-Boot Archiv)

diving team looked for the wreck of *UC50* in 1918. They found nothing, because they were looking in the area of HMS *Zubian's* attack. Of the 'known' losses of U-boats in the minefield area, this was the only one Damant did not find. Undoubtedly, this is another reason why historians discounted the attack.

In the most likely instance, this is the wreck of *UC50*. She had clearly been delayed on patrol for unknown reasons and was destroyed at the location given above whilst hurrying back to base.

No 6/5, *UB103* - Dover's Last Victim

Class: UBIII (UB103 series)	**Built at:** Blohm & Voss - Hamburg
Length: 55.30m	**Displacement:** 629t
Date sunk: 16th September 1918	**How sunk:** Depth charge
Historic Position: 50 52N; 01 27E	**Known Position:** 50 52.20N; 01 26.80E
Crew losses: 37 (all crew lost)	**Commander:** Klt. Paul Hindius

UB103 was one of the common UBIII-Class of U-boat. She was launched on 7th July 1917 and commissioned on 18th December. Under the command of Klt. Paul Hindius, *UB103* made four successful patrols before being sunk. During the course of these, she sank 15 ships for 28,746 tons including, the British vessels, *Eric Calvert* (1,862 tons) off St Anthony's Point on 22nd April 1918, the *Thorsa* (1,319 tons), *Elba* (1,081 tons), also on the same patrol. Her largest victim was the *Kendal Castle* (3,885 tons) which *UB103* torpedoed off Brixham on 15th September 1918, the day before she was destroyed.

It seems that at some time during the course of her last patrol, *UB103* was damaged in some way. This is because of the way she was located. The submarine was spotted from the air by the airship SSZ-1 because she was giving off a seven-mile trail of diesel fuel. The airship drew the nearest drifters (*Young Crow, East Holme, Fertility, Calceolaria,* and *Pleasants*) to the scene. Whether depth charges from these vessels, bombs from the airship, or a mine destroyed *UB103* is not certain. However, when *UB103* dived to avoid detection, three explosions were heard over a half-hour period. These marked the end of the last U-boat to attempt to cross the Dover Barrage.

This vessel seems to have been one of several in the Dover area that was investigated by Cmdr. Damant's Navy divers. She was certainly the target of a lengthy search over the next few days. *UB103* would have been a week late returning from patrol if sunk on this date. The search by divers of the wreck in this location may have been an attempt to ensure that *UB103* had been destroyed. R. M. Grant states that the wreck of *UB103* was indeed located by divers in 1918 and that £1,000 was awarded for her destruction.

The location of a UB-Class wreck at the known position given above has been reported. However, the author has not confirmed this. Historically notable for being the last U-boat sunk by the legendary Dover Patrol, she would make a great find for divers.

UB103 was one of only around ten U-boats destroyed due to the presence of air cover during World War One. The involvement of airpower in her destruction was a harbinger for destruction of hundreds of U-boats by aircraft in World War Two.

No 6/6, *U109* – Drifter Victim

Class: U81 (U105 series)	**Built at:** Germaniawerft - Kiel
Length: 71.55m	**Displacement:** 1000t
Date sunk: 26th January 1918	**How sunk:** Gunfire and mine
Historic Position: 50 53N; 01 31E	**Known Position:** Unknown
Crew losses: 43 (all crew lost)	**Commander:** Klt. Otto Ney

Commissioned on 7th July 1917, *U109* was on her maiden patrol when she was lost with all hands. Her destruction occurred on 26th January 1918 on the French side of the Dover Barrage. The drifter *Beryl III* spotted the U-boat on the surface and although outgunned, immediately attacked *U109*. There appeared to be a poor watch being kept by the U-boat. However, the U-boat's crew was soon awakened to the presence of the drifter when a shell hit the base of the conning tower. *U109* immediately crash-dived - straight into the main Dover minefield.

Two hours passed before another drifter, *Elysian,* heard two massive explosions. Then, gushes of diesel oil appeared on the surface. *Beryl III* had sunk her quarry.

Mr. J. H. Bullock, the skipper of *Beryl III,* was awarded the DSC and £1,000 was distributed among the crew of the drifter. However, in an act of benevolence, the crew decided to donate half of the money to the relief fund set up in Dover for the children and widows of those who had died on the Dover Patrol. The recent destruction of several small craft by German destroyers prompted this act.

The death of *U109* has similarities with the destruction of the U-boats in the Channel in World War Two. Many of those were on maiden patrols with inexperienced crews, brought hastily into service to make up for growing losses toward the end of the war.

The author has not been able to ascertain whether sport divers have located the wreck of this U-boat. However, it was found and identified by Cmdr. Damant's Navy divers in 1918 and, therefore, should be able to be located.

No 6/7, *UC78* – Found by Cmdr. Damant

Class: UCII (UC74 series)	**Built at:** AG Vulcan - Hamburg
Length: 50.45m	**Displacement:** 493t
Date sunk: May 1918	**How sunk:** Mine
Historic Position: 50 55N; 01 34E	**Known Position:** 50 56.140N; 01 31.58E?
Crew losses: 29 (all crew lost)	**Commander:** Klt H. Kukat

UC78 was one of the last of the UCII-Class to be built. She was launched on 8th December 1916 and commissioned on 22nd January 1917. It seems she was transferred to the Flanders Flotilla after operating in the Baltic initially.

Under the command of Klt. H. Kukat, *UC78* destroyed at least two ships during her operational life. Her career was cut short in May 1918 when she failed to return from patrol. The initial cause of her sinking was attributed to a series of underwater explosions witnessed near Le Colbart on 2nd May 1918. Much oil came to the surface and it was presumed at the time that a U-boat had been destroyed. By supposition, it was determined that this must have been *UC78*.

However, by this stage in the war, the admiralty was using divers to try to find and identify many of the U-boats sunk in the shallows around the British Isles. This included a major effort by divers under the command of Cmdr. Damant.

On 7th August a UC-boat was located by Damant's diving team off Gris-Nez. She was overgrown and

UC78 seen from the stern. (U-Boot Archiv)

samples of the marine life were examined, placing the sinking before June. The only candidate must have been *UC78*. Therefore, the Admiralty concluded that *UC78* had been mined off Gris-Nez during May. However, the possibility also remains that this could be the wreck of *UC79*, which disappeared in April 1918 and remains unexplained (see No 6/15).

As far as the author is aware, sports divers have not located this wreck since. However, its proximity to shore means that French divers have most likely discovered her by now. The most likely location is the reported submarine wreck at 50 56.140;01 31.58E, however, this has not been confirmed, as far as the author is aware.

No 6/8, *UB38* – First Dived on in 1918

Class: UBII (UB30 series)	**Built at:** Blohm & Voss - Hamburg
Length: 36.9m	**Displacement:** 303t
Date sunk: 8th February 1918	**How sunk:** Mined
Historic Position: 50 56N; 01 25E	**Known Position:** 50 57.85N; 01 21.63E
Crew losses: 27 (all crew lost)	**Commander:** Olzs. G. Bachmann

UB38 was one of the small UBII Class of U-boat. Notable for their small size and limited duration, this type of U-boat, nonetheless, contributed significantly to the grievous losses suffered by the allied merchant navies. This was due to the fact that they were mostly operational before the convoy system was introduced in 1917 and, therefore, had lots of defenceless targets to pursue and destroy.

UB38 is an example of how successful many of these small UB boats became. Under four commanders and on more than two

UB38's conning tower with its helm and compass on the bridge. (U-Boot Archiv)

dozen patrols, *UB38* accounted for 49 allied merchant ships, totalling some 53,991 tons. One of her largest victims was the 3,829-ton *Claverley*, sunk off the Eddystone Lighthouse on 20th August 1917. Ten sailors were killed when she was torpedoed.

UB38 was destroyed while attempting to cross the Dover Barrage on 8th February 1918. At 9.30 pm, she was sighted on the surface by the drifter *Gowan II*. Forced to dive, she suffered the fate of many others in this area, by running into the awaiting minefield. It took only twenty minutes before the inevitable happened; *UB38* blew up in a triple explosion. The £1,000 bounty for the destruction of this vessel was given to the Mayor of Dover's relief fund for the families of those lost on the Dover Patrol.

Cmdr. Damant's diving team located the wreck of *UB38* in July 1918. A small UB-boat that had been sunk for some weeks, could only have been *UB38*. A wreck incorrectly designated on the chart as *UC78* (see No 6/7) has been located at the position given above. However, investigation by local divers, Bob Peacock and Dave Batchelor, revealed the location of a small submarine, possibly *UB38*. This was very close to where Cmdr. Damant stated he had found her. The wreck lies over on her port side. The deck gun and conning tower are still in place. The major damage to this wreck is noticeable where the stern has been entirely blown off.

No 6/9, *U8* - Dover Patrol's First Victim

Class: U3 (U5 series)	**Built at:** Germaniawerft - Kiel
Length: 57.3m	**Displacement:** 636t
Date sunk: 4th March 1915	**How sunk:** Sweep and gunfire
Historic Position: 50 56N; 01 15E	**Known Position:** 50 56.04N; 01 15.38E
Crew losses: 0 (from 25)	**Commander:** Klt. A. Stoss

The primitive U8 in peacetime. (U-Boot Archiv)

U8 is rare among the U-boats sunk in the Channel, in that she was built prior to hostilities breaking out in 1914. In fact, *U8* is also rare in the fact that she was powered by petrol engines and originally designed not to incorporate a deck gun. She is, by all measures, a historic wreck, marking a turning point in submarine development, from small quirky coastal craft to devastatingly effective weapon of war.

U8's operational history involved a sortie from Belguim, through the Dover Barrage, as far as Beachy Head. In her second patrol she sank the 2,026-ton *Branksome Chine*, 1,976-ton *Oakby*, 4,014-ton *Rio Parana*, 5,867-ton *Harpalion* and the 1,165-ton *Western Coast*; all off Beachy Head. She also made an

This extraordinary photo, taken on a glass plate negative, shows the crew of U8 abandoning her in sinking condition. It is probably the first such photo ever taken. (Imperial War Museum)

aborted attack on the hospital ship *St. Andrew*. The patrols made by these few operational U-boats at the start of World War One were harbingers of the huge harvest of death and devastation that their successors were to bring to the shores of the British Isles.

However, *U8* was not to have a long career. On her next patrol she became the first victim of the Dover Patrol. On 4th March 1915, she snagged the nets that extended across the northern end of the Varne. A drifter observed this and the destroyers of the Dover Patrol were summoned. During the pursuit, HMS *Viking* fired her sweep over a diving U-boat. Later, a periscope was seen and HMS *Ghurka* fired her sweep near enough to the U-boat for her to be put out of action, with engines stopped and main switchboard ablaze. Klt. Stoss ordered 'abandon ship' and the crew lined up on deck, to be photographed in the act of surrendering. This became one of the most celebrated pictures from the First World War at sea and the first ever photo taken of a U-boat in the act of sinking.

The survivors of *U8* were treated well and the officers dined with their captors in Dover that evening. During interrogation, it was revealed that HMS *Viking* had in fact attacked *U20*, which had left base with *U8*. She survived to successfully operate in the Channel. Moreover, a few months later, *U20* and her commander Klt. Walter Schwieger were to become notorious for sinking the Cunard liner *Lusitania* off the Old Head of Kinsale, with the loss of over 1,100 civilian lives.

The £500 bounty awarded for sinking *U8* was shared among all the vessels involved in the hunt for the U-boat.

The presence of a U-boat wreck at the position given above has been known about for many years. Local diver, Dave Batchelor, who has been interested in the submarine wrecks of the area has confirmed that this is the wreck of *U8*. She was positively identified by the collapsible columns on her deck, which were used to expel the exhaust gasses from her petrol engine. He reports that *U8* is upright on the seabed and very intact.

No 6/10, *UB33* - Mined

Class: UBII (UB30 series)	**Built at:** Blohm & Voss - Hamburg
Length: 36.9m	**Displacement:** 303t
Date sunk: 11th April 1918	**How sunk:** Mined
Historic Position: 50 55N; 01 17E	**Known Position:** 50 56.03N; 01 17.98E
Crew losses: 28 (all crew lost)	**Commander:** Olzs. Fritz Gregor

UB33 was launched on 4th December 1915 and commissioned on 22nd April 1916. During her career she made more than a dozen patrols and accounted for 14,152 tons of allied shipping. In this time, she had five different commanders. One of these was Claus Lafrenz, who was sunk nearby in *UC65* (see No 5/11) and was one of the more successful commanders of the Flanders Flotilla.

UB33's career is notable for the rare fact that she served in two theatres of the war. She was, at one point, subordinated to the 4th Torpedo Boat Flotilla to carry out a patrol into the Gulf of Riga. She also carried an anti-contraband sweep around Norway and Denmark, where she captured three ships. Later, she served in the Channel, sinking among other vessels, the British collier *Northville* (2,472 tons) off Start Point.

UB33, which was mined in the Straits and later found by Royal Navy divers (U-Boot Archiv)

She sailed into the Channel for her last patrol on 6th April 1918. U-Boat Command did not know what happened to her, since she never returned. This was confirmed to Admiralty interrogators after *UC75* was sunk in May and her commander stated that the loss of *UB33* was unexplained. However, the Admiralty knew the fate of *UB33* all too well. In fact, they knew quite considerably more about her too.

UB33 was seen striking a mine on the south side of the barrage in the early evening of 11th April 1918. She was located on 27th April and Cmdr. Damant's divers confirmed this on 6th May. They returned to the wreck on 21st May and were able to penetrate the wreck and remove several valuable items, including a steel box containing codes and other signal material. During these dives, the commander's body was also removed from the open conning tower, suggesting that an attempt to escape may have been made.

Today, this wreck is located at 50 56.03;01 17.98E. Local diver, Dave Batchelor, describes the wreck as being half buried in the Varne Bank. Interestingly, her conning tower is lying off to one side of the wreck. It is known that it was standard practice to remove the conning towers of submarines prior to divers entering them. This was done because the standard diving dress of the time was too cumbersome to be safely used in the confined spaces of U-boat conning towers. It seems that there is no doubt that this is the wreck which Cmdr. Damant's diving team systematically examined over 80 years ago.

No 6/11, *UB58* – Identified by Detective Work

Class: UBIII (UB54 series)	**Built at:** AG Weser - Bremen
Length: 55.85m	**Displacement:** 646t
Date sunk: 10th March 1918	**How sunk:** Mined
Historic Position: 50 58N; 01 14E	**Known Position:** 51 00.11N; 01 18.58E
Crew losses: 35 (all crew lost)	**Commander:** Olzs. Werner Lowe

Olzs. Werner Fürbringer commissioned *UB58* on 10th August 1917. Already a veteran of the U-boat war, Fürbringer brought several crew members from his previous commands with him. He had been watch officer on *U20* under Walter Schwieger, in the period just before he sank the *Lusitania*.

In April 1915, Fürbringer took command of his first U-boat, *UB2*. A year later he was given command of *UB39* (also possibly lost in the Dover area - see No 6/25) and also commanded *UC70* and *UC17* before taking command of *UB58*. During his tenure in command of previous boats, he had shown himself to be an excellent commander, with a knack for surviving some very tight situations.

His previous experiences were to serve him well while commanding *UB58*. It seems as if this U-boat was jinxed from the beginning. Certainly Fürbringer had no luck with her at all. His first patrol was beset with mechanical difficulties and his second and third patrols were dogged with malfunctioning torpedoes. When fired, they headed for the bottom and exploded under the U-boat. On the two occasions this happened to Fürbringer, the depth of water under the keel was the only thing that saved him. This mini torpedo crisis in late 1917 was to be repeated again in 1940, with another design.

The second premature explosion wrecked *UB58*, which then had to limp back through the Dover Barrage. Fürbringer described the process of crossing this stretch of water as being a very dangerous undertaking. On a calm night, when fully illuminated, crossing the minefield at periscope depth was the only option. Keeping trim was essential, as was a cool nerve and a great deal of luck.

After his third patrol on *UB58*, Fürbringer, suffering from nervous exhaustion was admitted to hospital for a period of recuperation. It was while in the hospital, he was told that Olzs. Werner Lowe had been given command of *UB58* and that she had been sent back into the Channel. Somehow, he knew she wasn't coming back and that his long-standing and loyal crew was doomed. Three weeks later, when he was told *UB58* was missing he wrote that: 'I felt a part of me die'.

Indeed *UB58* was lost. What Fürbringer could not have known was that it was the dreaded Dover minefield that claimed her. On 10th March 1918, the patrol vessel *P24* heard three underwater explosions. As day broke, wreckage was found. This included the battery log from *UB58*, loaves of bread and pieces of wood. *UB58* had been at sea less than 24 hours.

Because the battery log had identified her, Cmdr. Damant's divers were not used to search for the wreck. Although this policy made sense at the time, for historians and divers, it left a gaping hole in the record of U-boat losses in the Dover area. Importantly, when this was later re-examined, it caused a significant part of the post-war analysis of U-boat losses in this area to unravel.

Local diver, Dave Batchelor, decided to locate this wreck and finally complete the work of U-boat identification began by Cmdr. Damant. Using the original position given above, he dived the wreck nearby which was always thought to have been a U-boat. It turned out to be a small steamer carrying a cargo of bricks.

Undeterred, Mr Batchelor looked at the evidence. The original position given for the sinking was accredited because this was where the floating remains were found. However, it quickly became apparent that tidal factors had not been taken into consideration. When this had been factored in, Mr Batchelor calculated that the items would have drifted 3-4 miles to the southwest from where they initially reached the surface.

When plotted on a chart, it revealed that they probably came from an area where Cmdr. Damant reported finding two U-boats. The historian, R. M. Grant had subsequently tentatively identified them as *UB108* (see Appendix 1) and *UB54* (see No 5/10 and Appendix 1). Mr Batchelor has dived this position several times and has combed the area looking for a second U-boat, but there is definitely only one there. When the propellers on this wreck were examined underwater, they were both stamped '*UB58*'- the wreck had been found. Moreover, it is known that Damant's diving team removed the deck cannon from one of the 'two' wrecks they located here. The wreck of *UB58* does not have one, proving in all likelihood that this is the one Damant examined. Damant gave this position as 51 00;01 18.45E – exactly in the position where *UB58* has been identified. She was clearly mined, because her bows are extremely damaged, (as described by Damant) while the rest of the wreck is in good condition.

It remains a mystery as to why Damant's divers stated two wrecks lay at this location. Perhaps a combination of narcosis, visibility, tiredness and the confines of working in standard dress provide part of the answer.

This represents an outstanding and hugely successful piece of detective work carried out by an amateur diver, which has helped add to the list of correct positions for sunken U-boats. The problem for historians now, is where the wrecks of *UB108* and *UB54* may be.

No 6/12, *UB56* - Mined

Class: UBIII (UB54 series)	**Built at:** AG Weser - Bremen
Length: 55.85m	**Displacement:** 646t
Date sunk: 19th December 1917	**How sunk:** Mined
Historic Position: 50 57N; 01 23E	**Known Position:** 50 56.81N; 01 23.10E
Crew losses: 37 (all crew lost)	**Commander:** Olzs Hans Valentiner

UB56 had a short and tragically undistinguished career. She had been a 'frontboot' for less than six months when she became another victim of the Dover Minefield. Under the command of Olzs. Hans Valentiner, she had made three previous patrols that had accounted for four ships, amounting to 5,407 tons of allied shipping.

UB56 ventured out on her last patrol on 18th December 1917 and was destroyed before getting through the barrage. At 11.42pm on the 19th December, the British destroyer HMS *Gypsy* witnessed the explosion that destroyed her. During a search for wreckage, survivors were heard in the water. Only one of these was located. He was hauled on board, gave his name as Engineer Officer Bleek, and confirmed that the submarine was *UB56*. He died shortly thereafter.

As with several other U-boats lost in the minefield, Cmdr. Damant's Navy divers located the wreck in August 1918. She was badly damaged, with her stern blown in. Already she was full of sand. Although not positively identified, it seemed fairly certain from the diving evidence, that Cmdr. Damant's team had found *UB56*.

The wreck has been located at 50 56.81;01 23.10E. Local diver, Dave Batchelor, describes her as being largely intact, clearly a UBIII-Class U-boat which has been protected by the shifting sands and has many features on her, which would have usually corroded away by now.

No 6/13, *UC64* - Sunk Next to the Varne Bank

Class: UCII (UC61 series)	**Built at:** AG Weser - Bremen
Length: 51.85m	**Displacement:** 504t
Date sunk: 20th June 1918	**How sunk:** Mine and depth charge
Historic Position: 50 58N; 01 23E	**Known Position:** 50 58.530N; 001 23.213E
Crew losses: 30 (all crew lost)	**Commander:** Olzs. F. Schwartz

Before her destruction, *UC64* had, under three commanders, sunk 27 ships totalling 25,038 tons of allied shipping. This had taken her a year to accomplish, since her commissioning in February 1916.

Her last commander, Olzs F. Schwartz was less than a day out of port when he became yet another victim of the Dover Minefield. *UC64* was heading toward the Gironde area to lay her deadly cargo of 'eggs' when an allied example blew-up and gave away her position, which was just to the eastward side of the Varne Bank.

The incident was seen by the drifter *Ocean Roamer*, which, along with seven other vessels, rushed to the scene and began to depth charge the still moving submarine. The second attack made by the drifter *Loyal Friend*, probably accounted for the destruction of the U-boat.

With oil and air escaping from the wreck for many hours afterwards, she was not hard to locate. On 6th July 1918, Cmdr Damant's Navy divers examined the wreck. They found an extremely damaged UC-Class submarine. Her entire undersides had been blown inwards and her interior was a mass of bodies and wreckage. Only her stern section was instantly recognisable. Undeterred from their purpose, the Navy divers used explosives to gain entry into the wreck. By the removal of items from inside its identity was confirmed as *UC64*.

Local diver, Dave Batchelor, has visited this wreck site. It is clearly the wreck that Damant's divers worked on. He describes it as completely blown in the control room section, with the conning tower dragged off the wreck. The removal of the conning tower was standard practice for Damant's men. The rest of the damage to the submarine is as Damant's team described.

No 6/14, *UB55* - Escape

Class: UBIII (UB54 series)	**Built at:** AG Weser - Bremen
Length: 55.85m	**Displacement:** 646t
Date sunk: 22nd April 1918	**How sunk:** Mined
Historic Position: 51 01N; 01 20E	**Known Position:** 51 01.32N; 01 19.78E
Crew losses: 29 (from 35)	**Commander:** Klt. Ralph Wenninger

UB55 was commissioned on 1st July 1917. She was the third command of the veteran commander, Klt. Ralph Wenninger. Previous to commanding *UB55*, Wenninger had commanded *UB17* and *UC17* on some of their most successful patrols. On 30th March 1918 he had been awarded the prestigious 'Pour le Mérite' for outstanding performance in command of submarines and for excellent planning of patrols. Wenninger had also proven to be a lucky commander. Once when in command of *UC17*, he had become hopelessly stranded in Lyme Bay and was in the process of preparing to scuttle, when he was swept to safety on the incoming tide.

In command of *UB55*, Wenninger had operated on five patrols in the Channel and Bay of Biscay. During the course of these, he had sunk 25 ships. These included some notably large prizes, such as the 3,113-ton *Eastlands*, sunk on 25th January 1918, the 3,831-ton *Foylemore*, sunk on 16th December 1917 and the 3,070-ton *Begonia*, sunk on 21st March 1918.

However, Wenninger's largest victim was the 8,232-ton American steamer *Chattahoochee*, which was sunk on 23rd March 1918, south of Wolf Rock. She was carrying a cargo that included 120 lorries. Due to its size and importance, this vessel had been allocated a central spot in a well–supported

The forward torpedo room of UB55. (U-Boot Archiv)

convoy heading for Brest. Aside from surface ships, this convoy also had air cover. Wenninger attacked the convoy during the night. The massive *Chattahoochee* was the obvious target and although it took three torpedoes to despatch her, this was done over the course of two hours. During this time, *UB55* was being hunted by the escort ships, which plastered the area with depth charges. Such had the U-boat war changed by 1918, that great risks were now needed to find and sink merchant ships, which increasingly could only be found in escorted convoys.

UB55 sailed on its last patrol on 21st April 1918. Aside from the regular crew of 28, there were seven trainees on board. The patrol was abruptly cut short when *UB55* encountered a trawler and seven drifters just north of the Varne Bank. The U-boat dived to evade them and became entrapped in the mined nets that were laid in this area. A mine detonated against her stern and *UB55* sank to the seabed. The U-boat was filling with water and could not be raised from the bottom. Panic began to grip the survivors, 12 of whom were in the fore compartment and eight in the control room. Chlorine gas started to build up inside, as the seawater flooded into the battery compartments. During this time, two crew members shot themselves. However, as the water level reached three feet or more, the forward and conning tower hatches could be opened, due to the equalisation of pressure, and at least 18 of the crew were blown upwards. Several suffered embolisms and were found dead on arrival at the surface. The escape routine had been made worse by the fact that the escape lungs had all been stored in the flooded stern section. During the night, all but six of the survivors died of exposure. In the morning Wenninger was found to be among those who had endured the night hours swimming in the Channel.

Under interrogation, the survivors related how the incident had occurred. They also remarked about how surprised they were at being treated so well. Wenninger returned to the German Navy when the war ended and remained in naval service until 1939, when he transferred to the Luftwaffe. In 1945 he had reached the rank of General.

The wreck of *UB55* lies in the above position. The UBIII-Class wreck is in good condition and apparently has an extended periscope, which has been bent, probably after snagging a shot-line or fishing equipment.

No 6/15, *UB78* – Divers Rewrite History

Class: UBIII (UB75 series)	**Built at:** Blohm & Voss - Hamburg
Length: 55.3m	**Displacement:** 648t
Date sunk: 19th April 1918	**How sunk:** Mined
Historic Position: 51 01N; 01 17W	**Known Position:** 51 01.03N; 01 16.48E
Crew losses: 35 (all crew lost)	**Commander:** Olzs. Arthur Stossburg

This UBIII-Class U-boat seems to have been rather unlucky during its brief career. *UB78* had been commissioned on 20th October 1917 and became a 'frontboot' in December that year.

In a total of five operational patrols, *UB78* is credited with sinking three ships for 1,511 tons, hardly an inspiring tally. However, she serves to illustrate how the newer commanders of 1918 found attacking escorted ships and convoys much harder than their counterparts had found attacking unescorted merchant ships earlier in the war. The only vessel of notable tonnage was the British steamer *Polleon* of 1,155 tons, which was sunk in the entrance to the Tyne on 22nd March 1918.

In the spring of 1918, the German high command was desperate to try and stem the flow of men and materiel across the Channel. The German spring offensive, which was, in fact, the last roll of the dice for the German army, had to succeed and that meant supplies to the allies had to be stymied. *UB78* was one of many U-boats that were to operate in this area. However, it was the U-boat that was sunk, not the supply ships.

The traditional loss information recorded for *UB78* relates that; on the morning of 9th May 1918, the troop transport *Queen Alexandra*, under the escort of the patrol vessel HMS *P33* was finishing her run across the Channel to Cherbourg. She was loaded with troops destined for the front. HMS *P33* sighted a U-boat on the surface ahead of her, but to ram would have meant a certain collision with the troop transport. So, *P33* slowed and allowed *Queen Alexandra* to increase speed and ram. Captain Angus Keith steered his ship at 20 knots right into *UB78*'s stern compartment. HMS *P33* sped in to drop a depth charge, but there was no need because the U-boat was no more. Besides, *Queen Alexandra* needed assistance to get into Cherbourg, although the damage to her was not critical. A buoy was dropped and the troop transport was taken into port. On the following day, HMS *P33* returned to the buoy and located a seven-mile long trail of battery acid and oil.

There is much evidence to suggest that the analysis of the loss of *UB78* is, in fact, inaccurate. On the night of 19th April 1918, a mine explosion was spotted in the Dover Barrage at the position given above. This is noted in Sir Roger Keyes autobiography, where he claimed that it had accounted for *UC79*, but he also conceded that this wreck was searched for by divers and not located. However, a wreck exists very nearby. Her bows point southwest showing that she was on her way to the Channel (*UC79* would have been returning from the Channel). Importantly, *UB78* had left base on the evening of 18th April 1918 and would have been passing through this area at the time of the explosion. When divers examined this wreck, both her propellers were stamped '*UB78*' – the clinching piece of evidence. There can be little doubt, therefore, that she was destroyed here, and not off Cherbourg as originally thought.

So what of the ramming by *Queen Alexandra*? Certainly it would seem that a U-boat was critically damaged. Because no U-boat returned to base and reported the incident, it must be assumed that she was sunk, either there or somewhere else on the same patrol. There is no reported submarine wreck at the location of the ramming, as far as the author is aware. However, that does not necessarily mean one will not be found in the future. The loss of *UC79* still remains to be attributed. She left Zeebrugge on 20th March; it is just possible *Queen Alexandra* destroyed her, although Grant attributes her loss to unknown causes in the Bay of Biscay. However, she could be the mystery UC-Class located at 51 10.6;01 43.47E (see No 6/25).

No 6/16, *UB109* - Destroyed by Remote Control

Class: UBIII (UB103 series)	**Built at:** Blohm & Voss - Hamburg
Length: 55.30m	**Displacement:** 649t
Date sunk: 29th August 1918	**How sunk:** Mined
Historic Position: 51 04N; 01 14E	**Known Position:** 51 03.73N; 01 14.13E
Crew losses: 28 (from 36)	**Commander:** Olzs. Kurt Ramien

UB109 was of the later-type of UB-boat, the UBIII-Class. She was launched in Hamburg on 7th July 1917 and commissioned by Olzs. Kurt Ramien on New Year's Eve 1917. She became a 'frontboot' with the Flanders Flotilla and was on her third patrol when she was destroyed.

During her service life, *UB109* destroyed 5 ships for 13,610 tons. She operated in the North Sea, Channel and finally off the Spanish coast. On her last patrol, she sank the 4,037-ton British steamer *Zinal* near the Azores ten days before she was herself sunk.

While the Flanders Flotilla had become aware of the new minefield laid outside Folkestone, there was no way of being able to relate this information to Olzs. Kurt Ramien, as he made his way back up the Channel. *UB109* passed over the Folkestone Gate hydrophones at 3.05am. Shortly afterwards, a line of mines was detonated and *UB109* was destroyed. As she hit the seabed in 20 metres, the survivors made their escape from the control room and were picked up. Ramien was among the survivors.

Cmdr. Damant's diving team was well organised by this time. They were able to find the wreck within 12 hours of her being sunk. Over the next week, the divers were able to clear away bedding and bodies and penetrate from the forward compartment, right back through the submarine and into the control room. A very detailed search of the wreck was made and a great deal of valuable material was recovered. One item was the chart overlay for *UB109*'s last patrol, tracing her course around Gibraltar, Spain and the Azores. Interestingly, Damant commented that the water inside the submarine was warm when first investigated. The heat had come from the U-boat's batteries!

It is known that the wreck of *UB109* lies at 51 03.73;01 14.13E. She is badly damaged, being in two halves. Reports suggest that the identity of this site was confirmed by the removal of the propellers, one of which was stamped *UB109*, the other *UB104*. Due to the presence of survivors and items recovered, there is no possibility that this could be any other U-boat.

No 6/17, Unidentified Submarine Wreck?

Class: Unknown	**Built at:** Unknown
Length: Unknown	**Displacement:** Unknown
Date sunk: Unknown	**How sunk:** Unknown
Historic Position: Unknown	**Known Position:** 51 03.29N; 01 15.63E
Crew losses: Assume all	**Commander:** Unknown

A group of divers from Dover informed the author of the presence of an unidentified submarine wreck at the location given above in 1999. Sadly, due to poor weather, the diving planned on the site could not be carried out.

However, from the divers description of the wreck, she is in extremely poor condition. It is known that the obstruction charted at this location was swept and reduced in 1963 and this may well be the reason the wreck is so damaged. The divers report that she has been heavily salvaged.

Interestingly, the wreck had a 'Krupps' 50mm deck gun. This is not a diameter of gun associated with U-boats from World War One. Also, certain items seen on the wreck contain lettering that appears not to be German, but possibly of another Nordic language, thought to be Norwegian.

There is some speculation as to whether this is a victim of the Dover Patrol, or something entirely different. Much further research by an experienced submarine diving team will be needed to work out its class, age and possible identity.

One persistent rumour is that it was lost on tow to the breakers. The author has not found any evidence to support this theory.

No 6/18, *UB31* – Identified by Propellers

Class: UBII (UB30 series)	**Built at:** Blohm & Voss - Hamburg
Length: 36.9m	**Displacement:** 303t
Date sunk: 2nd May 1918	**How sunk:** Depth charge – *Lord Leitrim*
Historic Position: 51 01N; 01 16E	**Known Position:** 51 02.06N; 01 10.22E
Crew losses: 26 (all crew lost)	**Commander:** Olzs. der Res. Wilhelm Braun

Commissioned in March 1916, *UB31*, under two commanders, destroyed 29 allied ships for 84,350 tons in the two years she was operational. While this record is far from the most impressive of its class, it is interesting because of the number of large ships she sank.

In fact, German records credit *UB31* with sinking six vessels over 5,000 tons. These included three British vessels, the 5,870-ton *City of Corinth*, sunk on 21st May 1917, south of the Lizard and the 6,570-ton *Boorara* was sunk on 20th March 1918. However, the largest was the 12,350-ton P&O liner *Medina*. She was torpedoed off Start Point on 28th April 1917 while travelling to London. Fortunately, she had disembarked her passengers in Plymouth and there were only six casualties. Interestingly, only one torpedo was needed to sink her. To this day, the *Medina* remains one of the largest shipwrecks in the Channel.

On 16th April 1918, *UB31* departed on her last patrol. She successfully negotiated the Dover Straits and was active in the Channel until her destruction on 2nd May. On that day, her periscope was spotted in the waters between the Varne Bank and Folkestone. The drifter, *Lord Leitrim* dropped a depth charge on the spot and was rewarded with oil and bubbles coming to the surface. The hunt continued, being guided by the airship SSZ29. Two more drifters also joined in. Then, *Ocean Roamer* dropped her depth charge, which probably finally destroyed *UB31* with all hands.

There was originally some confusion as to whether the submarine destroyed was in fact *UC78*. This is because she disappeared on the same night, on the other side of Le Colbart Bank (see No 6/7). However, the evidence produced by Cmdr. Damant's Navy diving team in August 1918 proves that the wreck located off Folkestone was a UB-Class submarine, which Sir Roger Keyes thought was the one destroyed on 2nd May. The divers also found *UC78* in August 1918 on the eastern side of the Channel.

The submarine wreck at the above position was positively identified as *UB31*, because this was the number stamped on both of her propellers. She was also clearly identifiable as a UBII-Class by her size and general design.

No 6/19, *UC26* - An Unlucky Boat

Class: UCII (UC25 series)	**Built at:** Blohm & Voss
Length: 49.45m	**Displacement:** 480t
Date sunk: 9th May 1917	**How sunk:** Rammed by HMS *Milne*
Historic Position: 51 03N; 01 40E	**Known Position:** 51 01.70N; 01 41.32E
Crew losses: 24 (from 26)	**Commander:** Klt. Graf von Schmettow

Although attached to the Flanders Flotilla since August 1916, *UC26* had actually only spent around a month at sea up to the time she was sunk. This was because of a run of mechanical failures and an accident.

Shortly after her first patrol, *UC26's* main motors had to be extensively overhauled. This took two months to do. Then, after two short patrols in the North Sea, *UC26* was back at Ostend for more repairs. It was while undergoing these, that she was accidentally crushed against a pier by a steamship. This destroyed her fuel tanks on one side and badly damaged two of her torpedo tubes. She was laid up again for several months.

When *UC26* finally sailed for her fourth and final patrol, morale was low. Her fuel tanks on the damaged side were left empty and her damaged torpedo tubes where not properly repaired. Although she successfully torpedoed a vessel off Le Havre and laid mines in her target area, her other torpedoes, stowed in the damaged tubes, failed to fire accurately, blighting what would otherwise have been a successful patrol.

At the end of her operations, *UC26* attempted to run the Dover Barrage on the surface. She was spotted by the destroyer HMS *Milne* and dived too late to avoid being rammed. *UC26* was struck just forward of the conning tower and plummeted to the seabed 46 metres below.

The surviving crew managed to stem the flow of water into the submarine, but could not get her to rise. As the electric power failed, it became obvious that escape from the bottom was the only route to survival. The crew was divided into two groups, one in the after compartment and one in the control room. Pressure in the submarine was equalised with the external water pressure. The hatches were opened and the survivors blew up to the surface.

Of the eight crew members that survived the ascent (made without escape equipment), two were plucked from the water. Germany later claimed that the British had cruelly left the rest in the sea to their fates, as it was claimed had also been done in the case of the torpedo boat *S20*, off Zeebrugge.

The interrogation report on the survivors of *UC26* points to an unhappy crew, who seemed to have been in the command of an over-optimistic commander. The diary kept by the second officer was also retrieved and also supports this theory.

The wreck of this submarine is probably lying in the position given above. Local diver and archaeologist, Bob Peacock, located this wreck recently and with his diving team, were able to ascertain that the wreck is a UC-Class submarine, in poor condition.

No 6/20, *UC46* - Rammed

Class: UCII (UC46 series)
Length: 51.85m
Date sunk: 8th February 1917
Historic Position: 51 07N; 01 39E
Crew losses: 23 (all crew lost)

Built at: AG Weser - Bremen
Displacement: 502t
How sunk: Rammed by HMS *Liberty*
Known Position: 51 06.86N; 01 37.15E
Commander: Olzs Fritz Moecke

Since her commissioning in September 1916, *UC46* had been working up to full readiness. She sailed on her only patrol on 25th January 1917 and successfully managed to break through the Dover Straits and into the Channel.

The details of this patrol are unclear, but it was assumed by the Admiralty that she operated

The shipyard model of UC46. (U-Boot Archiv)

initially in the Bristol Channel and then in the Channel. She is supposed to have laid the minefield off Breaksea Light Vessel, which claimed the British minesweeper HMS *Longset*. Her operations after this date are most unclear. Some reports suggest that she sank the British Steamer *Crown Point* off the Scillies on 6th February, but this is generally accredited to *U83*, which was sunk by the Q-ship *Farnbourough* later that month.

However, *UC46* attempted to make the crossing of the Dover Straits on the night of 8th February. It was undoubtedly the inexperience of the new commander that contributed to the loss of the boat. *UC46* came to the surface (presumably without a periscope sweep) on a very clear night. The destroyer, HMS *Liberty*, saw the submarine emerge half a mile in front of her. Initially the guns were fired, but this blinded the bridge, so the order to ram was given. HMS *Liberty* hit *UC46* at a speed of 24 knots. Her bows knifed into the U-boat's hull forward of the conning tower; she lurched to a standstill momentarily, before her momentum took her over the doomed U-boat. A depth charge was dropped as the stern passed over. Nothing more was ever seen of *UC46*.

HMS *Liberty* was severely damaged in the collision and limped into Dover. Analysis of her bows showed that at least four feet of her must have been embedded in the U-boat at the time of maximum impact. Lt. Cmdr. King was awarded the DSO for this sinking.

Local divers, and Dave Batchelor and Bob Peacock, have probably located the wreck of *UC46* at the position given above. They report that this is the wreck of a UC-boat. Her position so near to the reported sinking point of *UC46* makes her the ideal candidate. She lies over on her port side and is heavily netted. It is clearly the wreck of a UC-boat returning from patrol, because the mine chutes are empty, making it possible to peer straight through the hull, down onto the seabed.

No 6/21, *UB35* - Depth Charged to Destruction

Class: UBII (UB30 series)
Length: 36.9m
Date sunk: 26th January 1918
Historic Position: 51 03N; 01 46E
Crew losses: 21 (from 23)

Built at: Blohm & Voss - Hamburg
Displacement: 303t
How sunk: Depth charge HMS *Leven*
Known Position: Withheld upon request
Commander: Olzs. Kurt Stöter

The veteran, *UB35*, had been with the Flanders Flotilla for over a year when she was sunk in the first month of 1918. During this time, she had been under the command for four different officers and had sunk 39 ships for 47,216 tons.

The loss of *UB35* is unique among the submarines lost in the Channel, because when she was sunk, two members of her crew were not on board. They had fallen into British hands the previous day. They confirmed the submarine's destruction from the items collected from the sea that were later shown to them.

UB35 was on her 26th patrol when she was destroyed. She had been operating in the Channel and had claimed her biggest prize to date on 20th January. *UB35*'s victim was the 9,044-ton *Mechanican*. Two torpedoes where fired at the ship, which later sank while being towed to Portsmouth. The U-boat had not been able to ascertain whether the target had been sunk. This was due to the proximity of its escort vessels, which she wisely avoided tangling with.

On 25th January, *UB35* was in the process of boarding the Greek steamer *Epstatios*, off Portland, when the British patrol boat, *P34*, appeared in the distance. The U-boat immediately crash-dived and four members of the steamer's crew and two from the U-boat were left stranded in the water. The patrol boat picked them up. She then dropped a depth charge over the position where the submarine dived. At least one of the survivors thought it was here that *UB35* was destroyed, although on that occasion she actually escaped.

During the following night, *UB35* attempted to run the Dover Barrage. She surfaced in order to navigate through a series of net buoys at the north-east end of the minefield and was spotted by the destroyer HMS *Leven*. The following depth charge attack destroyed *UB35*. A survivor, who later died on they way back to Dover, confirmed the submarine's identity. The survivors of the *Epstatios* incident identified a letter from one crew member of *UB35* and an item of clothing from another.

The wreck of *UB35* has been positively identified by Belgian diver, Tomas Termote, by the U-boat number stamped on her propellers. Interestingly, her position is considerably to the east of the official position given by the allies in 1918. The wreck is in generally poor condition, however, several of her key features could be identified. These included ready-use ammunition containers lying next to the deck gun, on the seabed.

No 6/22, *U37* - Undiscovered

Class: U23 (U31 series)	**Built at:** Germaniawerft - Kiel
Length: 64.7m	**Displacement:** 878t
Date sunk: 1st April 1915?	**How sunk:** Mined?
Historic Position: 51 04N; 01 48E	**Known Position:** Unknown
Crew losses: 32 (all crew lost)	**Commander:** Klt. Erich Wilke

U37 under construction at Germaniawerft. (U-Boot Archiv)

U37 was on its maiden patrol when she was lost with all hands. The loss of this U-boat happened early in World War One, being only the 11th U-boat that had sunk up to that time. *U37* is thought to have been the fourth mine casualty.

She had left base for a patrol in the Channel on 20th March 1915 and had operated in co-operation with *U34*, under the command of Olzs. Claus Rücker (see No 1/20) and *U28*, under the command of Olzs. Freiherr von Förstner. Aboard *U34* was also the senior officer of the second half-flotilla Klt. Arno Spindler, who went on to become Germany's official historian of the submarine war against commerce in World War One.

Together, these submarines patrolled the Channel and sank several ships. *U37* is credited with the destruction of three steamers. The *Delmira* of 3,459 tons, sunk on 25th March, the *Emma* of 1,617 tons, sunk on 31st March and the *Seven Seas*, of 1,194 tons, sunk on 1st April 1915.

Because it has been generally accepted that the last two vessels on this list were victims of *U37*, it means that the two original sinking explanations for the loss of *U37* can be discounted. She was claimed sunk by the British steamer *Lizze* on 25th March, by ramming and claimed sunk again by the French vessel *St. Jehanne* by the same fashion on 30th March.

With both of those attacks ruled out, the final resting place of *U37* is far from certain. However, both German and allied sources have estimated that it is most probable that *U37* was mined in the Dover Straits area, while attempting to return to Heligoland at the end of its patrol.

The historic position given here has been derived from German historical sources, but must be treated with extreme caution. It is quite likely that this U-boat will show up somewhere entirely different in the Channel, in the years to come. An early example of the longer-range U-boat class of World War One, she would make an excellent find.

No 6/23, *UB39* - Mistaken Identity

Class: UBII (UB30 series)   **Built at:** Blohm & Voss
Length: 36.9m   **Displacement:** 303t
Date sunk: 15th May 1917   **How sunk:** Mined?
Historic Position: 51 07N; 01 47E   **Known Position:** Unknown
Crew losses: 24 (all crew lost)   **Commander:** Olzs Heinrich von Küstner

UB39 which sank 93 ships before she was destroyed (U-Boot Archiv)

UB39 marks another successful example of the small UBII-boats based in Flanders. Like others of her class, she initially sailed against Britain when there were rich pickings to be had. These came in the shape of unescorted merchant ships, plying the shipping lanes converging on Britain.

Under two commanders, *UB39* sank a very creditable total of 93 ships for 89,810 tons of allied shipping. Her first commander was the highly successful Werner Fürbringer, who was to survive the appalling 83 percent casualty rate of the Flanders Flotilla in World War One. Fürbringer commanded *UB39* on her first six patrols. On the fifth patrol, *UB39* was in the process of sinking a ship called the *Pronto* by the use of explosives, when a destroyer arrived on the scene. *UB39* was just able to rescue the prize crew and crash-dive to avert disaster. As *UB39* submerged, she made contact with the *Pronto*, completely wrecking the bridge.

The fragility of these small UBII-class boats was aptly demonstrated on Fürbringer's last patrol in command. While operating in the Western Approaches, *UB39* encountered a hurricane that blew for nearly 24 hours. The small submarine was totally unsuited to survive such an ordeal. Even at her maximum diving depth of 40 metres, she was tossed around like a cork. After 12 hours, the boat surfaced. The sea was so monstrous that Fürbringer and his helmsman had to be lashed to the bridge. Both compasses had failed and the boat could only proceed on electric motors, as the diesels needed the conning tower hatch open to draw air. At one point during this ordeal, the little submarine was washed past a freighter, combat being impossible. As the storm subsided, a gun action on another steamer was attempted, but the gun crew was washed off the foredeck and only luckily rescued. Fürbringer returned to Bruges. Unlike him, *UB39* was not to survive the war.

Under her next commander, Olzs Heinrich von Küstner, *UB39* made another eight patrols and claimed several noteworthy prizes. These included the 4,525-ton *Clan Macmillan*, torpedoed off Beachy Head in March 1917.

When *UB39* failed to return from its 14th patrol, the Admiralty was sure it was lost because she had been sunk by the British Q-ship *Glen,* off the Isle of Wight. The attack by the Q-ship was a good one, with the submarine being close when the order was given to open fire. She was seen to be hit more than once as she went underwater. With the admiralty convinced that a U-boat was destroyed, Lt. Cmdr. Turnbull was awarded a medal and the ship's crew was awarded £115.

However, that was not the end of the matter. A few days later, *UB18* limped into Bruges to tell of her lucky escape from a Q-ship off the Isle of Wight. She had been hit, but had survived.

UB39 was posted missing, shortly thereafter, with the Germans initially not knowing what had happened to her. Then, the commander of *UB12* reported seeing a massive underwater explosion on the morning of 15th May near the 'No Three Buoy' (British buoy 9A). Sadly the position given for the location of this buoy in the official history is incorrect, placing it too far to the south. Sir Roger Keyes places the British No 9 buoy at the position given above. *UB39* may well be in this area, although the position must be considered extremely doubtful at the present time. It is possible that the German No Three Buoy was somewhere north of the Varne.

It is also possible that *UB39* will be found somewhere else in the Channel area. Time will tell.

No 6/24, *UB29* - Depth Charged to Destruction

Class: UBII (UB30 series)	**Built at:** Blohm & Voss - Hamburg
Length: 36.9m	**Displacement:** 303t
Date sunk: 13th December 1916	**How sunk:** Depth charged by HMS *Landrail*
Historic Position: 51 09N; 01 46E	**Known Position:** Unknown
Crew losses: 22 (all crew lost)	**Commander:** Olzs Erich Platsch

UB29 was a commissioned U-boat for 360 days before she was sunk. In that time, under two commanders she sank 29 ships for 39,378 tons. The largest ships sunk were the British steamers, *Braunton* of 4,575 tons, sunk off Beachy Head on 7th April 1916 and *Torridge* of 5,036 tons, sunk in the Western Approaches on 6th September 1916. In a most peculiar coincidence, both these ships belonged to the Tatem Steam Navigation Company, which lost seven ships to U-boats during World War One.

On 24th October 1916, *UB29* survived a fight with the plucky British Q-ship, *Helgoland.* During the course of this engagement, the Q-ship suffered severe damage, which forced her to fire early and *UB29* escaped.

UB29 was known to the Admiralty because she had been involved in the beginning of the resumption of unrestricted submarine warfare in 1916. Under her first commander, Olzs. Pustkuchen, *UB29* had been ordered to resume the campaign of sinking ships without warning. In a similar event to the well-known case of the *Lusitania* in May 1915, *UB29* attacked the cross Channel packet steamer *Sussex* without warning on 24th March. Although the ship did not sink, the torpedo claimed the lives of 50

Destroyed in the Straits, the wreck of UB29 has not been located. (U-Boot Archiv)

passengers and crew. With Americans on board, this episode quickly blew-up into a diplomatic row, which brought about the abandonment of unrestricted submarine warfare by Germany for the second time.

Interestingly, Pustkuchen, one of the most successful commanders the Flanders Flotilla produced, was not listed as a war criminal by the allies for the 'Sussex outrage', as it became known.

UB29 sailed on her final patrol on 27th November. She successfully negotiated the Dover Barrage and was active in the western Channel for several days. In fact, the Admiralty thought the destroyer, HMS Ariel, had destroyed her in the Western Approaches on 6th December. However, this attack claimed UC19 (see No1/2) and UB29 went on to sink its final ship the following day.

UB29 was destroyed on 13th December as she negotiated the Dover Barrage. The British destroyer, HMS Landrail spotted her conning tower. As the U-boat frantically tried to escape, two well-placed depth charges brought about her destruction. There were no survivors.

Today, the wreck of UB29 remains to be found.

No 6/25, Unidentified UC-class

Class: Unknown	**Built at:** Unknown
Length: Unknown	**Displacement:** Unknown
Date sunk: Unknown	**How sunk:** Unknown
Historic Position: Unknown	**Known Position:** 51 10.6N; 01 43.47E
Crew losses: Assume all	**Commander:** Unknown

Local Ramsgate diver and archaeologist, Bob Peacock, has located the remains of a UC-boat at the position given above. This is a mystery because she does not fit into the official history of losses of World War One U-boats for this area.

However, there could be two reasons for this. First, dead-reckoning navigation was not particularly accurate during this period, especially under combat conditions. This would mean that the wreck is a UC-boat thought to have been sunk in this area and not yet identified. Second, the submarine was lost without anyone noticing. This could then be a mystery submarine loss, one already attributed as 'lost position unknown'. In either case, candidates could include UC6, UC9, UC21, UC79 (see No 6/15) and UC77 (see Appendix 1) among others.

Further detailed diving research is needed to work towards a possible identity to this mystery U-boat.

No 6/26, HMS B2 – Collision

Class: B-Class	**Built at:** Vickers - Barrow
Length: 43.01m	**Displacement:** 316t
Date sunk: 4th October 1912	**How sunk:** Collision with SS Amerika
Historic Position: 4 miles E. of Dover	**Known Position:** Withheld on request
Crew losses: 15 (from 16)	**Commander:** Lt. P.B. O' Brien

HMS B2 was the second of the British B-Class submarines to be launched and completed. There were a total of 11 built during 1904-6. The B-Class marked a significant improvement on the older A-Class, being almost twice the size. However, submarine design was still in its infancy in the UK and these boats were intended for operations in home coastal waters, protecting harbours and other vital points along the British coast.

The simplicity of HMS B2's design is evidenced by the fact that she was petrol-powered, had no living space at all and was essentially a one-compartment vessel. These features were the same as the

Holland-Class launched five years earlier. It is interesting to note that submarine command considered the endurance of the crews in this class to be three days!

During World War One, the B-Class had a chequered career. HMS *B11* was the most famous, because of her penetration of the Chanak Narrows, during the Dardenelles campaign, where she torpedoed and sank the Turkish battleship *Messudieh*. This action won Lt. N. D. Holbrook the Victoria

HMS B2 – sunk in a collision with a surface vessel. (Royal Navy Submarine Museum)

Cross. However, the B-Class was essentially obsolete by 1914 and only one was in commission at the end of the war. Interestingly, five of the class were converted into patrol craft, having their conning towers removed and a wheelhouse added as replacement.

HMS *B2* was one of only two to be sunk; the other, HMS *B10*, was salvaged and scrapped. As such, HMS *B2* is the only example of this class in existence today. HMS *B2* was on exercise off Dover in October 1912, operating with the fleet, during a practice defence of the Dover Straits. She cleared harbour at around 05.30 on 4th October and was on her way to join the fleet when she was struck by the 22,500-ton Hamburg-Amerika liner, SS *Amerika*. The huge ship penetrated deeply into HMS *B2*'s hull, just forward of the conning tower. The small submarine sank immediately. Since there were no compartments in her hull, there was little chance that any of the crew would survive.

However, Lt. Richard Pulleyne had been on the bridge at the time of the disaster and after being sucked down with the sinking submarine, was able to kick for the surface. When he emerged, he saw the vast liner going past, firing distress flares. He was later plucked from the sea by the submarine HMS *C16* that had been sent to investigate what had happened. Lt. Pulleyne went on to command the submarine HMS *E34*, winning both the DSC and DSO. His luck finally ran out in July 1918 when HMS *E34* was lost with all hands. SS *Amerika* was later to collide with and sink the British steamer *Instructor* in 1918, killing sixteen.

During 1912, HMS *A3* and *Holland 5* were also lost in the Channel (see Nos 4/18 and 5/13). HMS *A3* was salvaged, which gave encouragement to the possibility of doing likewise with HMS *B2*. Navy divers located her and an attempt to raise her was made. However, due to the weather at the time and the significant damage she had sustained, these plans were later abandoned.

It may have been because of these salvage attempts, that it took so long to locate the wreck of HMS *B2*. Divers finally located her in 1999. Local archaeologist and diver, Bob Peacock, says that she is upright, in good condition with all major features, as you would expect to see them. One of the nicest features was her single bronze propeller.

Appendices

Appendix 1

Submarines lost in the Channel, position unknown

This appendix examines the cases of submarines that are definitely known to have been lost in the Channel, but where there is no substantive positional information available to suggest where they may be.

There are two primary reasons why this occured. Firstly, many submarines on patrol never returned to base. Subsequently, no plausible explanation has ever been discovered to explain how they were lost. The only positional data that historians can go on is the patrol area that was assigned to them on their last patrol. Secondly, archival records can be poor, misleading or non-existent. In the case of the French submarine, *Diane*, the loss position remains a source of speculation.

UC36

In May 1917, the minelayer *UC36* was ordered from Zeebrugge to lay mines in the Channel. She is believed to have been successful in a laying a clutch of her 'eggs' off the Nab Tower. Her second field of mines was intended for the waters around the Needles. It appears that these were never laid.

All that can be said for certain, is that there is a UCII minelayer waiting to be discovered in the Isle of Wight area.

U93

In January 1918, *U93* either disappeared in the western Channel or on her way there. Much confusion seems to exist between the identities of *U93* and *U95*. Both were at sea in the same area at the same time and neither returned from patrol. The sinking of *U93* has been attributed to ramming by SS *Braeneil* (see No 1/16). However, this could also have accounted for *U95*.

At present there is no known explanation for the loss of this U-boat. However, she may well be located in the western Channel in the future.

Diane

The French submarine, *Diane*, was sunk on 11th February 1918. She was on escort duty with a convoy when she exploded and sank. Either an internal explosion, drifting mine, or a U-boat could have been responsible. There seem to be no records that give a position where this occurred, although it was witnessed by the convoy, which included the five-masted sailing ship *France*.

UB54

UB54 was lost while operating in the Channel sometime around mid-March 1918. Although R.M. Grant believed she had been located in the Dover Straits (see No 6/11), this has now been disproved. One possible position for *UB54* is the unidentified UBIII-Class submarine off Brighton (see No 5/10).

UB108

UB108 left Zeebrugge on 2nd July 1918 to operate in the Channel. Nothing more is known of what happened to her. Sir Roger Keyes believed that she was destroyed in the Dover minefield, but as yet the wreck has not been located. Certainly R.M. Grant's assertion that Navy divers located her is incorrect (see No 6/1). It is possible that she will be located in the Dover area. Also she may turn out to be the UBIII wreck off Brighton (see No 5/10).

UC77

UC77 was ordered to lay mines off Portland in July 1918. She did not return from this patrol. It is most likely that this submarine was lost on the outward journey, probably in the Dover area. The unidentified UC-Class submarine (see No 6/25) may well be *UC77*. Sir Roger Keyes thought she was destroyed in the Dover area either on 10th or 14th July. However, it is also possible that this submarine will be unearthed somewhere in the middle of the Channel.

Appendix 2

Submarines that may have been sunk in the Channel

This section lists all of the submarines that may possibly have been sunk in the Channel. As far as is known, the wrecks of these submarines have not been positively located elsewhere. These submarines are thought to have been en route to the Channel and its environs, although little information exists to aid the historian to attempt to identify where they may be found.

UB104

UB104 was lost in September 1918. She is known to have been active in Lyme Bay, but she never returned to base. By that stage in the war, U-boats took the northerly route back to their bases. *UB104* sank somewhere en route during her return run.

UB113

UB113 disappeared in October 1918. She had been ordered to operate in the Channel. There is no evidence to suggest she actually arrived in her patrol area, although some historians have suggested this. In all probability, she was mined before arriving in the Channel.

UB32

UB32 was destroyed in September 1917. It is most likely that she was sunk by an aircraft off Zeebrugge on 22nd September. However, this has not been substantiated. *UB32* was ordered to operate in the Channel and it is possible that she may have been sunk on the 11th by a motor launch in the eastern Channel. Then again, both of these reported attacks could be erroneous. Therefore, it is only safe to assume that *UB32* could be found in the Channel at some point in the future.

UB63

UB63 disappeared in January 1918. She was heading for Ireland, via the Dover Straits. She never made any signals on this patrol and did not return. Therefore, it is possible that she was lost by some unknown cause in the Channel.

UC16

UC16 was lost in early October 1917. She laid mines off Boulogne and did not return to port. It is possible that she lies in Channel waters.

UC21

UC21 failed to return from patrol in October 1917. She had been ordered to lay mines off the French coast. It is possible that she was lost in the Channel. A more likely explanation is that she was mined off Zeebrugge on her outward leg.

U1055

Ordered to patrol in the Channel, U1055 was posted missing after the cessation of hostilities in 1945. No information has been found to explain what may have happened to her.

U325

It is most likely that U325 is one of the three Type VIIC U-boat wrecks located off North Cornwall in the last few years. This was supposed to be her patrol area. There is only the slightest of chances that she may be found further south in the future.

U683

In late February 1945, U683 was ordered into the Channel to operate off Cherbourg. She never returned. No further information relating to this submarine has ever been unearthed. It is quite possible that she will be located in the western Channel in future years.

U740

U740 was ordered into the Channel after D-Day to operate off Plymouth. She did not return and no sinking report of the period can be reliably attributed to her loss. Clearly, in the western Channel somewhere, this wreck will undoubtedly be identified in the future.

U322

U322 was ordered into the Channel in November 1944. Although her loss is attributed to an air attack off Scotland, this remains unconfirmed. It is just possible that the wreck of U322 will be found in the Channel area in the future.

U650

Ordered into the Channel in December 1944, nothing was ever heard from U650. It is possible that she reached her patrol area. In the future, U650 may be located in the Channel, although it is more likely that she perished en route to her assigned area.

Appendix 3

Submarines sunk in the Channel and later salvaged

This section lists all of the submarines which have been wrecked in the Channel and, subsequently, have been broken-up or salvaged. The criteria for inclusion here is the fact that there is no wreckage of these vessels to be found or searched for in the waters of the Channel, although they did sink there.

Please note that some submarines sank in the Channel, were later raised, only to be sunk somewhere else in the Channel. Because of this, the following submarines have been omitted from this list and their full stories have been told in the main part of this book. They are: HMS *A1* (see No 4/16), HMS *A3* (see No 4/18), HMS *Sidon* (see No 3/20), and HMS *Narwhal* (see No 1/31)

HMS A4

This submarine sank on tow to be repaired in the deep dock at Gosport in October 1905. She was later raised and returned to service.

HMS A8

15 submariners were killed when HMS *A8* foundered while changing crews. The accident occurred off Plymouth on 8th May 1905. It seems as if the submarine accidentally dived. HMS *A8* was later raised. She was sold for scrap in 1920.

Algerien

On 17th January 1907, this French submarine sank at her mooring in Cherbourg harbour. She had been tied up in such a way, that as the tide rose, she tilted over and was swamped. She was raised and re-commissioned soon after.

Pluvoise

On 26th May 1910, the French submarine *Pluvoise* was sunk in a collision near Calais. She sank after being hit by the cross-Channel ferry *Pas-de Calais*. All of the 27 crew were killed. The *Pluvoise* was later salvaged.

Holland 4

In 1912, *Holland 4* was sunk during explosives testing (see No 5/13). She was later raised and towed to Chatham. At some point after this she was expended as a gunnery target, presumably in the North Sea or Thames Estuary.

Holland 1

On 29th October 1913, *Holland 1* sank while on tow to the breaker's yard. She was located in 1981 and raised in 1982. She underwent an overhaul, followed by submergence in a specially built tank, to remove harmful salts from her hull. She is now on display in a dedicated building at the Royal Navy Submarine Museum.

HMS C14

HMS *C14* was sunk in a collision with Admiralty Hopper No 27 on 10th December 1913. The accident occurred between Devil's Point and Drake Island in Plymouth Sound. All 20 of the crew swam to safety. HMS *C14* was later raised.

UB26

On 5th April 1916, *UB26* was destroyed in shallow water off Le Havre. Divers located her and within eight days she was raised. Much interesting intelligence material was found within the submarine. She was reconditioned and commissioned into the French Navy as the *Roland Morillot*. She was broken up in 1931.

UC61

UC61 ran aground off Gris Nez on 26th July 1917. The crew scuttled her and were later captured by French cavalry. This wreck yielded much useful intelligence information. The crew also seemed quite willing to answer questions during interrogation. The wreck was later broken up where she lay.

U118

After the end of World War One, *U118* was allocated to the French Navy. She was on tow to France on 15th April 1919, when her tow parted and she drifted ashore on Hastings beach. For some days she was an attraction for sightseers. She was scrapped on the beach. This submarine has been confused in the past with *UB118* (see No 2/7).

U118 wrecked on Hastings beach. (U-Boot Archiv)

UB131 ashore near Beachy Head, before being broken up. (U-Boot Archiv)

HMS A2

When HMS *A2* was decommissioned she was used as a lighting platform in the Gosport submarine base. At some point (probably January 1920) she foundered in Bomb Ketch Lake. *A2* was then sold to Mr H. G. Pound and is thought to have been raised and scrapped shortly thereafter.

UB131

On 21st January 1921, *UB131* was washed ashore near Beachy Head. The above photograph of her ashore clearly shows the outline of a UBIII-Class submarine. However, there is some confusion as to whether she was dragged off and dumped, or broken up on the beach. In the waters nearby, lies the wreck of a UBIII-Class submarine which had *UB130* stamped on one of her props (see No 5/12). In all likelihood this was mere simple coincidence. However speculation has arisen in the past that somehow the wrecked *UB131* became the wreck of *UB130*. The author has found no evidence to support this contention.

HMS K15

HMS *K15* sank alongside Portsmouth harbour on 25th June 1921. The hot weather was blamed for causing an expansion in the hydraulic oil that caused the vents to partially open. There were no casualties. HMS *K15* was later raised.

HMS H29

On 9th August 1926, HMS *H29* sank at her mooring in Devonport dockyard. Five dockyard workers and one submariner were drowned. HMS *H29* was raised the following day.

Minerve

This French submarine washed ashore on the west side of Portland on 19th September 1945. She had been under tow when the cable parted. The submarine was broken up where she lay and little remains of her today.

HMS Truant

Britain's second most successful submarine of World War Two met an ignominious end in December 1946. She was on her way to be broken up at Briton Ferry when her tow cable parted. She finally went ashore on the Normandy coast, north of Cap Flamanville. The author has not been able to ascertain for certainty what happened after this. It is most likely that she was broken up in situ.

HMS Artemis

This British submarine sank at Fort Blockhouse, Gosport on 1st July 1971, while refuelling. There were no casualties and she was later re-floated. This was the last submarine accident to befall the Royal Navy.

XE8 (ex HMS Expunger)

This XE-Craft sank while being towed into the Channel to be used for underwater exercises. Like so many other submarines on tow, she foundered only three miles out of Portland. Diver, Peter Cornish, located her in 1971. In 1974, she was raised by the Royal Navy and after conservation was put on public display. She is owned by the Imperial War Museum and presently on display at Chatham.

Bibliography

Primary sources

Public Records Office, Kew London

Proceedings of the Anti-Submarine Assessment Committee 1944-45. ADM 199/1786. There are 141 assessments within this file which relate to ASW attacks in the Channel. Where referenced they are:

AUD 1023/44, D 1213/44, D 1055/44, D 1033/44, D 1010/44, D 1031/44, D 1491/44, D 1032/44, D 1041/44, D 1491/44, D 1044/44, D 1334/44, D 1491/44, D 1078/44, D 1117/44, D 1154/44, D 1156/44, D 1076/44, D 1079/44, D 1093/44, D 1173/44, D 1088/44, D 1122/44, D 1128/44, AUD1186/44, AUD 1227/44, D 1135/44, D 1326/44, D 1327/44, D 1170/44, D 1190/44, D 1160/44, D 1180/44 and AUD 1302/44, D 1192/44, AUD 1172/44, AUD 1198/44, M07743/44, AUD 1183/44, AUD 1230/44, AUD 1352/44, AUD 1220/44, AUD 1185/44, AUD 1202/44, AUD 1203/44, AUD 1297/44, AUD 1201/44, AUD 1221/44, AUD 1241/44, AUD 1219/44, AUD 1250/44, AUD 1245/44, AUD 1265/44, AUD 1256/44, AUD 1329/44, AUD 1369/44, AUD 1287/44, AUD 1311/44, AUD 1318/44, AUD 1310/44, AUD 1289/44, AUD 1493/44, AUD 1403/44, AUD 1288/44, AUD 1350/44, M 08929/44, AUD 1390/44, AUD 1392/44, AUD 1465/44, M 09124/44, AUD 1454/44, AUD 1516/44, AUD 1561/44, AUD 1543/44, AUD 1465/44, AUD 1798/44, AUD 1836/44, M 012058, M 012871, AUD 1991/44, AUD 2010/44, AUD 36/45, AUD 16/45, AUD 55/45, AUD 28/45, AUD 50/45, AUD 98/45, AUD 177/45, AUD 287/45, AUD 356/45, AUD 149/45, AUD 366/45, AUD 380/45, AUD 425/45, AUD 425/45, AUD 353/45, AUD 326/45, AUD 437/45, AUD 437/45, AUD 468/45, AUD 627/45, AUD 550/55, AUD 591/45, AUD 623/45, AUD 379/45, AUD 910/45, AUD 454/45, AUD 742/45, AUD 780/45, AUD 925/45, AUD 639/45, AUD 785/45, AUD 35/45, M 04647/45, AUD 627/45

Summaries of U-boat losses in WW2	ADM 199/1789
Disposal of surrendered World War One U-boats	ADM 1
Interrogation of the crew of UC61	ADM 137/3898
Charts of search for HMS M1	MP1/500
Final report on search for HMS M1	ADM 116/2922
Chart of search for HMS Affray	ADM 116/8567
Questions and answers as to condition of wreck of HMS Affray	ADM 116/8567
Inquiry into sinking of HMS D3	ADM 137/3598
Interrogation of survivors of U40	ADM 186/805
Sinking of U373	AIR 15/277
Report of the sinking of U399	ADM 1/18013
Interrogation of survivors of UB26	ADM 137/3897
Reference to UC69 crew member	ADM 137/3898
Sinking of U629	AIR 15/277 84404
Report of attack on U740	AIR 27/912
Interrogation of survivor from U741	ADM 199/498
Interrogation of the survivors of UB19	ADM 137/3899
Patrol Log of HMS D4, detailing attack on UB72	ADM 173/1069
Anti U-boat minefields around the UK in WW2	ADM/116/6082
Records of the Salvage Department of the Admiralty	ADM/116/1632, 1590, 1596,

1630, 1596, 1634, 1510A, 1597, 1598, 1638, 1639, 1641.

National Archives, Washington DC

Interrogation of survivors of *U48*	CB 01398B
Interrogation of survivors of *U103*	
Examination of the crew of *UC61*	
Interrogation of survivors of *UC65*	CB 01379
Sections of the KTB of *U86*	
Submarine activities in the western Atlantic May – Oct 1918	
UB35 Interrogation of Prisoners	CB 01414
UB55 Interrogation of Prisoners	CB 01437

U-Boot Archiv, Altenbruch

A huge amount of material relating to all aspects of the history of the U-boats lost in the Channel. Each U-boat has a specific file. The material yielded from these could only be specifically listed in a separate volume. Much invaluable information lies within these files.

Naval Historical Branch, London

Interrogation of survivors from *U971, U269, U672*	NID.1/PW/REP/6/44
Hydrographics Office of the Navy, Taunton	
Disposal of U-boats at sea	D/M 31695/21

Royal Navy Submarine Museum, Gosport

Monthly Anti-Submarine Reports for World War One
Review of signals heard by submarines during search for HMS *Affray*
Individual boat files for each submarine lost in the Channel. Each file contains a myriad of useful information.

Published primary sources

Campbell	Admiral Gordon	My Mystery Ships	Hodder & Stoughton 1929
Chapman	Paul	Submarine Torbay	Robert Hale 1989
Cremer	Peter	U-Boat Commander	Naval Institute press 1995
Dickison	Arthur P	Crash-dive	Sutton 1999
Doenitz	Admiral Karl	Memoirs	Wiedenfeld & Nicolson 1958
Fürbringer	Werner	FIPS – Legendary U-Boat Commander 1915-1918	Leo Cooper 1999
Hashagen	Ernst	The Log of a U-Boat Commander	Putnam 1931
High Command of the Navy		U-Boat Commanders Handbook – 1943 Edition	Thomas 1989
Hirschfeld	Wolfgang	The Story of a U-Boat NCO 1940-46	Leo Cooper 1996
Keyes	Admiral Sir Roger	The Naval Memoirs of (2 volumes)	Thornton Butterworth 1935

Koenig	Captain Paul	The Voyage of the Deutschland	Hearst's International Library 1916
Macintyre	Donald	U-Boat Killer	Wiedenfeld & Nicolson 1956
Niemoller	Martin	From U-Boat to Pulpit	William Hodge & Co 1936
Syrett ed.	David	The Battle of the Atlantic and Signals Intelligence: U-Boat Situations and Trends 1941-1945	Ashgate 1998
Tirpitz	Admiral Von	My Memoirs	Hurst & Blackett 1919
Topp	Erich	The Odyssey of a U-Boat Commander	Preager 1992
Werner	Herbert A	Iron Coffins	Holt, Rinehart and Winston 1970
Whinney	Bob	The U-Boat Peril	Blandfords Press 1986

Secondary Sources:

Akermann	Paul	Encyclopaedia of British Submarines	Akermann 1989
Archive Committee		Submarine memories & More Submarine Memories	Gatwick Submarine Archive
Bacon	Admiral Sir Reginald	The Concise History of the Dover Patrol	Hutchinson 1932
Beesly	Patrick	Room 40 – British Naval Intelligence 1914-18	Hamish Hamilton 1982
Bendert	Harald	Die UB-Boote der Kaiserlichen Marine 1914-1918	Mittler 2000
Blair	Clay	Hitler's U-Boat War – The Hunters 1939-1942	Wiedenfeld & Nicolson 1997
Blair	Clay	Hitler's U-Boat War – The Hunted 1942-1945	Wiedenfeld & Nicolson 1999
Brown	David	Warship Losses of World War Two	Naval Institute Press 1990
Busch	Rainer	German U-Boat Commanders of World War II	Greenhill 1999
Chalmers	Rear Admiral WS	Max Horton and the Western Approaches	Hodder & Stoughton 1954
Chatterton	E Keeble	Q-Ships and their Story	Sidgwick & Jackson 1922
Chatterton	E Keeble	Beating the U-Boats	Hurst & Blackett 1943
Chatterton	E Keeble	Danger Zone	Rich & Cowan 1934
Cocker	MP	Royal Navy Submarines 1901-1982	Frederick Warne 1982
Coles	Alan	Three Before breakfast	Kenneth Mason 1979
Compton-Hall	Richard	Submarine Boats	Conway 1983
Compton-Hall	Richard	Submarines and the War at Sea 1914-18	Macmillan 1991
Davis	Robert H	Deep Diving and Submarine Operations	Siebe Gorman Company 1995
Evans	AS	Beneath the Waves	William Kimber 1986
Everitt	Don	K Boats	Airlife Publishing Ltd. 1999
Franks	Norman	U-Boat Versus Aircraft	Grub Street 1998
Gibson	RH	The German Submarine War 1914-1918	John Constable Ltd. 1931
Grant	Robert M	U-Boat Intelligence	Archeron Books 1969
Grant	Robert M	U-Boats Destroyed	Putnam 1964
Gray	Edwyn A	The Killing Time	Charles Scribner 1972
Gray	Edwyn A	Captains of War	Leo Cooper 1988

Gray	Edwyn A	Few Survived	Leo Cooper 1986
Gray	Edwyn A	The Devils Device	Naval Institute Press 1991
Groner	Erich	German Warships 1815-1945 Volume 2	Conway 1985
Guske	Heinz	The War Diaries of U764	Thomas 1992
Hadley	Michael L	Count Not the Dead	Naval Institute Press 1995
Herzog	Bodo	Deutsche U-Boote 1906-1966	Karl Muller Verlag 1993
Hinchcliffe	John & Vicki	Dive Dorset	Underwater World Publications 1999
Hogel	Georg	Embleme Wappen Malings	Koeler 1996
Howarth	Stephen	The Battle of the Atlantic - The 50th Anniversary International Naval Conference	Greenhill 1994
Hoy	Hugh Cleland	40 O.B. How the War Was Won	Hutchinson 1934
Humphreys	Roy	The Dover Patrol	Sutton 1998
Jackson	Robert	Churchill's Moat	Airlife 1995
Jane's		Fighting Ships of World War 1	Studio Editions 1993
Jones	Geoffrey	Defeat of the Wolf Packs	William Kimber 1986
Kemp	Paul	British Submarines of World War One	Arms & Armour Press 1990
Kemp	Paul	The T-Class Submarine	Arms & Armour Press 1990
Kemp	Paul	British Submarines of World War Two	Arms & Armour Press 1987
Kemp	Paul	U-Boats Destroyed	Arms & Armour 1997
Knowles	Richard Morris	John P. Holland	University of South Carolina Press 1998
Kurowski	Franz	Knight's Cross Holders of the U-Boat Service	Schiffer 1995
Lambert	John	The Submarine Alliance	Conway 1986
Le Masson	Henri	Les Sous-Marins Francais	Cite Brest 1980
Lipscomb	Commander FW	The British Submarine	Adam & Charles Black 1954
Madsen	Chris	The Royal Navy and German Naval Disarmament 1942-1947	Frank Cass 1998
Mallmann Showell	Jak P	U-Boats under the Swastika	Naval Institute Press 1987
Mars	Alistair	British Submarines at War 1939-1945	William Kimber 1971
Maw	Neil	World War One Channel Wrecks	Underwater World Publications 2000
McDonald	Kendall	Dive Wight and Hampshire	Underwater World Publications 1991
McDonald	Kendall	Dive Kent	Underwater World Publications 1994
McDonald	Kendall	Dive Sussex	Underwater World Publications 1989
McDonald	Kendall	Dive South Devon	Underwater World Publications 1987
McDonald	Kendall	Dive Sussex	Underwater World Press 1999
Messimer	Dwight R	The Merchant U-Boat	Naval Institute Press 1988
Milner	Marc	The U-Boat Hunters	Naval Institute Press 1994
Ministry of Defence (Navy)		The U-Boat War in the Atlantic 1939-45	HMSO 1992
Morison	Samuel Eliot	The Atlantic Battle Won May 1943 - May 1945	Little, Brown 1990

Mulligan	Timothy P	Neither Sharks Nor Wolves	Conway 1999
NARA		Records Relating to U-Boat Warfare	NARA 1985
NARA		U-Boats and T-Boats	NARA 1984
Newbolt	Henry	Submarine and Anti-Submarine	Longmans, Green & Co. 1918
Niestlé	Axel	German U-Boat Losses During World War Two	Greenhill 1998
Padfield	Peter	Dönitz - The Last Fuhrer	Gollancz 1984
Ritchie	Carson	Q-ships	Terence Dalton 1985
Rohwer	Jurgen	Allied Submarine Attacks of World War Two	Greenhill 1997
Rohwer	Jurgen	Axis Submarine Successes of World War Two	Greenhill 1999
Rohwer	Jurgen	Chronology of the War at Sea 1939-1945	Naval Institute Press 1992
Rossler	Eberhard	The U-Boat	Naval Institute Press 1989
Savas	Theodore P	Silent Hunters	Savas Publishing Co. 1997
Schoenfeld	Max	Stalking the U-Boat	Smithsonian 1995
Sharpe	Peter	U-Boat Fact File	Midland Publishing 1998
Shelford	Captain WO	Subsunk	George G Harrap 1960
Sims	Rear Admiral WS	The Victory at Sea	John Murray 1920
Smith	Peter C	Hold the Narrow Sea	Naval Institute Press 1984
Stern	Robert C	Battle Beneath the Waves	Arms & Armour Press 1999
Stern	Robert C	Type VII U-Boats	Naval Institute Press 1991
Sternhell	Charles M	Antisubmarine Warfare in World War II	Aegaen Park Press (undated)
Syrett	David	The Defeat of the German U-Boats	University of South Carolina 1994
Tarrant	VE	The U-Boat Offensive 1914-1945	Naval Institiue Press 1989
Tarrant	VE	The Last Year of the Kriegsmarine	Naval Institute Press 1994
Tennent	AJ	British Merchant Ships sunk by U-Boats in the 1914-1918 War	The Starling Press 1990
Termote	Tomas	Verdwenen in de Noordzee	Uiteverij De Krijer 1999
Terraine	John	Business in Great Waters	Leo Cooper 1989
Thomas	Lowell	Raiders of the Deep	Naval Institute Press 1994
Treadwell	Terry C	Submarines with Wings	Conway 1985
Warren	CET	The Admiralty Regrets	White Lion 1972
Watts	Anthony	The U-Boat Hunters	McDonald and Janes 1976
Wiggins	Melanie	U-Boat Adventures	Naval Institute Press 1999
Wingate	John	The Fighting Tenth	Leo Cooper 1991
Wynn	Kenneth	U-Boat Operations of the Second World War - Volumes 1 & 2	Conway 1998
Young	Edward	One of Our Submarines	Rupert Hart-Davis 1952
		Naval Who's Who 1917	J B Hayward 1981

Index

10th Flotilla, 44
A.T.O (Airship), 136, 137
A1, HMS, 47, 77, 99, 115, 116, 167
A2, HMS, 169
A3, HMS, 47, 77, 78, 88, 163, 167
A4, HMS, 167
A7, HMS, 19, 42, 47, 48
A8, HMS, 167
Abwher, 55
Aeolian Sky, SS, 78
Affleck, HMS, 70
Affray, HMS, 31, 59, 71, 72, 76, 80, 85, 86, 87, 88, 120, 171, 172
Afric, SS, 33
AG Neptun - Rostock, 31
AG Vulcan - Hamburg, 52, 63, 65, 146
AG Weser - Bremen, 35, 52, 54, 56, 73, 109, 111, 134, 151, 152, 153, 158
Alberich, 99, 100
Alberni, HMCS, 100
Aldebaran, SS, 54
Alderney, 37, 88, 105
Algerien, French Submarine, 167
Ambush, HMS, 86
Amerika, SS, 162, 163
Amfitriti, 119
Amy, (barque), 46
Ans, SS, 20
Ariadne, HMS, 133
Ariel, HMS, 20, 21, 162
Artemis, HMS, 170
Asdic, 71, 100
Audacious, HMS, 36
Audic, Lt. de V., 88
B10, HMS, 163
B11, HMS, 163
B2, HMS, 141, 162, 163
Bachmann, Olzs. G., 147
Bacon, Admiral Sir Reginald, 135, 141, 173
Baie de Seine, France, 31, 103
Bailey, Ian, 103
Balfour, HMS, 67, 68, 70
Banstead Sub-Aqua Club, 78
Barten, Klt. Wolfgang, 143, 144
Barton, Lt D H, 79
Batchelor, Dave, 6, 148, 149, 150, 151, 152, 153, 158
Beachy Head, 66, 133, 134, 136, 148, 161, 169
Begonia, SS, 153
Behrend, SS, 62
Ben Lawer (Trawler), 25
Bergen, Norway, 25, 127
Berwick Castle, SS, 116
Beryl III, (Drifter), 146
Bethlehem – Quincy, Mass, 74
Bethlehem Steel Corporation, 46

Bhlom & Voss – Hamburg, 20, 104
Bickerton, HMS, 71, 72
Bird, Simon, 6, 78
Bishop Rock, 19
Black Hawk, SS, 73
Blackburn, Lt John, 76, 85, 86
Blackman, Lt. Chas., 20
Boch, Karl, 44
Bombala, Q-ship, 109
Bonetto, Tim, 6, 123
Boorara, SS, 156
Braeneil, SS, 32, 164
Branksome Chine, SS, 148
Braun, Olzs der Reserve Wilhelm, 156
Braunton, SS, 161
Bremer Vulcan & Schiffbau, 39
Brest, France, 22, 26, 67, 100, 124, 126, 128, 130, 154, 174
Bright, Nick, 6, 61
Brighton, 5, 123, 137, 164, 165
Brissenden, HMS, 129
Britannic, HMHS, 35, 55
Britton, Gus, 6, 78, 80, 117
Brownsill, Flt. Lt. Anthony G., 31
Bryant, Commander Ben, 75
BSAC, 127
BTC81, Convoy No., 30
BTC108, Convoy No, 29
Burmeister, Klt. Walter, 29
Buxton, Dr Ian, 6
C14, HMS, 168
C15, HMS, 132, 133
C16, HMS, 163
CADW, 15
Calceolaria, (Drifter), 145
Calgary, HMCS, 73
Cammell Laird – Birkenhead, 80, 85
Campbell, Captain Gordon, 37, 62, 112
Canaris, Klt. Wilhelm, 54
Carolina SS, 121, 174, 175
Carrie, Lt-Cmdr Alec M, 40, 42
Cawsands Bay, 38
Cayton Wyke, HMS, 142
Champlain, SS, 54
Chasseur II, FS, 138
Chattahoochee, SS, 153
Chatterton, E. Keeble, 65
Chatterton, John, 6, 121
Cherbourg, France, 23, 36, 40, 101, 103, 105, 119, 120, 121, 138, 154, 155, 166, 167
City of Corinth, SS, 156
City of Glasgow, SS, 56
Claussen, Hans-Georg, 23
Claussen, Oblt. Friedrich, 25
Claverley, SS, 148
Conrad, Olzs. Gerhard, 66

Cooke, HMS, 31, 66, 67
Cordes, Klt. Ernst, 101
Cornish, Peter, 170
Corvus, SS, 30
Council for British Archaeology, 15
Cox, Ernest, 83
Crown Point, SS, 158
Cuba, SS, 102
Curzon, HMS, 124
Cyclops, 51, 53
D3, HMS, 16, 33, 123, 136, 137, 138, 171
D4, HMS, 59, 171
Dakar, North Africa, 109
Dalegarth Force, SS, 52
Damant, Commander G.C.C., 11, 141, 145, 146,
    147, 148, 150, 151, 152, 153, 155, 157
Dandier Weft - Dazing, 28
Dankleff, Olzs. Walter, 69
Danziger Werft - Danzig, 126
Day, John, 19, 48
D-Day, 30, 48, 67, 123, 127, 130, 143, 166
Deepquest Sub Sea, 81
Degetau, Olzs. H., 59
Delmira, SS, 159
Deutsche Shiff und Maschinenbau - Bremen, 143
Deutsche Werft - Kiel, 99
Deutschland (submarine), 106, 107, 108, 109, 120,
    121, 173
Devonport, 40, 51, 56, 169
Diane, French Submarine, 164
Dobberstein, Olzs. Erich, 30, 31
Dodman Point, 51
Dolphin, Lt. E.H., 133
Dommet, HMS, 31
Dönitz, Admiral Karl, 22
Dover, 5, 19, 20, 21, 25, 33, 61, 63, 132, 133, 141,
    142, 143, 145, 146, 148, 149, 151, 152, 155, 156,
    157, 158, 159, 160, 162, 163, 164, 165, 166, 173,
    174
Dowd, Gerry, 6, 136
DSEA, 42, 83
Duckworth, HMS, 28, 29, 31, 100
Dunois, 64
Dunraven, Q-ship, 112, 113
Dunster, Alan, 6
Dwinsk, SS, 121
E13, HMS, 79
E22, HMS, 24, 133
E34, HMS, 163
E35, HMS, 109
East Holme, (Drifter), 145
Eastlands, SS, 153
Ebert, Klt. Jurgen, 31
Eddis, Lt-Cmdr P L, 78
Eddystone Lighthouse, 45, 46, 136, 148
Ekins, HMS, 124
Elba, SS, 145
Elysian, (Drifter), 146
Empire Portia, SS, 30
English Heritage, 15
Environment and Heritage Centre, 15

Epstatios, SS, 159
Eric Calvert, SS, 145
Eskimo, HMS, 26
Essington, HMS, 29, 31
Exmouth, HMS, 47
Falmouth, 5, 31, 49, 51, 55, 56, 61
Fame, HMS, 69
Farnbourough, Q-ship, 158
Farsund, Norway, 23
Fertility, (Drifter), 145
Fisher, Admiral Jackie, 46, 82
Flensburger Schiffsbau, 120
Forester, HMS, 126
Förster, Olzs. Hans-Joachim, 99
Förstner, Olzs Freiherr von, 159
Forward, Keith, 6
Foylemore, SS, 153
France (5-masted sailing ship), 25, 56, 64, 164
Fritzoe, SS, 104
FTM69, Convoy No., 128
Fürbringer, Olzs Werner, 133, 151, 160
Galster, Olzs. H., 38
Ganilly (Trawler), 103
Gebauer, Olzs. Werner, 19, 20
George Hawley, SS, 25
George Parnell Company, The, 83
Germaniawerft – Kiel, 22, 32, 34, 37, 38, 60, 107,
    108, 120, 124, 130, 141, 144, 146, 148, 159
Germaniawerft AG – Kiel, 66
Ghurka, HMS, 149
Gibson, R.H., 11, 59, 173
Giessler, Olzs. Heinz, 103
Glen, Q-ship, 17, 161
Goetting, Klt. Gernot, 109
Gold beck, Loss. Heinz, 28
Goldbeck, Olzs. Heinz, 28
Goodson, HMS, 71
Goodwin Sands, 142
Gosport, 77, 85, 105, 115, 116, 137, 169, 170, 172
Gowan II (Gowan), 148
Grant, R.M., 11, 32, 38
Grau, Olzs. Peter, 70
Gray, Edwyn, 6, 48
Great Yarmouth, 24
Gregor, Olzs. Fritz, 150
Gregynog, SS, 52
Grenfell, Captain, F.H., 37, 62, 63, 99
Gröner, Erich, 11
Gunther, Olzs. Paul, 105
Gyllyngvasse, 51
H29, HMS, 169
H52, HMS, 45, 46
Hagene, Klt. Georg, 21
Haida, HMCS, 26, 27
Harpalion, SS, 148
Hashagen, Klt. Ernst, 104
Hastings, 56, 134, 168
Havelock, HMS, 28, 69
Hawke, HMS, 36
Hazard, HMS, 77
Hegewald, Klt. Wolfgang, 127

Helene, SS, 52
Helgoland, Q-ship, 161
Herbert, Lt. Godfrey, 33
Hesperus, HMS, 28
Hessler, Güther, 11
High Wycombe BSAC, 127
Hilgrove, Tony, 6, 34
Hindius, Klt. Paul, 145
Historic Scotland, 15
HM Dockyard - Chatham, 116
HM Dockyard - Pembroke, 45
HMS Dolphin, 117
HMS *Mignonette*, HMS, 25
Hofmann, Horst, 68
Holbrook, Lt. N D, 163
Holland 1, 136, 167
Holland 4, 136, 167
Holland 5, 116, 134, 135, 136, 163
Holland, John Philip, 134
Hollenden, Lord, 65
Horten, Norway, 19, 29, 30, 34
Horton, Max, 3, 83, 173
Hotspur, HMS, 69
Howaldtswerke - Hamburg, 67, 127
Howaldtswerke –Hamburg, 19
Hulsenbeck, Olsz. Ewald, 23
Hydrographic Office, 17
Hyronimus, Olzs. Guido, 123, 124
Icarus, HMS, 25, 69
Inconstant, HMS, 69
Instructor, SS, 163
Ireland, 14, 16, 19, 20, 26, 34, 35, 67, 134, 137, 166
Isle of Wight, 5, 17, 40, 67, 99, 105, 108, 114, 117,
    119, 127, 128, 137, 161, 164
Izac, Lt. Edward, 114
James Eagan Layne, SS, 28, 29
K13, HMS, 119
K15, HMS, 169
Kaiserliche Werft - Danzig, 40, 113
Kashmir, SS, 20
Kendal Castle, SS, 145
Kennet (Patrol Vessel), 57
Keyes, Admiral Sir Roger, 141, 155, 157, 161, 165,
    172
Kiel, Olzs. W., 64
King, Richard, 47
Kiotschka, Klt. Siegfried, 44
Knott, Graham, 6, 43, 59
Kootenay, HMCS, 123, 124
Kophamel, Klt., 121
Korte, Olzs., 106
Kraft, Otto, 42
Kriegsmarine, 11, 175
Kriegsmarinewerft - Wilhelmshaven, 69, 72
Kristiansand, Norway, 21, 26, 31
Krupp Germaniawerft - Kiel, 141
Kukat, Klt H., 146
Kukenthal, Olzs. H., 61
Kursk (submarine), 59
Küstner, Olzs Heinrich von, 160, 161
L'Escarmouche, FS, 102

L17, HMS, 42
L22, HMS, 42
L23, HMS, 42
L24, HMS, 59, 78, 79, 80
Lady Olive, Q-ship, 64
Lafrenz, Klt. Claus, 132, 133
Lakin, Lt. R B, 76
Landrail, HMS, 161, 162
Lanfranc, SS, 60, 131
Langley, Lt M A, 116
Latron, Lt de V, 138
Lauban, HMS, 24
LC Hill, Lt. Comdr., 67
Le Colbart, 147, 157
Le Havre, 60, 123, 128, 138, 157, 168
Leathes, Lt. Cmdr John D de. M., 82
Leuwer, Leo, 129
Leven, HMS, 158, 159
Liberty, HMS, 158
Lindberg, Lennart, 70
Lizze, SS, 160
Llandovery Castle, HMHS, 131
Loch Fada, HMS, 24, 29, 30
Loch Killin, HMS, 34
Lois (Trawler), 35, 38
Longset, HMS, 158
Lord Leitrim, (Drifter), 156
Lorient, 31
Lorna, (Yacht), 65
Lornaston, SS, 125
Lough Swilly, 36
Lovas, Uwe, 99
Lowe, Olzs Werner, 151
Loyal Friend, (Drifter), 153
LST404, 128
Lusitania, SS, 149, 151, 161
Lyme Bay, 5, 59, 153, 165
M1, HMS, 14, 19, 40, 41, 42, 43, 47, 82, 171
M2, HMS, 41, 42, 43, 59, 82, 83, 84
M3, HMS, 41
Macintyre, Captain Donald, 71, 72, 173
Magnus, Olzs Alexander, 109
Maid of Orleans, SS, 30, 31
Maitland-Dougall, Lt. W, 136
Mallmann-Showell, Jak, 5, 6, 7
Maria (submarine), 6, 19, 48
Marine Salvage of Penzance, 51
Maritime and Coastguard Agency, 15
Marviken, Norway, 69, 123
Matheson, Lt. Commander, 38
Matschulat, Olzs. Gerhard, 22
Mechanican, SS, 159
Medina, SS, 156
Mesaba, SS, 56
Mesnil, Lt. de V. A Couespel du, 119, 120
Messudieh (Battleship), 163
Metzger, Ewald, 35, 38
Milne, HMS, 157
Minerve, French Submarine, 169
Moecke, Olzs Fritz, 158
Mourne, HMS, 69

Nantucket lightship, 36
Narwhal, HMS, 49, 167
NAS, 15
New Era Productions, 46
New Zealand, HMS, 79
Newhaven, 144
Ney, Klt. Otto, 146
Niemayer, Olzs. G, 24
Niemöller, Martin, 55
Niestlé, Dr Axel, 6, 11, 12, 21, 24, 28, 70, 129, 130
Nitzsche, Olzs. Alfred., 20
Nollman, Klt. Rolf, 25
Noodt, Olzs. Erich, 62
Northville, SS, 150
O' Brien, Lt. P.B., 162
Oakby, SS, 148
Oates, Silas, 43
Ocean Roamer, (Drifter), 153, 156
Oldenburg (submarine), 120, 121
Olympic, SS, 35, 36, 139
Olzs Heinz Buhse, 28
Olzs. der Res. Wilhelm Braun, 156
Onslaught, HMS, 129
Onyx, HMS, 47
Operation Deadlight, 16, 39, 67
Operation Husky, 76
Operation Pedestal, 75
Operation Training Spring, 85
Opossum, HMS, 61
Orchis, HMS, 128, 129
Oribi, HMS, 129
Ormond, Lt. F T, 77
Ottawa, HMCS, 124
Ottowa, HMCS, 123
Oushla, SS, 105
Ovenden, John, 6, 65, 88
P32, HMS, 113
P33, HMS, 154
P65, HMS, 118
P555, HMS, 74
Pacific, SS, 29, 75
Palmgren, Olzs. Gerhard, 128
Parnell Peto, 83
Patia, HMS, 61
Patzig, Olzs. Conrad, 131
Peacock, Bob, 6, 143, 144, 148, 157, 158, 162, 163
Pendennis Point, 51
Penshurst, Q-ship, 59, 62, 99, 105
Persier, SS, 29, 30
Petz, Klt W., 37
Pink, HMS, 30, 31
Platsch, Olzs Erich, 161
Pleasants, (Drifter), 145
Pluvoise, French Submarine, 167
Plymouth, 19, 27, 29, 33, 38, 47, 48, 60, 61, 67, 71, 156, 166, 167, 168
Poel, Klt. Gustav, 126
Polleon, SS, 154
Port Colbourne, HMCS, 22
Pound, Gifford, 6, 24, 25, 27, 29, 30, 49
Pour le Mérite, 36, 112, 153

Prairial (submarine), 123, 138, 139
Prendergast, Maurice, 11, 59
President Lincoln, SS, 114
Prinz, Klt A., 32
Privet, Q-ship, 37
Prométhée (submarine), 99, 119, 120
Pronto, SS, 160
Public Records Office, Kew, 43, 111, 137, 171
Puffin, HMS, 142
Pulleyne, Lt Richard, 163
Puskuchen, Olzs, 161
Pustkuchen, Olzs. Herbert, 33
Pygmy, HMS, 47
Q-Ships, The (film), 13, 45, 46
Queen Alexandra, SS, 154, 155
Ramien, Olzs Kurt, 155
Receiver of Wreck, 20
Reclaim, HMS, 86
Reiherstieg – Hamburg, 107, 108
Remy, Klt. Walter, 114
Resolution, HMS, 78, 79, 80
Reuss, Heinrich XXXVII Prinz, 134
Rhein, Klt. Wilhelm, 54
Ried, Bill, 35
Rio Parana, SS, 148
Risdon Beazley Co., 27
Rocket, HMS, 42
Ropp, Klt. Dietrich von der, 141
Roskill, Stephen, 11
Rowley, HMS, 29, 100
Rücker, Klt. Claus, 35, 36, 159
Russell, HMS, 55
S24, 74
Safari, HMS, 75, 76, 81
Saint Egonat, SS, 126
Saint-Rémy, Lt., 137
Salcombe, 34, 35, 39
Saltzwedel, Klt Reinhold, 99, 111, 112, 113
San Bernado, SS, 62
Santa Isabel, SS, 109
Saywell, Dave, 6, 76
Schase, Olzs. Dietrich, 126
Schichau – Danzig, 21, 23, 25, 70, 101, 128
Schmettow, Klt Graf von, 157
Schmietenknop, Walter, 69
Schmitz, Olzs. M., 73
Schwartz, Olzs F., 152
Schwieger, Klt Walter, 149
Sea King (Trawler), 33
Sea Porpoise, SS, 103
Seahorse (Tug), 78
Seuffer, Klt Rudolf, 144
Seven Seas, SS, 160
Seymour, HMS, 129
Sidon, HMS, 80, 81, 167
Sieder, Olzs. Heinz, 130
Smith, Andy, 6, 80, 87
Spindler, Arno, 11, 17, 159
St Jehanne, SS, 160
St John, HMCS, 22
St Louis (warship), 88

St. Andrew, SS, 149
St. Vincent, HMS, 78
Start Point, 25, 31, 35, 38, 40, 43, 45, 60, 67, 68, 150, 156
Statice, HMS, 123, 124
Stayner, HMS, 127
Steinbrink, Otto, 24, 132, 133
Steindorff, Olzs E., 65
Stoss, Klt. A., 148
Stossburg, Olzs Arthur, 154
Stöter, Olzs Kurt, 158
Sturgeon, HMS, 116
Sussex SS, 33, 63, 161, 162, 174
Swansea, HMCS, 22
Swordfish, HMS, 16, 81, 99, 116, 117, 136
Talybont, HMS, 129
Tambach Castle, 11
Tatem Steam Navigation Company, 161
Tavy, HMS, 103
TBC 128, Convoy No., 34
Tein, Erich, 103
Termote, Tomas, 6, 159
The National Trust, 15
Thetis, HMS, 119
Thielmann, Olzs H., 111
Thomas, Lowell, 111, 121
Thorsa, SS, 145
Ticonderoga, USS, 108
Titanic, SS, 35
Torridge, SS, 161
Tottenham, Lt. C.L., 65, 66
Tropic, SS, 138, 139
Truant, HMS, 169
Turnbull, Lt. Cmdr, 161
Turpin, HMS, 80
Tyneside, SS, 83
U8, 141, 148, 149
U12, 141, 142
U16, 142, 143
U28, 143, 159
U34, 159
U37, 159, 160
U40, 134, 143, 144, 171
U48, 68, 143, 172
U53, 108
U73, 35, 55
U85, 37, 38
U86, 114, 123, 130, 131, 172
U90, 113, 114
U93, 32, 61, 164
U95, 32, 164
U96, 12, 111
U103, 35, 36, 64, 172
U109, 146
U110, 105
U118, 56, 168
U121, 106, 121
U122, 106, 107
U123, 107
U135, 40

U151, 106, 108, 120, 121
U152, 107, 108, 109
U153, 108, 109
U154, 109
U155, 108
U161, 39, 40
U212, 19, 124
U214, 66, 67, 68
U242, 28
U247, 22
U260, 67
U269, 70, 71, 72, 172
U275, 124, 125, 126
U322, 166
U325, 166
U327, 24
U390, 103
U399, 28, 29, 171
U413, 126, 127
U441, 71, 73, 129
U480, 12, 21, 99, 100, 130
U650, 24, 71, 73, 166
U671, 127, 128
U672, 12, 67, 68, 172
U678, 123, 124, 125
U681, 19, 20, 23
U683, 21, 24, 166
U740, 24, 166, 171
U741, 12, 128, 129, 130, 171
U763, 101
U767, 69, 70, 71
U772, 72, 73, 74
U927, 21, 31
U971, 26, 27, 172
U983, 30
U984, 71, 130
U988, 30, 31, 129
U1018, 28, 29, 30
U1055, 24, 71, 73, 166
U1063, 34, 43
U1105, 99
U1107, 100
U1169, 27, 28, 29
U1191, 70, 71, 72
U1195, 101, 102
U1199, 24, 25
U1208, 21, 24
U1209, 23, 24
UB10, 60
UB17, 153
UB18, 17, 24, 25, 35, 133, 161
UB19, 59, 62, 63, 72, 105, 171
UB21, 104, 105
UB26, 168, 171
UB29, 21, 33, 161, 162
UB31, 156, 157
UB32, 165
UB33, 150
UB35, 158, 159, 172
UB37, 63, 99, 105
UB38, 147, 148

UB39, 17, 151, 160, 161
UB54, 132, 151, 152, 164
UB55, 153, 154, 172
UB56, 152
UB58, 151
UB60, 25, 35
UB63, 132, 166
UB72, 59, 63, 64, 111, 133, 171
UB74, 65, 66
UB78, 154, 155
UB81, 99, 111, 113
UB86, 52
UB97, 52, 53
UB103, 145, 146
UB104, 132, 155, 165
UB106, 53
UB108, 151, 152, 165
UB109, 111, 155
UB110, 133
UB112, 54
UB113, 132, 165
UB118, 51, 56, 168
UB122, 109
UB128, 54, 55
UB130, 134, 144, 169
UB131, 134, 169
U-Boat Archive, Altenbruch, 6, 172
UC6, 162
UC9, 162
UC16, 166
UC17, 32, 151, 153
UC18, 64, 65
UC19, 20, 162
UC21, 162, 166
UC26, 157
UC36, 164
UC46, 158
UC49, 60, 61
UC50, 144, 145
UC51, 25, 35, 38, 39
UC61, 168, 171, 172
UC62, 73, 74
UC64, 152, 153
UC65, 63, 123, 132, 133, 150, 172
UC66, 27, 33, 137
UC68, 59, 60
UC69, 12, 99, 111, 171
UC70, 151
UC71, 112
UC77, 162, 165
UC78, 146, 147, 148, 157
UC79, 144, 155, 162
UC92, 55
UC110, 110
Uhl, Olzs. Georg, 71
Union Republicaine, SS, 114
Unseen, HMS, 44
Untiring, HMS, 44, 45, 119
Upstart, HMS, 44, 45, 118, 119
Usk, HMS, 117
Valentiner, Olzs Hans, 152

Varne Bank, 149, 150, 152, 153, 154, 156, 161
Vegesacker Werft - Vegesack, 71, 125
Vendémiaire, (submarine), 59, 88
Versailles, Treaty of, 106, 121
Vickers - Barrow, 77, 78, 82, 115, 134, 136, 162
Vickers – Barrow-in-Furness, 40, 44, 47, 49, 75, 118
Vickers Armstrong – Barrow in Furness, 75
Victoria Cross, 163
Victoria, FV, 36
Vidar, SS, 40, 42, 43
Vidette, HMS, 126
Viking, HMS, 149
Volger, Klt. Helmut, 124
Von Nostitz, Klt., 121
Vulcan, 39, 52, 53, 63, 65, 121, 146
Wanderer, HMS, 103, 104
war criminals, 19, 131, 162
Warilda, SS, 60, 61
Warren, Ivan, 6, 123, 125
Warwick Castle, SS, 126
Warwick, HMS, 126
Watchman, HMS, 101, 102
Webb, Peter, 6
Webster, Mark, 6
Wehrkamp, Olzs. Helmut, 125
Wellner, Klt. Hannes-Horst, 142
Welman, Lt G M, 47
Wendes, Dave, 76
Wenninger, Klt Ralph, 153
Wensleydale, HMS, 126, 127, 129
Western Coast, SS *t*, 148
Westwood, SS, 54
Weymouth, 43, 46, 49, 65, 73, 75, 78, 143
Whitesand Bay, 47
Wild Goose, HMS, 24
Wilke, Klt Erich, 159
Wilkins, Dave, 6
Winkler, Otto, 144
Wolf Rock, 23, 69, 153
Woodward, Martin, 6, 16, 99, 102, 114, 116, 117, 118, 131
Woonda (Tug), 134
World War One, 10, 11, 12, 13, 15, 17, 19, 24, 25, 32, 35, 37, 39, 40, 46, 51, 55, 59, 60, 61, 62, 72, 74, 79, 82, 88, 99, 106, 109, 110, 111, 112, 113, 114, 117, 123, 131, 132, 134, 135, 136, 138, 139, 141, 143, 144, 146, 149, 156, 159, 160, 161, 162, 163, 168, 171, 172, 174
World War Two, 9, 11, 12, 15, 19, 22, 27, 28, 29, 44, 51, 67, 68, 71, 72, 75, 80, 85, 99, 116, 126, 132, 141, 143, 144, 146, 173, 174, 175
XE8 - HMS *Expunger*, 170
Xifias, 44, 45
Young Crow, (Drifter), 145
Zeebrugge, 20, 24, 33, 60, 61, 65, 155, 157, 164, 165, 166
Zeplien, Olzs. Walter, 26
Zinal, SS, 155
Zubian, HMS, 144, 145

A range of books and videos for the naval enthusiast

Books

The German Submarine War, 1914-1918 - by R H Gibson and Maurice Prendergast

The British account of the German submarine campaign, which became the standard history on the subject when originally published. It relates how an underestimated weapon, the U-boat, came to almost starve Britain out of the war. All theatres and incidents, such as the sinking of the Lusitania are covered in detail. The adoption of the convoy system and final defeat of the submarine menace is also fully related.

14x22cm paperback 438 pages with 31 b&w photos and 10 maps ISBN No 1904381081

£19.99 + £2.50 UK postage

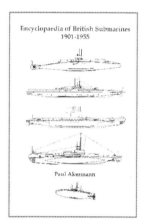

Encyclopaedia of British Submarines, 1901-1955 - by Paul Akermann

This excellent technical history of HM Submarines is the most comprehensive history of British submarine development ever published. From the little Holland 1 to the mighty pre-nuclear submarines, this encyclopaedia covers them all. Each class is treated to its own history and the fates of each individual submarine are shown too. It is profusely illustrated, giving a fascinating insight into some of the greatest submarine designs ever built.

20x29cm paperback 522 pages with 31 b&w photos and over 100 line drawings ISBN No 1904381057

£35.99 + £4.00 UK postage

My Mystery Ships - by Rear Admiral Gordon Campbell VC DSO

One of Britain's most famous heroes of World War One, Campbell destroyed three U-boats while in command of three different Q-ships. He developed the desperate tactic of allowing himself to be torpedoed in order to lure the U-boat to the surface, where he could then open fire. No less than five Victoria Crosses were awarded to his crew during the war. This book is his story of those heroic deeds. A global best-seller.

14x22cm paperback 300 pages with 28 b&w photos and illustrations ISBN No 1904381073

£14.99 + £2.00 UK postage

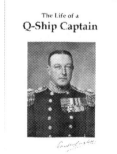

The Life of a Q-Ship Captain - by Rear Admiral Gordon Campbell VC DSO

The most successful Q-Sip captain of all time, Gordon Campbell became a national hero. His stature can be measured by the fact that he led the honour guard during the entombing of the Unknown Warrior. This engaging autobiography relates Campbells life from boyhood to election as MP for Burnley.

14x22cm paperback 352 pages with 11 b&w photos ISBN No 1904381065

£14.99 + £2.00 UK postage

A Submariner's Story - by Joel Blamey DSC DSM

The autobiography of Britain's oldest submariner. Joel Blamey joined HM Submarines in 1926, survived peacetime accidents and the Second World War. He endured some of the worst depth-charge attacks from which British submarines escaped.

This book represents a remarkably candid recollection of a 28-year career as a submariner, written from the perspective of an engineer officer.

Already widely acclaimed as a classic, Joel has been on television and radio in 2002 promoting this fascinating book.

16x23cm paperback 278 pages with 14 b&w photos ISBN No 1904381022

£17.99 + £2.50 UK postage

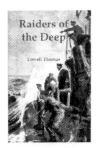

Raiders of the Deep - by Lowell Thomas

The only oral history of the U-boat men of the First World War. It is one of the timeless classics of naval history. Lowell Thomas interviewed the surviving U-boat officers in the 1920's and told their story of how they nearly won the war at sea. This book became a worldwide bestseller when released in 1931. It is available again uniquely from Periscope Publishing Ltd. This edition contains a portrait and mini-biography of Lowell Thomas, who was equally famous for his association with Lawrence of Arabia.

14x22cm paperback 364 pages with 27 b&w photos ISBN No 1904381030

£14.99 + £2.00 UK postage

U-Boats Destroyed - by R M Grant

"R.M. Grant's 'U-Boats Destroyed' is quite simply a classic. This edition will no doubt enthral military enthusiasts again, as one of the most significant landmarks of naval literature." JAK MALLMAN-SHOWELL

The first of Grant's books deals with the physical destruction of U-boats; how it was planned and executed and the lessons learned throughout the First World War. Unavailable since 1964.

14 x 22cm paperback 172 pages with 61 photos & ills ISBN No 1904381006

£14.99 + £2.00 UK postage

U-Boat Intelligence - by R. M. Grant

The second of professor R M Grant's books on the defeat of the U-Boats in World War One. This book examines the role played by allied Intelligence in hunting down and destroying German submarines. It includes the breaking the German naval codes, radio interception, the role of secret agents and naval divers. Unavailable since 1969, it remains the defining book on the subject.

14 x 22cm paperback 196 pages with 24 ills & photos ISBN No 1904381014

£14.99 + £2.00 UK postage

Forthcoming Books

"U-Boat Hunters" by R. M. Grant	available March 2003	£14.99
"Fear God and Dreadnaught - Britain's First Nuclear Submarine" by P. Boniface	available June 2003	£17.99

Videos *(in PAL and NTSC formats)*

"U-Boat Wrecks of Operation Deadlight", *U2511, U155, U218, U637, U778, U281*, etc.	£14.99
"U-Boat Wrecks of The English Channel", *U772, U741, U678, U1195, U413, U480*	£14.99
"The Mystery of HMS Affray"	£14.99
"The Wrecks of the Battle of Jutland", *Queen Mary, Invincible, Lützow, Black Prince*	£14.99
"Titanic's sister - HMHS Britannic", sunk by a mine from *U73*	£14.99

UK customers please add £2.00 postage per video

Order from:
Periscope Publishing Ltd.
33 Barwis Terrace, Penzance, Cornwall TR18 2AW UK
tel/fax: +44 (0) 1736 330769
sales@periscopepublishing.com
order online at www.periscopepublishing.com